God's Wisdom for Navigating Life

REDEEMER

God's Wisdom for
NAVIGATING
LIFE

A Year of
Daily Devotions
in the Book of Proverbs

TIMOTHY
KELLER

with KATHY KELLER

VIKING

VIKING

An imprint of Penguin Random House LLC
375 Hudson Street
New York, New York 10014
penguin.com

ISBN 9780735222090 (hardcover)
ISBN 9780735222106 (e-book)

Printed in the United States of America
5   7   9   10   8   6

Set in Warnock Pro
Designed by Cassandra Garruzzo

To Bruce and Missy Terrell
Wise leaders and friends
whose wisdom and love have guided both us
and Redeemer Presbyterian Church for many years.

INTRODUCTION

There may be readers picking up this book who profited from our earlier yearlong devotional book, *The Songs of Jesus*. In that case especially, it is helpful to reflect on the differences between Psalms and Proverbs. The Psalms are filled with expressions of emotion, of pain, joy, and praise. They show us how to process our experiences before God. Proverbs is a very different book. It calls us to study, to think, to learn the practical discipline of centering all our thoughts and actions on God. Indeed, one of the main messages of Proverbs is—*you've never really thought enough about anything.* Psalms is about how to throw ourselves fully upon God in faith. Proverbs is about how, having trusted God, we should then live that faith out. If the Bible were a medicine cabinet, Psalms would be the ointment put on inflamed skin to calm and heal it. Proverbs would be more like smelling salts to startle you into alertness. Here are a few pointers for studying the book of Proverbs with profit.

Proverbs as Poetry

Proverbs is not a set of "simple steps to a happy life" for quick consumption. A proverb is a poetic art form that instills wisdom in you as you wrestle with it. As English readers we cannot receive the full force of the original, and yet we can still learn enough about the features of Hebrew poetry to discern layers of meaning that we would otherwise miss. Perhaps the most fundamental mark of Hebrew poetry is parallelism. Two phrases, clauses, or sentences are brought into close connection with each other so that they modify and expand on each other. The second may magnify and extend the thought of the first, or it may instead offer a counterpoint that limits and softens the first idea.

In each case the two thoughts mutually clarify each other, sharpening our understanding. So Proverbs 13:6 says, "Righteousness guards the person of integrity, but wickedness overthrows the sinner." The first clause helps us understand "wickedness" in the second clause more specifically as a lack of integrity. Because of parallelism, the words "wicked" and "righteous" and "wise" and "foolish," which show up constantly and (seemingly) repetitiously, actually mean somewhat different things in each proverb. We miss much of the meaning of a proverb unless we compare the clauses very closely and watch for the interplay between words.

Another prominent feature of Hebrew poetry, as in all poetry, is the importance of vivid images. A beautiful but foolish woman is like a gold ring in a pig's snout (Proverbs 11:22); a lazy employee is like vinegar to the teeth (Proverbs 10:26). Images and metaphors are always invitations to think out the many ways that "this is like that." A thoughtful reader can list five, then ten, then more ways that the image explains the principle.

Proverbs as Puzzle

Goethe once said of languages that "whoever know only one, knows none," and that is likely true, but it is even more true of proverbs.[1] If one proverb says, "The morally good *always* have a good life," and later another says, "Sometimes the morally good suffer," we modern readers think we've found a contradiction. That's because we think of proverbs either as individual standalone promises or commands. But usually they are neither. Each is a description of some aspect of how life works. One proverb on marriage, taken all by itself, seems to apply to every instance. A later proverb, however, reveals that there are some marriage situations in which a different practice is required. Only taken and fitted together, with each one modifying the others as the parallel clauses do, do the proverbs yield a full, multidimensional picture of a particular topic.

Proverbs, then, give up their meaning only cumulatively. No one saying gives you the whole picture. Proverbs 29:19 says that servants simply can't understand the reason they should do things, so you just have to be very strict with them. This seems to be a sweeping statement about their capabilities, but Proverbs 17:2 tells us that a wise servant can end up being better than a family member. Only when the two are placed together can we see that 29:19 is not talking about all servants and employees but rather about those with an unresponsive, sullen attitude.[2]

So if we read Proverbs' various statements on a subject all together, we can see many larger points. In chapter 12 we are told that the path toward disaster can seem to be the right one to a fool, but in chapter 16, that the disastrous road can appear to be right to *any*one. In other words, sometimes, even if you have done due diligence, your choices may still go wrong, because it is a broken world. The wise know that sometimes "all paths may run ill." As we will see, there *is* an order God put into things when he created the world and by which we must abide. But on the other hand this is a fallen world, distorted by sin, and the wise know that the created order does not always work, nor is it always easy to discern.

Only all together do the proverbs bring us a wise, nuanced, theologically rich, many-faceted view of the world.

Proverbs as Pedagogy

Many have concluded that the book of Proverbs was originally a manual for the instruction of young men. The addressees are always "sons." If that is the case, then it makes sense that we should have warnings against predatory, adulterous women in chapters 5 through 7 but no analogous warning about predatory, adulterous men.[3] Modern readers sometimes chafe, therefore, at how male oriented the book is. We should not conclude from this, however, that Proverbs is more negative about female character than male, or that women should not be instructed in wisdom while men should be.

We have seen that the creation and dissemination of proverbs took a great deal of artistry and deep learning. Yet in Proverbs 1:8; 4:3; 10:1, and elsewhere it is both father *and* mother who are instructing their son. The mother was "an authoritative voice along with the father."[4] This surely means that daughters as well as sons must have been trained in the terse poetry and epigrammatic wisdom of proverbs. Indeed, the idealized wife of Proverbs 31:26 "speaks with wisdom" and "faithful instruction is on her tongue." These are technical terms meaning she speaks at length with great solemnity and imparts the wisdom of the ages.[5] So while the original readers of Proverbs were male, not female, the wisdom and training of this book nevertheless applies to everyone.

We should, however, never forget that Proverbs was written not for private reading but as a manual to be worked through in a community of learners, with older, wiser mentors. At the very least, then, we would like to urge you to use this daily devotional together with a group of friends. Here is a suggested way to do this.

Choose one or more friends and agree to use the devotional together, each reading the same reflection individually, in private, on the same day. At the end of each reflection there is a question that helps you think more personally about how the teaching applies to your life. Write the answer to the question in a journal. Then write answers to two additional questions about the day's proverb(s) in your journal, unless your response to the first query has already included them.

1. Where in your life or the life of someone else have you seen this observation illustrated?
2. How can you put this observation into practice— in thought, attitude, word, or deed?

After completing your journal entry, pray the prayer at the end of each page. These short prayers are just "on ramps"—suggested ways to begin talking to God personally about what he is teaching you in his Word. Put the prayer in your own words if you wish, and then continue speaking to him about how the particular Scriptural teaching should play out in your life. This should be your daily routine—read, meditate using the journal questions, and pray.

Then meet with your friends who are doing the same daily exercise as often as you can. Share your best insights, discuss them together, encourage one another to apply the insights to your lives, and report to one another on how your efforts are going.

Proverbs as Part of the Whole Bible

While we call Proverbs a "book," it really is one chapter in a much larger book—the Bible—which presents, through all its various parts and narratives, a single, coherent story. That story is that the human race has marred God's good creation through sin and now needs salvation, and that this salvation has been accomplished and can be found only in Jesus Christ. Therefore, like every other part of the Bible, Proverbs will give up its fullest and richest meaning only when it is read in the light of the person and work of Jesus. Jesus dazzled his listeners with his wisdom (Luke 2:40,47; Mark 6:2). He claimed to be the new Solomon with the ultimate wisdom (Luke 11:31). The personified Wisdom that created the world (Proverbs 8:22–31) is finally revealed to be Jesus, the Word of God, with whom God created the world (John 1:1–4.) Paul calls Jesus the wisdom of God (1 Corinthians 1:24, 30), the one in whom all God's wisdom is hidden (Colossians 2:3).

Remember, too, that "the fear of the Lord" (Proverbs 1:7, 9:10) is the beginning of wisdom. A living, vital relationship with God is wisdom's absolute prerequisite. This "fear," as we will see, is not cringing terror but an attitude of awe and wonder before the faithful, covenant love of God. The New Testament shows us that the kind of relationship with the Lord that Proverbs calls for can be fully realized only through faith in the gospel of Jesus Christ.

The Themes of Proverbs

Perhaps the most challenging aspect of the study of Proverbs is the task of synthesizing all that it says on a particular subject. In this devotional book, the first weeks of the year examine the general teaching on the subject of wisdom in the first nine chapters of Proverbs. After that, however, I have grouped the daily readings into sets of topics, enabling the reader to accumulate the various insights on a specific theme, piecing together the wisdom that the book offers on the subject. Readers should expect that some proverbs recur in more than one daily reading. The reason is that many proverbs do not speak strictly to one topic, but have implications for practice under several headings of wise living. The themes are listed below.

Knowing wisdom: January 1–February 7

What is wisdom?
What is foolishness?
How do we become wise?
The case for wisdom

Knowing God: February 8–March 23

The fear of the Lord
God's order perceived
God's order disrupted (Ecclesiastes)
God's order hidden (Job)

Knowing the heart: March 24–June 12

Understanding the heart
Reordering desires
Understanding temptation
Understanding emotion
The Seven Deadly Sins

Knowing others: June 13–August 10

Friendship
Words
Gossip
Listening
Conflicts

Knowing the times and seasons: August 11–September 3

Guidance, planning, and decision making
Insights for our age

Knowing the spheres: September 4–December 14

Marriage
Sex
Parenting
Money and work
Power
Justice

Knowing Jesus, the true wisdom of God: December 15–December 31

In each day's reflections, text references for Proverbs will be cited only by chapter and verse numbers. (So "10:13" rather than "Proverbs 10:13.") Text references for every other book of the Bible will have chapter and verse numbers accompanied by the name of the book. (So "Psalm 37:29.") Also, words and phrases taken from that day's biblical text that are quoted in the body of the reflection will be in italics rather than within quotation marks.

KNOWING WISDOM

What Is Wisdom?

January 1

> The proverbs of Solomon son of David, king of Israel . . . for understanding proverbs and parables, the sayings and riddles of the wise. (1:1,6)

WHAT IS A PROVERB? A proverb (Hebrew *masal*) is a poetic, terse, vivid, thought-provoking saying that conveys a world of truth in a few words. Modern people do not have a category for proverbs. They are neither absolute commands nor promises, and often they are partial. That is, they need to be put beside other proverbs on the same subject to get the full picture. They are observations about how life works. The point of a proverb, then, is to get rightly related to reality through hard thinking and sustained reflection. A proverb is like hard candy: If you just bite down on it, you get little out of it and may even get a broken tooth. Instead you must meditate on it until the sweetness of insight comes.

Wisdom is not only for "deep thinkers." It is how you get through daily life. It helps you know what to do when your child comes home from school with a black eye, or when you suddenly come into unexpected money, or when you lose your job. What do you do that won't make things worse? Our wisdom will guide us as we grow in the knowledge and image of his Son, Jesus, who is Wisdom itself.

In what area of life do you most need to grow in wisdom?

Prayer: Lord, I'd prefer if you would simply tell me what to do through some inner voice or some book of specific rules for every situation. Instead I hear you calling me to grow into a wise person who discerns what to do. Help me to answer that call, and give me understanding. Amen.

January 2

The proverbs of Solomon son of David, king of Israel: for gaining wisdom. (1:1–2a)

NOT JUST MORAL. The main word for *wisdom* in Proverbs (Hebrew *hokma*) includes being moral but goes beyond that. It is making the right choice even when there are no clear moral laws telling you explicitly what to do. Some decisions require only knowledge (like the proper medicine to take) and some only compliance with rules (like whether to commit adultery or not). But no Bible verse will tell you exactly whom to marry, which job to take, whether to move or stay put. Yet a wrong decision can be disastrous. And there are no explicit moral laws against character flaws such as abrasiveness, impulsiveness, emotional fragility, and disorganization, yet they can also damage the course of your life.[6]

If God had given us a hundred-volume set of rules for every situation, we would have relied on the book and our diligence. But when we see what wisdom truly is, we will be driven to look to Jesus, of whom it was said, "What's this wisdom that has been given him?" (Mark 6:2).

Have you ever seen an example of a good and moral person who was very unwise?

Prayer: Lord, I tend to be smug about my right beliefs. I love to think I know the truth, but even when I do, I don't know how to use it. Please bring into my life what is necessary for wisdom to grow, and then remind me that I received it from you. Amen.

January 3

The proverbs of Solomon son of David, king of Israel: for gaining wisdom and instruction. (1:1–2a)

DISCIPLINE. Surrounding the Hebrew word *hokma* in these early verses of Proverbs are many near synonyms that shed much light on what wisdom is. The Hebrew *musar* (*instruction* in 1:2–3) means training with strong accountability. It means being drilled under an instructor who often gets up in your face. So wisdom often comes through the pain of personal confrontation by friends (27:5), or from learning from one's mistakes (26:11), or from the suffering that God judiciously allows into our lives (3:11–12). Every time your car breaks down and you have to figure out how to fix it, you become "wiser" about cars. So it is with life. Proust wrote that wisdom can be discovered only "after a journey through the wilderness which no one can make for us, which no one can spare us."[7]

To become wise is to become a disciplined person, given not to impulsiveness but to self-examination, to circumspection, and to clear thinking. It is to become a resilient person who through hard knocks has become poised and resourceful. As an athlete becomes physically competent only after rigorous training, so wisdom is hard won.

Can you see in your own life how God has used difficulty to make you wiser?

Prayer: Father, children need discipline even though they may rebel and resist when they receive it. An undisciplined child, however, will have a miserable life. Forgive me for not recognizing the hard knocks and disappointments of my life as your fatherly discipline. Let me learn wisdom from them all. Amen.

January 4

For gaining wisdom and instruction; for understanding words of insight. (1:2)

DISCERNMENT. Another aspect of wisdom is *insight* (Hebrew *bina*). This means the ability to notice distinctions and shades of difference where others see only a blur. Kathy can see small but significant differences between the performances of ballet dancers that Tim can't perceive, and he can notice fine differences in the quality of a curveball that are lost on her. We are, as it were, wiser than each other in the fields of dance and sport.

Biblical wisdom, however, brings discernment to the skill of the daily living of life itself. To be wise is to recognize multiple options and possible courses of action where others can imagine only one or two. Wisdom discerns multiple dimensions to people's motives and character, rather than putting everyone into the binary categories of "good people" and "bad people." Discernment is also the ability to tell the difference not just between right and wrong but also among good, better, and best. Christians find that as Christ's love in our hearts grows, so does "depth of insight" (Philippians 1:9). His love heals the self-absorbed ego and enables us to notice and be sensitive to others around us.

Where has God been enabling you to see fine distinctions that you didn't see before?

Prayer: Lord, our world seems divided between the people who see everything as black or white and those who see everything as gray. Deliver me from both legalism and relativism—neither is wise. Give me the humility and discernment that is necessary for having a wise heart. Amen.

January 5

For receiving instruction in prudent behavior . . . for giving prudence to those who are simple, knowledge and discretion to the young. (1:3–4)

DISCRETION. The Hebrew words *haskel* (*prudent behavior*) *ormah* (*prudence*) and *mezimma* (*discretion*) all mean to plan and live strategically. Just as there are moral people who are not wise, so there are visionaries who see where we should go but have little idea of the practical steps for bringing the goal into reality. To be wise is to anticipate problems without falling into either the danger of overconfidence or the paralysis of overcaution. It is to know not only what to do but also when to do it. A blessing at the wrong time can have the effect of a curse (27:14). While discernment (January 4) is a form of *in*sight into hearts, discretion is a form of *fore*sight, knowing what kinds of behaviors will lead to what result (22:3).

Wisdom is, in one sense, knowing how to be "successful" at something. But it is wrong to mistake worldly sophistication for godly wisdom, as Adam and Eve did (Genesis 3:6). The ultimate wisdom was seen in Jesus, the suffering servant (Isaiah 52:13) whose success was absolute but not of a kind that the worldly sophisticates of his time could recognize.[8]

Remember a time when you had the discernment to know what to do but not the discretion to know how to accomplish it. What did you learn from that?

Prayer: Lord, I want to be successful, but for many wrong reasons. Do everything necessary—even bringing into my life humbling disappointments—that will teach me to care more about being faithful than about being successful. Only then will I be freed from the pride and fear that prevent true success. Amen.

January 6

Let the wise listen and add to their learning, and let the discerning get guidance. (1:5)

LEARNING. As we can be moral and still be unwise, so it is possible to be very knowledgeable and yet be foolish. A social scientist may know much about the empirical factors that lead to poverty. Yet in actually trying to help a poor family, she might make their lives far worse. So there's knowledge without wisdom. But can you have wisdom without knowledge? No. You have to be knowledgeable about a subject before you can apply it with the discipline, discernment, and discretion of wisdom. So Proverbs calls those who would be wise to *add to their learning.* The Hebrew word *leqah* means extensive study.

To be wise we must understand human nature, how human relationships work, suffering and death, and the character of God himself. Wisdom is wedding thought and experience to become "competent with regard to the realities of life."[9] And among all other things we should study, true wisdom requires deep knowledge of the Scriptures. Even Jesus based his every move on the Bible, quoting Scripture to face and explain his death (Matthew 27:46; Psalm 22:1). How can we be wise without being immersed in the Word of God?

How can you take steps to greatly increase your knowledge of the Bible? In what other areas of life should you be reading now?

Prayer: Lord, I spend far too little time studying and meditating on your Word, and I have no excuse. We always make time for the things we value most. So I ask your forgiveness for not loving your Word and you as you have loved me. Teach me your truth. Amen.

What Is Foolishness?

January 7

"How long will you who are simple love your simple ways? How long will mockers delight in mockery and fools hate knowledge?" (1:22)

THE OPPOSITE OF WISDOM. Throughout the book of Proverbs the opposite of wisdom is called foolishness. In English the word "fool" is little more than an insult. In Proverbs, however, *fools* are people so habitually out of touch with reality that they make life miserable for themselves and all around them. We can't treat our body any way we want without consequences. We can't treat people any way we want and expect to have good friends and a strong family. We can't all live selfish lives and expect the social fabric to remain intact. Fools, however, do all these things and therefore sow and reap discord and destruction.

There are various forms of foolishness, as we will see. But the ultimate foolishness is to make anything the center of our lives besides God. That will always lead to disappointment and breakdown. Jesus describes the "foolish man" whose home is built on sand instead of on the solid rock of Christ's word and wisdom (Matthew 7:24–26). Fools fail to see these boundaries embedded in reality—physical, psychological, relational, and spiritual. They step outside them and wonder why they sink.

Where have you seen most recently—either in your life or someone else's—the bitter fruit of foolishness?

Prayer: Lord, my heart so often wants to deny reality, but that is foolish. Reality in this fallen world is both wonderful and terrible. Help me see it for what it is, and teach me to walk wisely in it. Amen.

January 8

"How long will you who are simple love your simple ways? How long will mockers delight in mockery and fools hate knowledge?" (1:22)

THE MOCKER. Three kinds of fools are mentioned in this verse. The *mockers* (Hebrew *lesim*) prove it is not mental capacity but attitude that determines whether we become wise or foolish.[10] At the root of mockers' character is a high pride that hates submitting to anyone (21:24). Their strategy is to debunk everything, acting very smug and knowing in the process. Mockers, though fools, appear to most eyes as worldly-wise and highly sophisticated.

Some things, of course, deserve critique and even satire. Even God mocks sometimes. However, to "sit in the company of mockers" (Psalm 1:1) is to make cynicism and sneering a habitual response. Habitual mocking will harden you and poison relationships. "To 'see through' all things is the same as not to see."[11] We live in a postmodern age that encourages deconstruction and in an Internet age that makes mocking and scoffing easy and reasoned discourse difficult. So we must resist the enormous cultural pressure to become mockers. Contrast this with Jesus: "He will not quarrel or cry out. . . . A bruised reed he will not break, and a smoldering wick he will not snuff out, till he has brought justice through to victory" (Matthew 12:19–20).

When have you been tempted to roll your eyes and dismiss someone rather than engaging with them?

Prayer: Lord, help me to avoid the world's shortcuts to looking wise—the cynical air, the inside joke, the sighs and feigned sadness about how stupid everyone is. Let me despise no one and respect everyone, even if I am correcting them. Amen.

January 9

"How long will you who are simple love your simple ways? How long will mockers delight in mockery and fools hate knowledge?" (1:22)

THE SIMPLE. Every sort of fool is out of touch with reality, but each kind in a different way. The next fool in this list is the Hebrew *pĕthiy*—the *simple*. This kind of foolishness is gullibility. "The simple believe anything" (14:15). They are too easily led and influenced. Like children, they may be overimpressed by the spectacular and dramatic, or they may need approval too much and so be taken in by forceful personalities who give it to them. They will support dictatorial leaders who promise them peace and prosperity. They can be intellectually lazy, not wanting to ponder and think out a matter. They are also likely to fall for get-rich-quick schemes (12:11).[12]

The simple can change and learn sense (19:25) but they can also "inherit folly" (14:18)—graduate into being full-blown fools. Nevertheless, we should be careful not to equate credulity and naïveté with a lack of sophistication. We once pastored an entire congregation of somewhat unsophisticated people, but they were by no means simple. You can lack sophistication, as the world assesses it, and still be wise. And you can be sophisticated—well-off, well connected, and educated—but still be simple.

Whom have you met who you thought was rather simple but turned out not to be so? What traits did they reveal?

Prayer: Lord God, while I see the "mocker" in me, I also see the "simple." I certainly need human approval too much and I am also intellectually impatient, not wanting to think things out. I have often asked you to save me from my sin. Now, Lord, save me from my foolishness. Amen.

January 10

"How long will you who are simple love your simple ways? How long will mockers delight in mockery and fools hate knowledge?" (1:22)

THE OBSTINATE. The most common word used for fools in Proverbs is the Hebrew *kĕciyl*, the obstinate. The main mark of *fools* is that they are opinionated, wise in their own eyes, unable to learn knowledge or be corrected.

Child psychologist Jerome Kagan discovered that children are born with one of three basic temperaments that determine how they instinctively respond to difficulty.[13] Some respond with anxiety and withdrawal, some with aggression and assertive action, and some with optimism and an effort to win through by being social and cordial.[14] Each default works well in some situations. But Kagan argued that, unless parents intervene, children's natural temperament will dominate, and they won't learn how to act wisely in situations in which their habitual response is inappropriate or even deadly. In other words, we are naturally obstinate and unwise. Modern culture insists that we should let children be themselves, but what feels most natural to us might be disastrous (22:15). To become wise, the anxious must learn to be bolder, the bold to be cautious, and the chronically sunny to be more thoughtful. Only in Jesus do we see one who does not habitually assert or withdraw but always responds appropriately to the situation with perfect wisdom (John 11:23–25, 32–35).

Where are you most opinionated and least open to new ideas or criticism?

Prayer: Father, I see Jesus moving through life without a wrong word or false step. He knows exactly when to be quiet and when to speak, when to correct and when to affirm. How I want to be like him! Please begin to re-create his wisdom in me, through your Word and Spirit. Amen.

January 11

A troublemaker and a villain, who goes about with a corrupt mouth, who winks maliciously with his eye, signals with his feet and motions with his fingers, who plots evil with deceit in his heart—he always stirs up conflict. Therefore disaster will overtake him in an instant; he will suddenly be destroyed—without remedy. (6:12–15)

THE TROUBLEMAKER. Another kind of fool is the troublemaker. The mark of this person is constant *conflict* (6:14). This is the opposite of the peacemaker (Matthew 5:9), the bridge builder whose careful, gracious answers (15:1) disarm and defuse tensions. The troublemaker instead stirs them up. This is not the person who disturbs the false peace with an insistence on honesty. Rather, this is someone who always feels the need to protest and complain rather than overlooking a slight or wrong (19:11). When troublemakers do contend, they do not present the other side fairly. Their corrupt mouths produce deceptive omissions, half-truths, and innuendo. Their body language (winking, signaling) creates a hostile situation rather than one that leads to resolution.

Troublemakers tell themselves and others that they just like to "speak truth to power." But disaster will overtake the troublemakers (6:15). As time goes on, it becomes clearer that the troublemakers themselves are a reason that conflict always follows in their wake. They can be permanently discredited by events that expose them for what they are. But the ultimate reason for their downfall is that "the Lord hates . . . a person who stirs up conflict in the community" (6:16,19).

If you have been involved in a series of conflicts, is it because you have the traits of a troublemaker? Do you know any troublemakers you should confront?

Prayer: Lord, thank you for this warning. It is right to tell the truth, even to people who do not welcome it. But show me if I am speaking the truth in love or instead asserting it unnecessarily or harshly. I want to be valiant for truth, not a troublemaker. Give me the wisdom to discern the difference. Amen.

> Go to the ant, you sluggard; consider its ways and be wise! It has no commander, no overseer or ruler, yet it stores its provisions in summer and gathers its food at harvest. . . . A little sleep, a little slumber, a little folding of the hands to rest—and poverty will come on you like a thief and scarcity like an armed man. (6:6–11)

THE SLUGGARD. Another kind of fool in Proverbs is the sluggard. The wise are self-starters, needing only internal motivation, not threats, to do their work (6:7). They also are not impulsive, instead practicing delayed gratification (verse 8). In contrast, the sluggard makes constant excuses for apparently small lapses (*a little . . . a little . . . a little*) but then is surprised when he is assaulted by *poverty* (verses 10–11). "He . . . deceives himself by the smallness of his surrenders. So, by inches and minutes, his opportunity slips away."[15]

In *Hillbilly Elegy* the author tells of Bob, who worked with him at a tile warehouse with his girlfriend. Bob missed work once a week, was chronically late, and took many breaks each day, lasting over half an hour each. His girlfriend missed work every third day and never gave advance notice. When they were fired, after many warnings, Bob was furious. The author concludes, convincingly, that too many today are "immune . . . to hard work," and that what used to be thought of as good, reasonable jobs are now seen as demanding unreasonable standards.[16] The result is social decay, as Proverbs warned. Contrast this with Jesus, who said, "My Father is always at his work to this very day, and I too am working" (John 5:17).

Is there any area of your life that is "slipping away" because you are not getting to work on it?

Prayer: Lord, it is wrong to overwork, driven by a need to succeed and please others. But it is equally wrong and destructive to be lazy. Here, as in so many other areas, I need divine aid to strike the godly balance. Help me, Lord! Amen.

January 13

For their feet rush into evil, they are swift to shed blood. How useless to spread a net where every bird can see it! These men lie in wait for their own blood; they ambush only themselves! Such are the paths of all who go after ill-gotten gain; it takes away the life of those who get it. (1:16–19)

TRAPPING YOURSELF. No bird of the air would be stupid enough to fly into a visible trap (1:17). But even the birds are wiser than those who think they can get up the ladder by trampling on someone else. Those who do wrong to others are lying in wait for their own blood. They *ambush . . . themselves*—something the stupidest animal would not do.

The New Testament makes the same point, that gaining the world at others' expense means losing your soul (Mark 8:36). How does it happen? When you are ruthless to others, you unleash your heart's capacity for cruelty and selfishness. Those appetites get out of your control and lead to bad decisions.[17] When you live to satisfy not others but only yourself, you will be eternally unsatisfied. Jesus, the ultimate teacher of wisdom, tells us we must lose our lives in service to God and others in order to find them (Matthew 16:25).

Have you ever done something selfish that ricocheted back onto you? How did that incident illustrate the gospel principle "Lose yourself to find yourself"?

Prayer: Lord, my heart tells me that I have to make the pursuit of my happiness the primary thing. But then my heart stays empty. Instead of seeking happiness, I will seek you and say, "Come what may." And only then will I be happy in the end. Amen.

"Since you disregard all my advice and do not accept my rebuke, I in turn will laugh when disaster strikes you; I will mock when calamity overtakes you." (1:25–26)

ABSURDITY. When disaster strikes the foolish, Wisdom *laughs*. Is this cruel? No. Wisdom here is a representative figure, and the laughter is not coldheartedness but a way to convey "the absurdity of choosing folly."[18] Albert Camus argued that our hearts long for love without parting, but a universe without God gives us only "the conscious certainty of death without hope."[19] This chronic lack of fulfillment Camus called "the Absurd." He saw life as one long black comedy of incurably, unchangeably seeking things out of life that it simply cannot provide.

Camus thought there was no God. Proverbs knows there is, but it agrees that life lived without God will bring futility, because the things of the world cannot fulfill the deepest heart longings. You can never get out of romance, money, and accomplishment the fulfillment that only a relationship with God can bring. So life in a world without God will indeed feel futile and absurd. "The expectation of the righteous ends in joy, but the hopes of the wicked come to nothing" (10:28).[20]

Are you experiencing frustration and futility, even a sense of meaninglessness? Is there something in this world that has failed to satisfy? What can you do about that?

Prayer: Lord, older books and movies ended with good defeating evil, but today they depict life as dark and ambiguous, with no happy endings. Both views of the world are simplistic and foolish. You assure me that my life's story will contain beauty and absurdity and will end in eternity. Renew that assurance in me today. Amen.

January 15

> "For the waywardness of the simple will kill them, and the complacency of fools will destroy them; but whoever listens to me will live in safety and be at ease, without fear of harm." (1:32–33)

COMPLACENCY. As we have seen, the mark of the fool is to be wise in his own eyes. This leads to the deadly spiritual condition of smug *complacency*. There is nothing more foolish than to think you have life under control when it is not controllable. The classic example is Jesus' parable of the Rich Fool (Luke 12:19–20). No matter what type of designer life you think you have put together for yourself, bereavement, illness, betrayal, and financial disaster happen to everyone. No amount of wealth, success, power, or planning can make you impervious to them.

Fools live in a dream of metaphysical self-sufficiency. They think they have everything sorted, and the complacency leads to disaster. But the opposite of complacency—anxiety—is no solution. We can lose our overconfidence and still be at ease, without fear if we remember that we have the omnipotent, sovereign Lord of the universe as our father. Christians also remind their hearts that if God did not spare us his own Son, how will he not give us whatever we need (Romans 8:32)?

If things are going pretty well for you, are you getting complacent? If things are not going well, are you getting anxious? How can you avoid both?

Prayer: Lord, I have been so often whiplashed back and forth between thinking I have everything under control and feeling panic that everything is out of control. Neither is the case. You are in control, and until I rest in that, I'll be a miserable fool. Amen.

January 16

He mocks proud mockers but shows favor to the humble and oppressed. (3:34)

MOCKING THE MOCKERS. The mocker "wears a perpetual sneer."[21] His talent for cutting insults and invective looks like intellectual sophistication. Behind the mask of witticisms, however, is a vastly inflated confidence in his own opinion and intelligence. That is why here proud *mockers* are contrasted with the humble.

Mockers are especially influential with the simple, among whom they often rise up to become ringleaders. In our current cultural atmosphere, the most socially sought after people are the greatest scoffers and debunkers. But there is nothing worse than looking up to mockers, who make it impossible for you to develop loyalty or reverence for anything. They do so not with heartfelt arguments but with sighs, snarky comments, and arched eyebrows.

The final judgment on them is deadly and fitting: [The Lord] mocks proud mockers (3:34). He "opposes the proud but shows favor to the humble" (1 Peter 5:5). The ultimate example is how God came into the world, not as a proud mocker but as one who is "meek and lowly in heart" (Matthew 11:29, KJV).

Do you have any friends or people you admire who are mockers? Are you in any way drawn to them for this trait?

Prayer: Lord, the world tells us that the superconfident and self-promoting are the ones who get respect, but it's only temporary. Actually, we reap what we sow. Lovers are loved, and mockers are mocked. Help me to remember this all day today. I so need it! Amen.

How Do We Become Wise?

January 17

> If you call out for insight and cry aloud for understanding, and if you look for it as for silver and search for it as for hidden treasure, then you will understand the fear of the LORD and find the knowledge of God. For the LORD gives wisdom; from his mouth come knowledge and understanding. (2:3–6)

UNDERSTAND THE PARADOX. In Proverbs chapters 2 through 4 there's much teaching on how wisdom develops and grows within us. At the start we are confronted with a paradox. Wisdom is something we should seek. Just as Wisdom cries out to us (1:20–21), so we are to *cry aloud* for wisdom (2:3). But after 2:3–4 calls us to the greatest of effort, likening it to searching for hidden treasure, verse 6 tells us that ultimately wisdom is a gift from God. This idea runs through the whole Bible. Philippians 2:12–13 calls us to "work out your salvation with fear and trembling" but immediately adds, "for it is God who works in you to will and to act in order to fulfill his good purpose."

The paradox itself is wise. If it were all up to us, we would labor under crushing anxiety and burn out. But if God only worked apart from us, we would lose all sense of initiative. The paradox gives us enough incentive *and* enough assurance to pursue the knowledge of God all our life long.

Are you pursuing wisdom as you should? If you are, are you being as patient with God as you should? He gives out wisdom in his wise time.

Prayer: Lord, you give us the opportunity to do something and the desire to do it—so when it is accomplished we must admit it was all from you. Yet you require our utmost effort, and in that exertion we grow into the likeness of your son, Jesus. How brilliant you are, my God. Amen.

Thus you will walk in the ways of the good and keep to the paths of the righteous. For the upright will live in the land, and the blameless will remain in it; but the wicked will be cut off from the land, and the unfaithful will be torn from it. (2:20–22)

BE RIGHTEOUS. When Proverbs speaks of the *righteous* and the *wicked,* we think it means the "moral" and the "immoral." That is only partly right. The Hebrew words for righteous—*tzedeq* and *mishpat*—have a strongly social aspect. Bruce Waltke writes: "The righteous are willing to disadvantage themselves to advantage the community; the wicked are willing to disadvantage the community to advantage themselves."[22]

The righteous say, "Much of what I have belongs to the people around me, because it all comes from God and he wants me to love my neighbor." The wicked say, "I can do what I want with my things." Go through Proverbs, reading "righteous" and "wicked" now with this fuller definition in mind, and it will become like a whole new book. It will move you toward living a truly righteous and just life—being not merely personally moral but also committed to social justice. It will also point you to the one who came "not . . . to be served, but to serve, and to give his life as a ransom for many" (Mark 10:45).

In what ways are you disadvantaging yourself, in time and money, for the good of the community in which you live?

Prayer: Lord, I earned my money through the capacities and opportunities that all came from you. Help me to see my time, money, and social connections as given to me by you for the good of those around me. This will be hard, because my culture makes me think I'm poor and don't owe anyone else. Don't let me believe that. Amen.

January 19

My son, if sinful men entice you, do not give in to them. If they say, "Come along with us; let's lie in wait for innocent blood, let's ambush some harmless soul . . ."—my son, do not go along with them, do not set foot on their paths. (1:10–11,15)

DON'T RELY ON PEDIGREE. Here parents warn their son not to take up a life of violence (1:8–19). Middle-class people will think such an alarm is unnecessary for *their* children. Certainly a mother on Chicago's South Side might need to say this, but not us! Proverbs, however, knows that anyone has the potential to become cruel. When someone is revealed to be a shooter or bomber, the neighbors often say to interviewers, "But he came from such a good family."

The Bible never assumes that family pedigree is any insurance against evil. Nor does it teach that only the poor are prone to violence. The well-off can also "grind the heads of the poor" through legal but ruthless economic practices (Amos 2:6–7). Your middle- and upper-class children "might be tempted to join a firm whose profits rest on exploitation of laborers, on destruction of the environment, or on success at the expense of justice and truth."[23] Don't think that a life of wrongdoing can be avoided just because you come from "a good family."

Are there any ways in which you may be participating in an arrangement that benefits you but is cruel to someone else?

Prayer: Lord, it is so self-serving to imagine that *our* friends and family could never do anything *that* bad. Yes they can, and so can I. Help me create a community that "exhorts one another daily," lest we be "hardened by the deceptive nature of our own sin" (Hebrews 3:13).[24] Amen.

January 20

Out in the open wisdom calls aloud, she raises her voice in the public square; on top of the wall she cries out, at the city gate she makes her speech. (1:20–21)

GET EXPERIENCE. Here Wisdom invites people to learn from her, but she does so not from the ivory tower but outside, in the *public square* and public places of the city. Wisdom is developed only in experience. No matter how hard they study, the graduates of medical school, law school, and business school will become truly wise in their fields only out in the open, that is, in real-life experience.

Proverbs is not an "inspirational" book with statements that immediately jump off the page at you. Wisdom cannot be conveyed by a series of TED talks or "executive briefings." It is inaccessible to people too busy for its method. It comes through first with experience and then with deep, honest reflection on that experience. It emerges only as we ask searching questions: When did I last see this illustrated in my life or someone else's? Where do I need to practice this? How would my life be different if I did? What wrong thinking and attitudes result when I forget this? Remember how often Jesus, our teacher, spoke in parables and answered questions with other questions, trying to get us to reflect, think, and grow in wisdom (Matthew 13:10; Luke 20:4; John 16:29).

What has happened to you recently that was significantly good or difficult? Have you reflected on it with others to learn wisdom from it?

Prayer: Lord God, I know far too much about the Bible that I have not prayed and obeyed into my life. Rescue and help me. Keep me from being just a hearer of your Word and not a doer of it. Don't let me deceive myself (James 1:22). Amen.

> "Then they will call to me but I will not answer; they will look for me but will not find me, since they hated knowledge and did not choose to fear the LORD." (1:28–29)

DON'T DELAY. Because wisdom comes not through acquisition of knowledge but through long experience and reflection, it takes years to produce. What happens, then, if suddenly you come to a crisis that demands great discernment and self-control? If you haven't learned the hard-won habits of wisdom—of resting in Christ when other comforts are removed, of discerning choices among the bad, the good, and the best—you cannot suddenly develop them overnight, any more than you can get ready for the Olympics overnight.

John Newton wrote, "The grace of God is as necessary to create a right temper . . . on the breaking of a china plate as on the death of an only son."[25] That is, only if we learn grace and wisdom in smaller daily disappointments will we be ready for the great ones. In the crisis, you will long for wisdom, but it will not answer. "There are points of no return; when the storm is upon us, it is too late to seek shelter. Moments of decision pass and are gone forever. Timing is all."[26]

Are you devoting time to developing wisdom? Begin by assessing how much planned time you give to, first, Bible study and, second, personal accountability with Christian friends.

Prayer: Lord, I know you won't give me more than I can bear (1 Corinthians 10:13). But *I* can fail to put on all the spiritual armor you give me (Ephesians 6:10–18) and thereby put myself in harm's way. Give me the real thing, the hard-won wisdom. I'm ready to do what is necessary to receive it. Amen.

January 22

> Trust in the LORD with all your heart and lean not on your own understanding. (3:5)

IDENTIFY YOUR IDOLS. Proverbs chapter 3 lists six things that can serve as the marks of a wise person and at the same time are the means for growing in wisdom. The first is *trust in the Lord.* You can believe in God yet still trust something else for your real significance and happiness—which is therefore your real God. We hide how we do this from ourselves, and it is only when something goes wrong with, say, your career or your family, that you realize it is much more important to you than the Lord himself.

What does this have to do with wisdom? Everything. There are excessive emotions surrounding things you make the functional trust of your heart, whether it's your career, wealth, spouse, children, or some romantic relationship. You will be inordinately shaken, anxious, angry, or despondent if anything threatens them. They cloud your judgment, distort your vision of yourself and the world. Idolatries of the heart lead to foolishness in the life. The ultimate remedy for idolatry is the gospel. We won't need to justify ourselves by works—by success or romance or achievement—if we are freely justified by faith in Jesus (Romans 3:21–24).

What is the best candidate in your life for an alternate "god"?

Prayer: Lord, when the Israelites prayed to you for help you did not respond, but when they "put away their idols," you began work in their lives (Judges 10:10–18). I too have run to you with my requests without the willingness to root out my deep, false gods. O Lord, "help me find my All in Thee" and in nothing else. Amen.

January 23

Trust in the Lord with all your heart and lean not on your own understanding; in all your ways submit to him, and he will make your paths straight. (3:5–6)

SUBMIT TO HIS WORD. A second mark and means of wisdom is to submit to God *in all your ways*—every area of life—and *not on your own understanding.* Our culture tells us to submit everything to our understanding, to question everything including the Bible. But everyone must choose something to not question. Modern people don't question their right and ability to question everything. So everyone is living by faith in some ultimate authority. Proverbs calls us to make it God's Word, not our reason and intuition.

The Bible can guide you in all your ways, even when there is not a specific verse for every life situation. As you immerse yourself in the Bible's story of a personal God who made us and saved us for a relationship with him, it makes every part of life—how you spend your money, relate to people, allocate your time, and see yourself—look different than if you didn't believe the story. Then wisdom grows as you live daily life shaped by the biblical narrative and divine realities.

Are you seeking to understand the Bible's main themes and "big picture" story rather than merely seeking inspiration from individual Bible verses?

Prayer: Lord, I want to not just study your Word like a book but to inwardly digest it, making it part of me. Let your Word "dwell richly" within me so I can have your wisdom to guide myself and my loved ones (Colossians 3:16). Do this for the sake of Jesus, the Word made flesh. Amen.

January 24

Do not be wise in your own eyes; fear the LORD and shun evil. This will bring health to your body and nourishment to your bones. (3:7–8)

BE TEACHABLE. The third mark and means of wisdom is a willingness to take advice. Fools are *wise in [their] own eyes.* Some take no advice at all. Other fools listen to only one kind of advice. For example, teenagers tend to be very averse to the advice of older people but rely primarily on the counsel of their peers. Many of us listen only to people of our own race or class or political persuasion and not to others.

Wisdom is to see things through as many other eyes as possible, through the Word of God and through the eyes of your friends, of people from other races, classes, and political viewpoints, and of your critics. Wise women and men create a company of counselors around them—mentors and advisers and friends and people from whom they can get a "second opinion." The gospel is the greatest resource for creating teachability. It shows us that we are sinners, yet its deep assurance of God's unconditional love for us in Christ makes it possible to face our flaws without denial.

Is there a person or kind of person you should be listening to but have not made the effort to do so?

Prayer: Lord, I have a heart that does not love correction, and I live in a society that tells me to trust only my own, inmost feelings. All things inside and outside of me seem to conspire against my efforts to become a teachable student of your Word and of life. I seek a broken and contrite spirit. Amen.

January 25

Honor the LORD with your wealth, with the firstfruits of all your crops; then your barns will be filled to overflowing, and your vats will brim over with new wine. (3:9–10)

BE GENEROUS. The fourth mark and means of wisdom is generosity. Inordinate love of money and confidence in its power blind us, and the best way to break money's power over us is through giving lots of it away. The *firstfruits* of a crop were to be given to God and the poor even though it wasn't certain how big the harvest would actually be.

A farmer told his pastor that one of his cows had unexpectedly given birth to two calves, "and when I sell them, I'll give the proceeds I make on one of them to the church." A few weeks later the man informed his pastor, "I'm sorry to say it, Reverend, but the Lord's calf died." For many of us, it's always the Lord's calf that dies. We don't give to God in a planned, committed way. We wait to see if we have the money to do everything we want and then give to God only when there is excess. In contrast, though he was infinitely rich, Jesus gave not just the excess but all of his wealth and even his life to save us (2 Corinthians 8:9).[27]

Can you devise a plan in which you could increase the percentage of your income that you give away over the next three years?

Prayer: Father, help me to think out how I should practice the "firstfruits" principle with my wealth. Help me to give away deliberately, not impulsively. Let my giving be sacrificial, not a token. And let me do it gladly, not begrudgingly, remembering how Jesus gave not just his possessions but his own blood. Amen.

January 26

My son, do not despise the LORD's discipline, and do not resent his rebuke, because the LORD disciplines those he loves, as a father the son he delights in. (3:11–12)

LEARN FROM ADVERSITY. The fifth mark and means of wisdom has to do with adversity and trouble in life. Often a generous heart and life can lead to increasing financial prosperity (3:10). But verses 11–12 show this is by no means an absolute rule. The world is "riddled with evils, mysteries, and troubles beyond human grasping and fixing."[28] The mark of wisdom is to be ready for suffering. If you aren't, you aren't competent with regard to the realities of life. But suffering is also a *discipline* for growth in wisdom. It can drive you toward God into greater love and strength or away from him into hardness of heart.

Given that suffering is inevitable, and it's going to make you either wiser or more foolish, what should you do? You should accept your troubles as means for spiritual growth and part of the plan of our loving heavenly Father. If you can do nothing else, you can always glorify God by having a trusting attitude toward him as you suffer, rather than becoming bitter. And the best way to do that is to look at God the Son suffering infinitely for you. That will help you trust him as you suffer.

Are you ready for adversity? Why or why not?

Prayer: Lord, when things are going wrong for me, the last things I want to do are to pray and to trust you. Yet I've come to see that if I just cling to you in prayer during the stormy times, I'm spiritually stronger, not weaker for it. Please remind me of what I am saying today when the next time comes! Amen.

January 27

> Do not withhold good from those to whom it is due, when it is in your power to act. Do not say to your neighbor, "Come back tomorrow and I'll give it to you"—when you already have it with you. (3:27–28)

DO JUSTICE. The sixth mark and means of wisdom in Proverbs chapter 3 is a concern for justice. The *good* that we must give to our neighbor means practical aid for an economic or physical need. It is striking that the text adds that this is not simply a matter of charity but is your neighbor's *due.* To not care for them when they are in need is not merely a lack of charity; it is injustice.[29] Put bluntly: If you have things your neighbor doesn't have, share them, because he or she has a right to the part of the world over which God has made you a temporary steward.

John Calvin wrote, "We are not to consider what men merit of themselves, but to look upon the image of God . . . to which we owe all honor and love. . . . You will say, 'He has deserved something far different of me.' Yet what has the Lord deserved?"[30] Verse 28 goes even further and tells us not to delay doing good. Jesus' parable of the Good Samaritan (Luke 10:27–36) defines our neighbor as anyone we encounter who is in need.

If you are involved with your needy neighbors, it will teach you wisdom. Are you?

Prayer: Father, I live in the most competitive society ever, and so I get fixated on what people "merit of themselves." Let me remember that every human being, even the most flawed and broken, is of infinite value to you. Let me go beyond the platitudes to truly love my neighbors with my worldly goods. Amen.

January 28

The beginning of wisdom is this: Get wisdom. Though it cost all you have, get understanding. Cherish her, and she will exalt you; embrace her, and she will honor you. (4:7–8)

JUST GET IT. Proverbs chapter 4 is filled with the repeated exhortation "do not forsake" wisdom. The message is clear: Never, ever give up in your pursuit of wisdom. Do absolutely anything to get it, whatever it costs you. Why? Because it is more costly to not have it. You will make decisions that lead to one difficulty and disaster after another. So do whatever it takes.

Already we have seen some of what that entails: identification of your heart trusts, immersion in and obedience to the Word of God, friendships and openness to critique, patient learning in adversity, and personal involvement in real service to others, especially the most needy. These must be practiced reflectively through long experience, within a community of people seeking the same wisdom. They will lead to knowing God, knowing yourself, knowing the human heart and its ways, and knowing the times and seasons. And your decisions and choices will become wiser. We can paraphrase verse 7 like this: "Here's how you get wisdom: Just get it!" Wisdom comes not to the most fortunate or intelligent but to those most determined to find it.

How determined are you to get wisdom—really?

Prayer: Lord, I have set my heart on wisdom, but I confess that my spiritual resolve in the past has often flagged. My will is weak. So, to help me seek wisdom, capture my heart with a vivid view of Jesus setting his face to go up to Jerusalem to die for me (Isaiah 50:7; Luke 9:31). Amen.

The Case for Wisdom

January 29

> "To you, O people, I call out; I raise my voice to all mankind. You who are simple, gain prudence; you who are foolish, set your hearts on it." (8:4–5)

FOR EVERYONE. Proverbs chapter 8 makes a grand case for the supreme importance of godly wisdom. True wisdom cries out to *all* people (verse 4), including even the *simple*—those who are extremely gullible and clueless (verse 5). No one needs to remain a fool.

Perhaps the greatest encouragement in this passage is easily missed. Wisdom is literally seeking us. Proverbs 8 depicts Wisdom as an actual person, "so that our own search, earnest as it has to be . . . is a response, not an uncertain quest."[31] Who is that person? The New Testament reveals it to be Jesus himself, "the power of God and the wisdom of God" (1 Corinthians 1:24). The Greek philosophers believed that behind the universe there was a cosmic principle, the *Logos*, that only the educated and cultured could discover. But the Gospel of John reveals that the *Logos* behind the universe is Jesus—a cosmic person—who can be known and loved. In the end, the main way to become wise is to have a personal relationship with him to *set our heart* on him. And anyone can do that, regardless of status or education.

How can you make your relationship with Jesus Christ less formal and more personal?

Prayer: Lord, I thank you for being a God for *all* people. Your wisdom is not just for the mystics and philosophers. It is for anyone who can believe in Jesus Christ. "I praise you . . . because you have hidden these things from the wise and learned, and revealed them to little children" (Matthew 11:25). Amen.

"I, wisdom, dwell together with prudence; I possess knowledge and discretion. To fear the LORD is to hate evil; I hate pride and arrogance, evil behavior and perverse speech." (8:12–13)

THE SAFETY. To be wise is to have the *prudence* and *discretion* that bring success (verse 12). Then verse 13 speaks of hating arrogance and pride. We must never divide verse 12 from 13. Why? David A. Hubbard notes that arrogance and conceit are faults "to which shrewd and clever persons are especially prone."[32] Without awe and wonder—fear before God—success can and usually does lead to a sense of superiority and hubris. Then the spiral begins. Pride moves you toward foolishness, such as overconfidence in your intuition, which ultimately results in bad decisions and downfall.

Moral character is to success as the safety is to a gun: It keeps you from shooting yourself with it. "True wisdom is canny and resourceful," writes Kidner, and that is the reason that only "being rooted in the fear of the Lord [can make it] free from the faults of worldly wisdom."[33] Don't miss the fact that the word *hate* is used twice, and the second time it is spoken by Wisdom. "What is repugnant to godliness is repugnant to wisdom: there is no conflict of interest."[34]

If you have been enjoying any success, have you been secretly taking credit for it? Are you seeing it as the gift of God that it is?

Prayer: Lord, my heart fears that if I am kind rather than ruthless, I will not be successful. But I see what your Word says, that humble goodness is the most practical in the end, because it walks in the same path that Jesus did, who triumphed through service and love. Amen.

January 31

Counsel and sound judgment are mine; I have insight, I have power.... [B]y me princes govern, and nobles—all who rule on earth. . . . With me are riches and honor, enduring wealth and prosperity. My fruit is better than fine gold; what I yield surpasses choice silver. (8:14, 16, 18–19)

BY-PRODUCTS. All the things that create success—the right plan (*counsel*), the strategic resourcefulness to carry it out (*sound judgment*), and the boldness to execute (*power*)—belong to wisdom (verse 14). All accomplishment that is not mere luck is grounded in the attributes of wisdom.[35]

The wise are practical. Yet true wisdom still sees success as only a by-product—not the main goal. Wisdom brings *enduring wealth*—a Hebrew term that means an inner richness of joy and divine favor that is better than fine gold (verse 19). Perhaps it would be best to say that real wisdom tends toward prosperity, but prosperity itself is never the wise person's ultimate goal. The wise do what they do not because it is satisfying or because it works but because it is right and loving to God and his creation. Success may come or not—but that is not the point. If you see success as a possible by-product, not the main goal of wisdom, then you will indeed be wise. Even if "your hands shall flow with gold," yet "over you gold shall have no dominion."[36]

Do you tend to be either too concerned with results and practical success or too unconcerned?

Prayer: Lord, I pray for my community, country, and society. There is no social order without your wisdom, and even those who do not acknowledge you are dependent on it. Give us wise leaders, not fools. Give us peace so we can joyfully serve you and our neighbor "in all godly quietness."[37] Amen.

February 1

I was there when he set the heavens in place, when he marked out the horizon on the face of the deep, when he established the clouds above and fixed securely the fountains of the deep, when he gave the sea its boundary so the waters would not overstep his command, and when he marked out the foundations of the earth. (8:27–29)

FOUNDATIONS. Wisdom was with God when he marked out the *foundations* of the world. The New Testament teaches the agent of creation was Jesus, the eternal Word and wisdom of God (John 1:1–14; Hebrews 1:1–4).

Because the Bible is the Word of our creator, it is our soul's "owner's manual." The things it commands are the very things we were created to do. So godly wisdom comes from relating to God not as just a general divine being but as our creator (February 22). But if God's wisdom is Jesus, then we must also understand the gospel in order to be wise (1 Corinthians 1:24). The logic of the gospel—that you are an undeserving sinner *and* yet an unconditionally loved child of God at the same time—brings a unique combination of humility and confidence that makes you wise in a way nothing else can (February 9). Biblical wisdom, then, takes us back to the very *foundations of the earth*. The only wisdom that works in daily life is that same wisdom that created and will redeem the world.

How can thinking of the Bible as your "owner's manual" help you better accept and use it in your life?

Prayer: Lord, I have been perplexed by Proverbs' dual call to not be "wise in my own eyes" and yet to face life with confidence and resolve. How can I do both? But the gospel is the answer. I am a loved failure, a righteous-in-him sinner. This is truly the beginning of wisdom. Amen.

February 2

Then I was constantly at his side. I was filled with delight day after day, rejoicing always in his presence, rejoicing in his whole world and delighting in mankind. (8:30–31)

WISDOM'S JOY. The Father and the Son delighted in the world they made and in us. We see beauty in things when they are rightly related to one another.[38] Thus an arch is more beautiful to us than a rock field, and love is more beautiful than hate. The more we discern how the parts of a piece of music, or of a flower, all fit together, the more we delight in the music and the flower, not for what it can do for us but for what it is in itself, as part of God's creation. Wisdom is essentially about discerning and forming the right relationships and *rejoicing* in them.[39]

God created us simply for the joy and love of it. He loves us not instrumentally—for what he can get out of us—but for us. So it is the height of wisdom to love God for himself alone, and to value human beings not simply for what we can get from them but as beings who reflect the image of our maker (Genesis 1:26).

Next time you face a case of unanswered prayer, ask yourself: Do you love God for God himself or for the things you get from him?

Prayer: Lord, I am startled by this teaching that the heart of wisdom is joy and delight in things for themselves. My modern life makes me too busy to stop and ponder "the work of thy hands" until it triggers praise to my maker and redeemer. Let me take time for beauty. Amen.

She has sent out her servants, and she calls from the highest point of the city, "Let all who are simple come to my house!" To those who have no sense she says, "Come, eat my food and drink the wine I have mixed. Leave your simple ways and you will live; walk in the way of insight." (9:3–6)

WISDOM'S BANQUET. The woman Wisdom calls us to find the way to her *house* where there is a feast waiting. Great food represents the desires and appetites of our hearts. "Over time, we grow in wisdom or folly according to the ultimate loves and commitments that move us."[40] We can't overcome workaholism if we love money and status too much. We can't overcome bitterness or slander if we love our reputation too much. It is not just willpower but a reordering of our desires that will bring wisdom.

The way of wisdom is not the way of quick fixes and dramatic turnarounds. It is the way of long training and discipline. But train the heart, not just the mind and will. Don't just believe in the goodness of God—savor it in worship and prayer. Christians know that the ultimate feast for the soul will be the wedding supper of the Lamb (Revelation 19:6–9), where Jesus, the Lord of the feast, will satisfy us fully, giving us the "best wine" of his saving love (John 2:1–11). Even the foretastes that we get now will heal our restlessness and so make us wise. "The hill of Zion yields a thousand sacred sweets [even] before we reach the heavenly fields and walk the golden streets."[41]

Does your prayer life include much praise and savoring of Jesus, or is it mainly a time of asking for things?

Prayer: Father, I have made many wrong decisions. As I look back on them, I now realize they were less a lack of know-how and more the result of an empty heart. Pour out your love into my heart by the Holy Spirit (Romans 5:5). Amen.

February 4

Whoever corrects a mocker invites insults; whoever rebukes the wicked incurs abuse. Do not rebuke mockers or they will hate you; rebuke the wise and they will love you. Instruct the wise and they will be wiser still; teach the righteous and they will add to their learning. (9:7–9)

WISDOM'S PROGRESS. Life *rebukes* us through the hard knocks of trials and troubles, which show us our weaknesses and foolishness. Friends help us grow through the bracing love of correction. These are the two versions of wisdom's main teaching method—the "comeuppance."[42]

The further you go down the road toward folly, the more you interpret all events as supporting what you always believed anyway. And when things go wrong, you blame others and circumstances for your problems. This hardens your heart rather than softening it, and it makes you less open to counsel than ever. *Instruct the wise and they will be wiser still*, but try to tell the mocker anything and it will make him worse than he was before you tried. In the New Testament, Jesus laid out this principle. "Whosoever has shall be given more" (Matthew 13:12–16). The more wisdom you have, the more wisdom you will gain in every turn in the road of life. The less wisdom you have, the less you will learn from anything. So learn from your mistakes and from criticism—at all costs.

When was the last time you let someone or something change your mind about a significant issue?

Prayer: Lord, when things go wrong—or when I do wrong—help me to drop all my defenses, my blame shifting, and my self-justifications. These are the tools of fools. Like a soldier let me say to you, "No excuse, sir!" and learn what I should learn. Help me start with what happened yesterday. Amen.

February 5

If you are wise, your wisdom will reward you; if you are a mocker, you alone will suffer. (9:12)

WISDOM'S FELLOWSHIP. Ancient wisdom taught that you would thrive as a person only if you put the needs of your family and community above your own self-interest. Our modern culture rejects that entirely. We are told to "be true to ourselves," to decide who we want to be and then to demand that our community and family recognize and honor that regardless of its impact on relationships. Today we sacrifice the good of the group for the absolute freedom of the individual. The result is an increasing number of people who feel disconnected and lonely.

Mockers sneer at the values and beliefs of any community. Thus the mocker has no real friends, and in the end he suffers *alone*. Christians absolutize not the will of either the individual or the community but the will of God. When we believe the gospel, the barriers of pride that divide us are taken away (Ephesians 2:14–16), and the lonely are put into families (Psalm 68:6; John 1:12–13). Salvation leads toward more and deeper relationships but sin toward being alone.

Are your good friendships growing in quantity and quality, or are you letting the busyness and mobility of modern life have their way?

Prayer: Lord, I praise you have made me part of a new people and a new family. It is not easy to be open, or to take the time to cultivate relationships. But I must, first, in order to honor you, my Father, and also so I will never have to suffer alone. Amen.

February 6

[Folly] sits at the door of her house, on a seat at the highest point of the city, calling out to those who pass by, who go straight on their way, "Let all who are simple come to my house!" To those who have no sense she says, "Stolen water is sweet; food eaten in secret is delicious!" (9:14–17)

FOLLY CAN ONLY SMUGGLE. Like Wisdom, Lady Folly also provides food in her house, but it is *stolen*. "Folly and sin are always parasitic of the good that God by Wisdom has made. Folly takes the goods and destroys their goodness by ripping them from their proper place in the coherence of things. . . . Folly has not built her house; she has stolen it."[43]

Many young adults are unreligious and relativistic, insisting that every person has a right to create their own moral values and no one can tell them how to live. Yet they have deep moral convictions against racism and sexism that they insist are true for everyone.[44] Such moral absolutes are smuggled—they don't make sense if there is no God and all morality is culturally relative. In Wisdom's banquet you have all the goods a human being wants—meaning, satisfaction, freedom, identity, and hope. But they are not stolen. They flow naturally out of a relationship with the Lord.

Do you have any friends who smuggle moral absolutes into a relativistic worldview? How can you speak to them about it?

Prayer: Lord, I have many friends who don't believe in God at all but believe intensely in human rights and in the importance of aiding the oppressed. They don't see that these "goods" have been stolen. Help me find ways of explaining that without unnecessarily offending. Open their hearts to their need for you. Amen.

February 7

"Stolen water is sweet; food eaten in secret is delicious!" But little do
they know that the dead are there, that her guests are deep in the
realm of the dead. (9:17–18)

THE WALKING DEAD. Proverbs tells us righteousness brings
life while wickedness leads to death. This may be literally true.
Many of the behaviors promoted in Proverbs—marriage, work,
prudence, emotional self-control—are associated with longer life
spans. "Accept what I say, and the years of your life will be many"
(4:10). However, usually "life" and "death" refer not to length but
to quality of life.[45] Sometimes "to live" refers to having loving relationships (15:27) or to the psychological well-being of a "heart
of peace" (14:30). And sometimes it means the spiritual life that is
fellowship with God (21:21).

To miss out on true life, then, is to enter the realm of death
before your physical life on earth is ended. To live a life cut off
from God, with ever-increasing spiritual blindness, brittleness,
and hardness, is to become a spiritual corpse. Folly's guests
reside *deep in the realm of the dead.* So we must choose life
(Deuteronomy 30:19).

Have you really grasped that having biblical wisdom is a matter of life or death?

Prayer: Father, before I put faith in Jesus I was outwardly alive
but inwardly dead in sin (Ephesians 2:1). Now, though physically
I weaken, inwardly I'm becoming more and more alive (2 Corinthians 4:16). I need to remember what true life and true death
are, especially when I face the inevitable challenges of sickness,
injury, and age. Amen.

February 8

> The fear of the LORD is the beginning of knowledge, but fools despise wisdom and instruction. (1:7)

GOD-CENTEREDNESS. *The fear of the Lord is the beginning* of wisdom the way the alphabet is the beginning of reading. There is no wisdom at all without it. But what is it? There is a kind of fear that is just the dread of punishment (Joshua 2:14). But there is also a standing in awe of someone (Joshua 4:24), with the resulting fear of doing anything to grieve or dishonor the person. It is in this second sense that we must understand the true "fear of the Lord," for it increases the more we admire and praise him in wonder (1 Chronicles 16:25).

There are, then, only two ways of thinking about life. You can "let [the Lord] be your fear" (Isaiah 8:13 KJV)—your life center—or something else will be. Either God's Word will be the unquestioned arbiter of truth or something else will serve that function (public opinion, your own feelings, or human scientific reasoning). Either God and your relationship with him will be the thing you esteem most—and every single other thing will be evaluated in light of that—or your relationship to some other thing (such as money) will define reality.

Do you follow the world's wisdom, namely, that you can understand the world and yourself without reference to God or his Word? Or have you thoughtfully rejected it?

Prayer: Lord, I want to make you "my fear" rather than be both intimidated and enticed by things in this world that can't hold a candle to your power and glory. Make yourself a living, bright reality to my heart. Amen.

February 9

The fear of the LORD is the beginning of knowledge, but fools despise wisdom and instruction. (1:7)

RESPONDING TO GRACE. To our surprise, *the fear of the Lord* increases the more grace and forgiveness are experienced (Psalms 42:2–3, 130:4). But this is key to Proverbs. All the advice for daily living assumes a holy God who nonetheless redeems by grace. A God who accepts only the most moral people will inspire slavish fear of punishment. A God who simply accepts everyone might evoke warm affection. Only a belief that we are lost but freely saved sinners creates a joyful yet awe-filled assurance of his saving love.

This is wisdom's *beginning*, its prerequisite. The deep consolation of his grace heals the heart of the arrogance, hurt feelings, jealousy, self-pity, anxieties, and fear of the future—all forms of self-absorption at the root of bad decisions and character. This fear is of the Lord, Yahweh, the name God revealed to Moses in the burning bush. So wisdom flows not from some god in general but from faith in the biblical God, who led us out of captivity by his power and grace, through the greater Moses, Jesus Christ (Hebrews 3:1–6).

Can you think about how a disbelief in God's grace may lie at the root of many of your problems?

Prayer: Lord, you revealed your burning, infinite beauty and glory to Moses in a simple desert bush. Now, through the grace of Jesus, may you begin to reproduce your holy character in me by allowing my heart to burn with a holy fear of you, my loving God. Amen.

February 10

The fear of the LORD is the beginning of knowledge, but fools despise wisdom and instruction. (1:7)

CHANGING DEEPLY. Faith in Jesus moves us from the dread of punishment to the godly fear that is *the beginning of wisdom*. In Christ we no longer fear God's judicial penalty (Romans 8:1,15). But wisdom requires a genuine hatred of wrongdoing, not just a calculated avoidance of it out of self-interest. The dread of punishment only makes us self-absorbed—worried about being hurt.[46] The true *fear of the Lord* serves him out of joy and high appreciation for who he is. "Even if there were no hell," this kind of loving fear "would still shudder at offending him alone."[47]

The difference between slavish, self-interested fear and the true fear of the Lord is the difference between a mere moralist and a real Christian. There is no wise living unless we have a relationship with him, one in which we obey him out of love for who he is. Only a faith sight of Jesus' sacrificial love for us both humbles us and yet affirms us into the joyful fear of the Lord.[48]

Do you refrain from sins mainly because you hate their consequences? Or do you refrain out of distaste for the sins themselves, as they grieve and offend God?

Prayer: Lord, "give me an undivided heart, that I may fear your name" (Psalm 86:11). Yes—when I do wrong it rebounds on me and I hate that. But make yourself so real to me that I long to do right and be holy for your sake, just to bring you delight. Then I will fear you truly and walk in wisdom. Amen.

February 11

The fear of the LORD leads to life; then one rests content, untouched by trouble. (19:23)

RESTING IN GOD. Those who fear God find God satisfying, and they are contented. The second phrase literally says that they "spend the night" *content,* meaning that God is like a haven for the storm tossed.

How is it possible to live life untouched by trouble? This does not say that we will not have trouble, only that it will not overthrow our contentment. Trouble can take anything away from you except God. Therefore, if God is to you a greater safety, a deeper security, and a more powerful hope than anything else in the world, you fear no trouble. Depending on God in trouble is a spiritual skill that can be learned only *in* trouble. Difficulties take away earthly comforts and then, through prayer and reflection on the Word, we are driven closer to God to get his unique consolations. The process is long and in many parts painful, but the fruit is a spiritual poise that no trouble can dislodge. Jesus promises it to all his disciples (Matthew 11:28–30).

Think of the last time you went through a very difficult season. Did it strengthen or weaken your intimacy with God? Are you more ready for trouble or less?

Prayer: Lord, St. Augustine said our hearts are restless until they find their rest in you. But I freely confess that though I believe in you, I am often discontent. Let your attributes—love, patience, power, justice, mercy—be not abstractions but comforts to me. By your Spirit make yourself real to my heart. Amen.

February 12

> Whoever fears the LORD has a secure fortress, and for their children it will be a refuge. (14:26)

TRUSTING IN GOD. On January 23 we saw that "trusting in the Lord" meant obeying his will whether we like it or not. But there is a second aspect to trusting the Lord. It means accepting what he allows to come into our lives, whether we understand it or not. It trusts him to "in all things work for the good" (Romans 8:28), even if we can't see the whole plan.

This kind of dependent trust in God is like a *secure fortress.* Other people may look to their own reason and talent to handle life. Or they may look to some great leader or a loved one they depend on for everything. The problem is that these "fortresses" are easily captured. Your intelligence and foresight are limited. Loved ones die. Then we are left defenseless. But when our greatest *fear* and ultimate hope is God and his loving, wise plan, then there is nothing that can overthrow us.

Is there some difficulty in your life now that you can accept, not as a good thing in itself but as part of God's wise plan for your life?

Prayer: Lord, when things go wrong for me, I get so angry at you. I don't know why you aren't supporting my brilliant plan for my life! But how dare I think that my plan could be smarter or more loving than yours? I repent. Amen.

February 13

> Whoever fears the LORD has a secure fortress, and for their children it will be a refuge. The fear of the LORD is a fountain of life, turning a person from the snares of death. (14:26–27)

ENJOYING GOD. God is both a *fortress* and *a fountain*, because "evil not only attacks but attracts us."[49] We are tempted to lie, be ruthless, and trample on others—for fear that if we are too virtuous, we will be passed by in the competition of life. But we are also tempted to greed, lust, gluttony—for fear that if we are too virtuous, we will miss out on much joy and pleasure. This means we must not simply know how to trust in God as a *fortress*. We must also learn to delight in him, enjoying his presence and love as a *fountain*. Some kinds of Christianity put the emphasis on the will and life actions, other kinds on the emotions, worship, and praise. The Bible never, ever emphasizes one over the other or pits them against each other.

When others, including our children, see us trusting God and not melting down before the problems of life—and when they see us actually delighting in God rather than being merely dutiful—that may be a refuge for them. It may attract them to a relationship with him.

When people who know you well watch you under pressure, what do they see?

Prayer: Lord, I rejoice in your justice, which is my security, and your love, which is my joy. What would I ever do without "thy justice like mountains, high soaring above; thy clouds which are fountains of goodness and love"?[50] Amen.

February 14

Ears that hear and eyes that see—the LORD has made them both. (20:12)

RADICAL GRACE. Wisdom requires practical experience but experience does not necessarily lead to wisdom. The fool sees and hears things but his *eye* and *ear* do not perceive them properly (17:24; 23:9). This proverb claims we are incapable of these things without God's help. We have seen that God offers a salvation by grace. Here we learn we can't even want or receive this salvation without his gracious help.

Unaided, the human mind and heart will distort what they see and hear. Any eye or ear that interprets reality truly is doing so only with God's help. He does not just supplement their power; he *makes* them. As Paul writes in Romans 3:11: "There is no one who understands; there is no one who seeks God." Unless God himself opens the eyes and ears, through unmerited grace, we can do nothing. Though Proverbs concentrates its teaching on principles for wise living, it is not moralistic. It does not teach that we can earn God's blessing by exerting our moral power. It assumes, in verses like these, that nothing at all can be accomplished without dependence upon the saving grace of God.

When you think of sharing your faith with a friend or relative, how does radical grace encourage you to have hope that literally *any*one can come to faith?

Prayer: Lord, I am not capable in myself of any spiritual good. And to even be able to say *that* is an insight given by you. Oh, it's all of grace, from first to last! It is by the grace of God that I am what I am (1 Corinthians 10:15). I bless your name for your unmerited mercy. Amen.

February 15

Blessed is the one who always trembles before God, but whoever hardens their heart falls into trouble. (28:14)

PRACTICING HIS PRESENCE. To *always tremble* before God is a way to talk about existentially, moment by moment, practicing the presence of God. It means to keep God consciously in mind as you move through your day. You never get mad at someone without remembering God is there, watching. This is the God who has come from heaven to earth to forgive you, who forgave his enemies from the cross. To the degree that you remain deliberately aware of this, you will maintain a soft heart toward those that wrong you, not a hard heart.

Jesus may have had this proverb in mind when he told the parable of the Unmerciful Servant (Matthew 18:21–35). The servant who owed his master an enormous amount of money was forgiven, but when he met a fellow servant who owed him a small amount, he was harsh and vicious. Failure to forgive others who have wronged you demonstrates that you have forgotten how much you have been forgiven, and at what cost to Jesus (Philippians 2:6–8).

How can you, today, discipline yourself to practice the Lord's presence?

Prayer: Lord, there could not be a more practical spiritual discipline than to keep you ever before me, to be always aware of your presence (Psalm 16:8). In every conversation, action, and event let me keep you in mind. That is the way of true wisdom. Amen.

February 16

Through love and faithfulness sin is atoned for; through the fear of the LORD evil is avoided. (16:6)

FAITH AND WORKS. Through God's covenant love (Hebrew *chesedh*) sin *is atoned for*. So our salvation comes not because of our *love and faithfulness* but because of God's. Yet verse 6b tells us that the fear of the Lord this salvation produces in us leads us to shun evil. This is what we see also in the New Testament. The Protestant Reformation summarized this biblical teaching about Christ's salvation. It denied that faith in God *plus* the shunning of evil merited salvation. But it also denied that true faith in God could bring a salvation that did not issue the shunning of evil.

Rather, the Reformation taught that we are saved by faith alone but not by a faith that remains alone. That is, we are saved by Christ's atonement, apart from any merit or goodness in us. But genuine faith in Christ will always result in a grateful joy that produces life change. Both legalism and relativism are foolish. The gospel is true wisdom.

Has your faith produced real life change? Would the people closest to you say that over the past two years you have become more loving, joyful, peaceful, patient, kind, humble, and self-controlled?

Prayer: Lord, the gospel appears foolish to the world (1 Corinthians 1:18–25), but it is the most sublime wisdom. I praise you for giving us a powerful incentive to serve you, but without crushing us under guilt. It is wiser than either the stifling moralistic cultures or the rudderless relativistic cultures of the world. Amen.

The LORD detests the sacrifice of the wicked, but the prayer of the upright pleases him. . . . The LORD is far from the wicked, but he hears the prayer of the righteous. (15:8,29)

DETESTABLE SACRIFICES. In Old Testament worship, a *sacrifice* was an offering that believers were to bring to God. In the New Testament, our financial gifts given as part of worship, as well as our charity to the poor, are also called "sacrifices" (Philippians 4:18; Hebrews 13:16). These proverbs reflect the teaching of the prophets (Isaiah 58:1–14), namely, that we may give large sums of money to church and charity, but if that is accompanied by being wicked, God *detests* it. If despite your financial generosity you conduct a life devoted to advantaging yourself by disadvantaging others, that is not true faith.

History is filled with figures who made money exploiting people and then sought to make a name for themselves through philanthropy. But God detests this. A ruthless business deal that hurts others to enrich yourself cannot be made up for through religiosity or philanthropy. These verses show us how intensely our daily social and economic behavior matters to God.

Are you generous within your work and business—to customers and employees? Is the company you work for exploiting people?

Prayer: Lord, like most people, I think of myself as fair-minded, but do I habitually disadvantage myself to advantage others? When I look at my life through this biblical standard, I fall short. Forgive me! And help me live in such a way that my life and prayer please you. Amen.

> Commit to the LORD whatever you do, and he will establish your plans. (16:3)

EVERY AREA OF LIFE. To trust God is to obey him in whatever he says (January 22) and to submit to his will in whatever he sends (February 12). Here we are challenged to do this across every arena of our life—in *whatever you do*. That includes our work, leisure, intellectual life, inner thought life and imagination, friendships, health and treatment of our body, marriage or romantic relationships, money and possessions, relationship to church and other Christians, emotional life, and personal identity. To *commit to the Lord whatever you do* is to deliberately go through each of these areas and list what trusting (obeying and submitting to) God would require. Then ask God for his help to implement the list.

The second clause says that, if we commit our lives to him, he will take care of our *plans*. As the rest of the Bible shows us, that does not mean he gives us whatever we want. Rather, the wise accept that "even if our human plans are subverted, we can recognize an even deeper plan at work in our lives," namely, the all-wise and good will of God (Romans 8:28).[51]

Have you systematically committed whatever you do to the Lord?

Prayer: Lord, even though I don't understand everything you tell me in your Word, I will obey it. Even though I don't understand everything you send into my life, I will accept your plan and learn from it. What I just said is an enormous commitment, and it frightens me. Fortify me and strengthen me to find my all in you. Amen.

February 19

To do what is right and just is more acceptable to the LORD than sacrifice. . . . If anyone turns a deaf ear to my instruction, even their prayers are detestable. (21:3, 28:9)

BRIBING SACRIFICES. We saw (February 17) that sacrifices and good deeds that are not backed up with a righteous life are detestable to God (21:3). But 28:9 goes deeper, telling us that even seemingly heartfelt *prayers are detestable* to God unless accompanied by a humble, teachable spirit. In 2 Kings 5, Naaman the Syrian seeks to be healed of leprosy by Israel's God. So he takes royal letters of petition and much wealth and presents them to the king of Israel to receive his miracle. He assumes the king controls the prophets. But the king of Israel tears his robes (2 Kings 5:7), and says, in essence, "Here the king doesn't tell the prophets what to do. The prophets tell the king what to do. God can't be bought off with sacrifices and prayers."

God is a person, not some cosmic principle, and there can be no "subpersonal transactions" with him.[52] We must love him with our whole heart and gladly listen to him. Only when we know our prayers and gifts merit nothing will they have worth in God's eyes.

Look at the last time you experienced a great disappointment. Did you feel God owed you? Why?

Prayer: Father, recently something very difficult happened to me, and I caught myself thinking, "What good is all this prayer and Bible study if God treats me like this?" Now I see how wicked and foolish it is to think I can put you in my debt. Forgive me and change me. Amen.

February 20

HIS WORD. The beginning of all wisdom is the "fear of the Lord." But how do we know if we are relating to the real God? The answer is there is no real knowing of God unless we know him through his Word. Otherwise we are creating a God out of our imagination. Proverbs assumes the truth of Scripture, but here is a strong claim that God's Word is *flawless*, that is, that it is perfect, sufficient, and without error. Of course Agur is thinking only of the prophecies and Scriptures that had been written up to his day. But there is a similar warning at the end of the entire Bible (Revelation 22:18–19) to not add to God's Words.

Taken together, Proverbs 30 verses 5 and 6 teach against two equal, opposite errors: either to think that some of God's words are outdated, obsolete, untrue or to treat one's own insights and "revelations" as equal to the Scripture. Modern skeptics make the first mistake. Many Christians make the second mistake, lifting up their religious traditions, or their inner feelings, or their cultural preferences to the level of revelation, so they are equal with the Bible. We must do neither.

Are you completely convinced of the full authority of the Bible—of every word? Are you committing either of the two main errors?

Prayer: Lord, "I have more insight than all my teachers, for I meditate on your statutes" (Psalm 119:99). I know some people with little formal education who through their knowledge of Scripture are wiser than worldly experts. Let your Word light my path as well. Amen.

February 21

The greedy stir up conflict, but those who trust in the LORD will prosper. (28:25)

ALL OTHER THINGS. To trust in the Lord means at least this: Even if you knew you could make a lot of money by lying, you would not do it. The *greedy*, however, will do whatever it takes to make the money. But this verse adds that the greedy end up inheriting *conflict* and those who trust will *prosper*. Jesus also said: "Seek first his kingdom and his righteousness, and all these things will be given to you" (Matthew 6:33).

What does that mean? Jesus said, "In this world you will have trouble" (John 16:33), so he could not have been promising that we would always be rich and at peace. In fact, making status, wealth, and popularity the ultimates in your life often causes you to lose those very things. Remember how the kids at school who were the most desperate for friends and popularity were the ones you avoided? Making God your supreme good will often lead to many good things in this life. So trust God and you will have what you need.

Have you seen this at work in your life or someone else's—that seeking prosperity and material safety too much led to its loss?

Prayer: Lord, it is one thing to believe in you—to believe that you exist and that you can save us through Jesus. It is another thing to trust you existentially, moment by moment, in the twists and turns of everyday life. Help me with your Spirit to graduate from belief to trust. Amen.

February 22

> There is no wisdom, no insight, no plan that can succeed against the LORD. (21:30)

THE SOVEREIGNTY OF GOD. At one level this proverb means that if you set yourself against God to defy his will, you will end up only accomplishing his will at your own expense, as did Pharaoh in Exodus and those who crucified Jesus (Acts 2:23).

At another level, this text expresses the negative side of Proverbs' great principle, that the fear of the Lord is the very beginning of wisdom. So "no true synthesis (*wisdom*), analysis . . . . (*insight*) or policy (*plan*) can be arrived at in defiance of God."[53] That is, without faith in God, even the most sophisticated and diligent thinker is going to leave out too much of reality to be genuinely wise about life. No one would trust a surgeon who had no medical training or a cook who could not tell salt from sugar. And why should we trust even our own thoughts and intuitions if they omit the one who created the fabric of the universe and holds it all together?

The next time you experience the pain of worry and anxiety, consider that it may be fueled by too much confidence that your plans are wiser than God's.

Prayer: Lord, I pray mercy for my friends who are indeed leaving you out of their plans and lives. No one is wiser or more just than you, and I have no right to tell you your business. But you want me to tell you my desires—and I desire that you would open their eyes and hearts to your truth. Amen.

February 23

The LORD works out everything to its proper end—even the wicked for a day of disaster. (16:4)

NO LOOSE ENDS. Here is another way we can trust God. We can trust him to be the sovereign judge of all people. That liberates us from having to do the job ourselves. Miroslav Volf argues that "the practice of non-violence requires a belief in divine vengeance."[54] He goes on to explain that it is virtually impossible if you have been the victim of an attack, not to pick up a weapon and try to settle the score—unless you have a strong belief that someday God will right every wrong.

Either Jesus will pay for your sins, if you trust in him to have paid for them all on the cross, or you will pay for them yourself. And that goes for everyone who has wronged you. That means we can leave things in God's hands. We do not have the knowledge, the right, or the power to judge others for their sins. A crucial component of a wise life is a conviction that God works out everything *to its proper end—even the wicked for a day of disaster.*

Is there anyone in your life you have trouble forgiving? Use the insights of today's devotional to help you.

Prayer: Lord, I praise you—though with fear and trembling—that you are the judge of all the earth. Deliver me from the temptation to want to sit in judgment on certain people. I cannot see into anyone's heart or into their past enough to know what they deserve. Help me put these matters into your hands. Amen.

February 24

> The fear of the LORD is the beginning of wisdom, and knowledge of the Holy One is understanding. (9:10)

THE HOLY ONE. The theme of Proverbs 1:7 is repeated here. Every person's wisdom—way of interpreting the meaning of things—*begins* with one's view of God. What is a cat? It depends. Are we in a godless universe, so every living thing is just the product of a violent process of survival of the fittest? Or is God the impersonal world-spirit, so that everything in the physical world is an illusion? Or are we created by God, put into this world to care for it, including the animals (Genesis 1:26)? Each view of reality would necessarily look at a cat—and perhaps treat a cat—differently.

This time, Proverbs adds that the one we *fear* is *the Holy One*.[55] There is no more threatening divine attribute. In light of his holiness we see our sin most clearly. Only Jesus' blood atones and makes it safe for us to be in the presence of the holy God (Hebrews 10:19–22). If we believe in Jesus, the contemplation of God's holiness actually enhances our joy. That we should receive the love of a holy God—is a miracle of grace.

Meditate on the holiness of God.[56] To love God's holiness will make you infinitely humbler and happier.

Prayer: Lord, you are so holy that in your presence men like Isaiah and Moses were thrown into trauma. Yet through Jesus you have become my Holy Father (John 17:11). Nothing changes me like direct meditation on your holiness and hatred of all sin. So that I may do this, strengthen me in my inner being by your Spirit. Amen.

February 25

> By wisdom the LORD laid the earth's foundations, by understanding he set the heavens in place; by his knowledge the watery depths were divided, and the clouds let drop the dew. (3:19–20)

GIVENNESS. God created the world with his divine Word and *wisdom* (February 1), and we are to live our daily lives according to his Word and wisdom. This is because "the only wisdom by which you can handle everyday things in conformity with their nature is the wisdom by which they were divinely made and ordered."[57] The very same divine wisdom that speaks to you in God's Word was the basis for the creation of the world.

So there is "givenness" to things—physically, socially, morally, and spiritually—that is built into the fabric of creation. As we said before (January 7), we can't treat our body any way we want without out consequences. We can't treat people any way we want and expect to have good friends and a strong family. We can't live selfish lives and expect our social fabric to remain intact. And there is also a spiritual order. If we try to center our lives on anything but God, it leads to fragile identity and psychological disorder. It is the essence of wisdom to perceive this divine order in life and to align one's life with it.

In which of these areas might you be pushing against the fabric of God's ordered creation?

Prayer: Father, when I'm tempted to do something wrong, I still tell myself that basically I can get away with it. But no one ever, finally, gets away with sin. It will find us out. Burn this truth into my heart that I might not sin against you. Amen.

February 26

My son, do not forget my teaching, but keep my commands in your heart, for they will prolong your life many years and bring you peace and prosperity. . . . The LORD detests all the proud of heart. Be sure of this: They will not go unpunished. . . . The violence of the wicked will drag them away, for they refuse to do what is right. (3:1–2, 16:5, 21:7)

RETRIBUTION. The owner's manual that comes with your car tells you when to change the oil and what fuel to use, so as not to damage the car. To ignore the owner's manual—written by the car's creators—is to violate the design of the car by doing things that the automobile was not built to withstand (February 1). No one will have to come and give you a fine or legal penalty. The consequences will be natural. You will ruin your own car.

Because of creation, there is a principle of "natural retribution" embedded in the world. Right living will be rewarded (3:1–2) and evil will not go unpunished (16:5), but notice it is not said exactly how this will happen. 21:7 indicates there is a natural boomerang effect to cruel behavior. Yet 16:5 hints that the Lord is behind it all. In short, consequences are inherent within our actions.[58] Sins "find you out" (Numbers 32:23; cf. Galatians 6:7). Behaviors that violate God's word also violate our created design, and thus we harm ourselves as we do them. Right living honors our design and leads to thriving (February 27).

When was the last time you experienced something of the natural retribution of the world?

Prayer: Lord, my culture tells me that I can be whatever I choose, but your Word and experience show me that is not the case. My body, my talents, my location in the world—all both limit me and serve as callings from you. Help me to become the person you made me to be. Amen.

February 27

Whoever gives heed to instruction prospers, and blessed is the one who trusts in the LORD. (16:20)

BLESSEDNESS. The Bible is filled with promises of "blessedness." The Hebrew word means far more than mere happiness. It means multidimensional flourishing. In Genesis 3 we see that sin put us in a condition where we are in contradiction with God, our true selves, other human beings, and even nature itself.[59] We are out of alignment with the creation order in all its dimensions, and so our normal human state consists of spiritual emptiness, inner anxiety and crises of identity, conflicts between nations, classes, and races, and the destruction of our natural environment.

To be blessed, then, is to know partial but substantial healing of each of these areas as God's salvation repairs our hearts and our behavior. Spiritually we reconcile with and grow closer to God. Psychologically we come to understand ourselves and find our feelings and actions coming more under the Spirit's control. Relationally we discover the added depth and dimension that common faith can add to human friendship. Socially we find ways to serve neighbors and the broader civic community, no longer captive to political ideologies. Salvation is not merely forgiveness and admission to heaven. It means life *is* healed, slowly but surely, in all its dimensions.

Take time to thank God for the dimension of life in which, lately, you have seen God bringing blessedness.

Prayer: Lord, how easily we Christians talk about "blessings." But when I ponder the power of the biblical promise, I do hunger for the blessed life. But let me remember, "Blessed are those who hunger . . . for" not blessedness but "righteousness" (Matthew 5:6). Amen.

> The LORD does not let the righteous go hungry, but he thwarts the craving of the wicked. Lazy hands make for poverty, but diligent hands bring wealth. (10:3–4)

LEVELS. There's an order to creation, and so natural consequences are embedded in life. But do good and bad behavior always lead to good and bad outcomes respectively? Most would answer, "Often but not always." What, then, do we say to statements such as those in 10:3–4? Derek Kidner argues they are true at four levels: "logical, providential, spiritual, and eternal."[60]

First, "sin . . . sets up strains in the structure of life which can only end in breakdown." Living selfishly can feel great but catches up to us physically, relationally, psychologically. Second, "however much rope God gives us, he remains in control." God allowed bad things in Joseph's life, but it was all for a purpose (Genesis 50:20). Third, "whatever their worldly state, the righteous are the truly rich." Even in a life filled with suffering, Christians are justified in God's sight, adopted into his family, indwelt by the Holy Spirit, and guaranteed a place in the new heaven and new earth—priceless things. Fourth, "in the world to come, justice will be complete."[61]

Think of something that you have done right but that has not been rewarded in worldly terms. How does this analysis help put it in perspective?

Prayer: Lord, I praise you that, like a wise father, you may allow painful things into our lives, but it is to help us learn and grow (Hebrews 12:11). And we grow into maturity when we recognize that we already have our real wealth in your love and regard. Amen.

March 1

A good name is more desirable than great riches; to be esteemed is better than silver or gold. (22:1)

ORDER DISRUPTED. Proverbs tells us that hard work and honesty lead to a prosperous and happy life. Yet here we learn virtue is *more desirable* than wealth. The clear implication is that there are times you must choose between wealth and integrity.[62] So there is an order to creation but it is partially broken, disrupted by sin. God's world still "runs with a certain reliability," so that honesty and industry may result in financial gain, but not always.[63] While work generally leads to prosperity (10:4), sometimes injustice sweeps the fruit of labor away (13:23, 28:6).

Proverbs stresses the continued existence of this order, while Ecclesiastes emphasizes more its confusion and broken nature, and Job tells us it is often hidden.[64] To be wise we must see all of these. For example, to think either that hard work will always create wealth or that it usually does not is foolish. The gospel of Jesus creates this wisdom. It avoids the naïveté of thinking we can earn a good life with our good works. It also prevents us from becoming discouraged, knowing that the Lord of the universe is our loving Father.

Is your natural tendency to be too sanguine about the outcomes of good living and hard work—or too cynical?

Prayer: Lord, like so many, I was naive about life. I did not think that I would ever have to choose between being comfortable and doing the right thing—but that is the world we live in now. Give me enough joy in you to always choose the right thing rather than the easy thing. Amen.

March 2

Her ways are pleasant ways, and all her paths are peace. She is a tree of life to those who take hold of her; those who hold her fast will be blessed. (3:17–18)

ORDER RESTORED. Wisdom is depicted as *a tree of life* (3:18; 11:30; 13:12; 15:4). The Tree of Life was in the Garden of Eden but is also mentioned in Revelation 22:2, in which the Tree of Life stands at the center of the renewed creation, paradise regained. In Genesis 3:14–19 God foretold the disruption of the created order—under sin, work and life will be filled with pain and futility. St. Paul says that the broken, "frustrated" creation will be finally put right only when Christ returns to glorify and perfects his own (Romans 8:19–22).

Until then, this proverb promises that when we walk in accordance with God's Word and wisdom we begin to get a foretaste of the Tree of Life—the fullness of life that will be restored to us on the last day. And we may approach the Tree of Life only because Jesus was hung on a tree of death (Galatians 3:13). As Jesus says in George Herbert's poem, "Man stole the fruit, but I must climb the tree; The tree of life to all, but only me."[65]

Do you ever lift up your eyes enough to see the far horizon—the future life that Jesus has secured for you at infinite cost to himself?

Prayer: Lord, our first ancestors' rebellion made us subject to death. And I confess that every day in my own sins I confirm that terrible choice. I praise you that you tasted death for me, that I might have this tree of life. Amen.

March 3

I said to myself, "This too is meaningless." For the wise, like the fool, will not be long remembered; the days have already come when both have been forgotten. Like the fool, the wise too must die! (Ecclesiastes 2:15–16)

BROKEN. No one book of the Bible gives us the whole picture of God's salvation and truth. Proverbs makes the case that because God is the creator, wise actions normally lead to good results in life. The key word, however, is "normally." There is much *ab*normal about our world, so that prosperous people often are not hardworking while many poor people are. The relationship between behavior and reward is—not completely but to a significant degree—disrupted.

It's possible to overread Proverbs to teach that "good things . . . happen to good people and bad things happen to bad people."[66] While Proverbs acknowledges the disruption of order, the books of Ecclesiastes and Job (also part of the Bible's Wisdom literature) explore it. Proverbs says that, in general, the godly are remembered and the wicked forgotten (10:7). But here Ecclesiastes 2:15–16 observes that often a good, wise person is no more honored than a *fool*. Ecclesiastes and Job, then, must be read together with Proverbs if we are to learn wisdom.

Does it surprise you that in our broken world good behavior does not always lead to favorable outcomes? Do you find yourself blaming God for this? Or are you learning to be wise in a broken world?

Prayer: Lord, I live in a world that you made good but that we have marred. How wrong it is for me to blame you for what doesn't "work" in life! Help me to trust in you and bide my time "until the world is mended."[67] Amen.

March 4

"Meaningless! Meaningless!" says the Teacher. "Utterly meaningless! Everything is meaningless." What do people gain from all their labors at which they toil under the sun? (Ecclesiastes 1:2–3)

VANITY. In older translations, Ecclesiastes begins, "Vanity, vanity—all is vanity." Modern editions translate "vanity" as "meaningless," though the older word might be better. The author is observing that we reach so few of our goals, and the goals we do reach are not nearly as fulfilling as we thought. There seems to be no *gain*. The point is so bleak that many ask, "What is this doing in the Bible?"

The answer is in the phrase *under the sun*. It is what today we'd call a thought experiment. The author asks us to imagine trying to live only under the sun—with no God or eternity beyond this world. If this world is all there is, can we find meaning? The experiment has two benefits. First, it will show us that, to a degree, this world *is* separated from God by the sin of the human race, so it does not function as it was created to, and that therefore even believers encounter a great deal of human life's "vanity." It also shows how rejection of God can make life even more pointless.

What would you consider vain or futile in your life? How would adding God to that situation change it?

Prayer: Lord, when the futility of my life begins to overwhelm me, I realize it is because I am looking only at what is "under the sun" and not at the eternal weight of glory being prepared for me (2 Corinthians 4:17). Help me to fix my eyes "not on what is seen, but on what is unseen" (2 Corinthians 4:18). Amen.

March 5

What has been will be again, what has been done will be done again; there is nothing new under the sun. Is there anything of which one can say, "Look! This is something new"? It was here already, long ago; it was here before our time. No one remembers the former generations, and even those yet to come will not be remembered by those who follow them. (Ecclesiastes 1:9–11)

INSIGNIFICANCE. Ecclesiastes asks us to imagine how fulfilling things can possibly be if what we see in this world and life is "all that is or ever was or ever will be."[68] If that was the case, the text says, nothing would be remembered. If this world is all there is, ultimately the sun will die and all human life will be wiped away by the sands of time and there will be no one to remember anything that ever happened.

This is a devastating insight. It means that if life under the sun is all that there is, then whether you spend your life helping people or killing people, in the end it makes not a whit of difference. If human beings really are going back to nothing, we should admit that nothing we do matters. Even believers today are shaped by the secular culture's complete emphasis on happiness here and now, in this-world benefits. But we should not be. The fleeting pleasures of life are senseless, useless, and insignificant if we try to live without reference and gratitude to God.

What circumstances in this life *under the sun* do you imagine would fulfill you if you had them? Are you sure?

Prayer: Lord, whatever I do "in the Lord is not in vain" (1 Corinthians 15:58). Because of Jesus' resurrection I know that I will be resurrected, and so it is not my status in this world but in the next that defines me. I praise and thank you for that. Amen.

March 6

So my heart began to despair over all my toilsome labor under the sun. For a person may labor with wisdom, knowledge and skill, and then they must leave all they own to another who has not toiled for it. This too is meaningless and a great misfortune. What do people get for all the toil and anxious striving with which they labor under the sun? All their days their work is grief and pain; even at night their minds do not rest. This too is meaningless. (Ecclesiastes 2:20–23)

THE VANITY OF ACHIEVEMENT. *Under the sun*, work and achievement fail on their own terms. First, they fail an objective test. Work does not actually, in the end, really achieve. Quickly or slowly the results of our toil are wiped away by history. The person who takes up your work after you may undo all you have done (Ecclesiastes 2:21). Second, work and achievement fail a subjective test—they never fully satisfy. Work brings *grief and pain*. You are up early and late to bed, often unable to sleep even at night and filled with the feeling that the work is not really all that well done.

Proverbs points to the satisfaction work can bring, but Ecclesiastes reminds us that we often feel the "thorns and thistles," the grinding frustration that is the curse on work in a fallen world (Genesis 3:17–19). Work and achievement, without the peace of God in our lives through the Spirit, will never be enough. We need the God whose labor led to real rest (Genesis 2:2) and the Savior who could even sleep through a storm (Mark 4:38).

Have you ever achieved a goal, only to find it unfulfilling? What goals would outlast the sun? Make a list.

Prayer: Father, help me to use the gospel on myself to weaken the perfectionism that makes my work a burden. Give me the deep rest of soul that comes to the degree I remember I am saved by faith in Jesus, not by the quality of my work. Amen.

March 7

I said to myself, "Come now, I will test you with pleasure to find out what is good." But that also proved to be meaningless. "Laughter," I said, "is madness. And what does pleasure accomplish?" . . . Everything was meaningless, a chasing after the wind. (Ecclesiastes 2:1–2,11)

THE VANITY OF PLEASURE. Now Ecclesiastes explores the way of hedonism and self-expression as a solution to the futility of life. *Laughter* is a word that refers to the kind of high spirits you experience at a sporting event or at a party with food, wine, and friends. *Pleasure*, the Hebrew *simha*, is a more reflective joy of appreciating the beauty or excellence of something. But in the end they are meaningless and vain; they fail on their own terms.

Why? One reason is that pleasure doesn't *accomplish* anything. Pleasure seeking can draw you into enormous expenditures of time and money, and at some point the sheer wastefulness of it dawns on you. Second, pleasure is a *chasing after the wind*; that is, it is trying to grasp something that cannot be grasped. In this world, pleasures are fleeting. Ironically, the more you look to the things of this world to give you your deepest pleasures and satisfactions, the more frustrating they will be. So a life devoted to pleasure actually does not deliver pleasure.

What pleasures do you look to for renewal and refreshment? Do you find the same refreshment from being in the presence of God in his Word? Why not?

Prayer: Lord God, "among the sundry and manifold changes of the world" let it be that my "heart may surely there be fixed, where true joys are to be found"[69]—even on Jesus Christ our Lord. Amen.

March 8

I applied my mind to study and to explore by wisdom all that is done under the heavens. What a heavy burden God has laid on mankind! I have seen all the things that are done under the sun; all of them are meaningless, a chasing after the wind. What is crooked cannot be straightened; what is lacking cannot be counted. I said to myself, "Look, I have increased in wisdom more than anyone who has ruled over Jerusalem before me; I have experienced much of wisdom and knowledge." . . . For with much wisdom comes much sorrow; the more knowledge, the more grief. (Ecclesiastes 1:13–16,18)

THE VANITY OF KNOWLEDGE. Ecclesiastes speaks of apply[ing the] mind to . . . wisdom—that is, seeking to understand the seen, material world. Since the author is considering doing this under the heavens it means trying to understand the world in terms of itself.[70] This almost by definition is the scientific enterprise—the effort to find a natural (not supernatural) cause for absolutely everything. But this project is proclaimed a failure. We can't fix human problems with mere technology and knowledge—*what is crooked cannot be straightened* (Ecclesiastes 1:15). Science can't change the heart. We may study racism, crime, and poverty and make some advances. But the view that every phenomenon has a natural cause and therefore a technological solution in the end fails because this simply isn't true.

There are supernatural, spiritual problems that need supernatural, spiritual remedies. In the end, the more we know the more we see how little we know. This can lead to a sense of helplessness—*the more knowledge, the more grief.* Human reason unaided by God's revelation will never give us the whole picture.

What problems do you have in your life or see in the lives of others that need spiritual solutions? How can you access those solutions?

Prayer: Lord, our society has rested its full hope for itself on unaided science and technology. But this will not be enough! Please preserve our social life and order with your help and grace, and let the knowledge of the Lord grow again in our country. Amen.

March 9

All share a common destiny—the righteous and the wicked, the good and the bad, the clean and the unclean, those who offer sacrifices and those who do not. As it is with the good, so with the sinful; as it is with those who take oaths, so with those who are afraid to take them. This is the evil in everything that happens under the sun: The same destiny overtakes all. The hearts of people, moreover, are full of evil and there is madness in their hearts while they live, and afterward they join the dead. (Ecclesiastes 9:2–3)

THE VANITY OF MORALITY. Ecclesiastes 9:2 depicts the good and evil, the religious and irreligious—and concludes, rightly, that under the sun *the same destiny overtakes them all.* If this world is all there is, when we die, we rot, and when all who know about us die, even our memory is gone.

Sinclair Ferguson says that the author's "thought experiment" is driving us to a conclusion. "Like the [rest of the] Bible (Isaiah 22:13; 1 Corinthians 15:32) [the author] sees there is only one logical conclusion to life if it has no post-mortem hope, no promise of a resurrection: let us eat, drink, and be merry. Tomorrow we die. Recognizing this . . . is no more than a matter of honest thinking."[71] And *the hearts of people . . . are full of evil.* The sinful human race does indeed have the world it deserves, in which good and bad behavior are not rewarded neatly and appropriately.

We have already experienced some of the blessings of renewal in our lives through the work of Christ on the cross as applied by the Holy Spirit. Make an inventory of all the areas of death, decay, and evil that still need to be addressed in your own heart.

Prayer: Lord, Ecclesiastes painfully provokes me to admit that you are all my hope and my only hope. Help me raise my eyes "above the sun," constantly remembering that, while you will one day make everything right, nothing will be fully right until then. Amen.

March 10

However many years anyone may live, let them enjoy them all. But let them remember the days of darkness, for there will be many. Everything to come is meaningless. You who are young, be happy while you are young, and let your heart give you joy in the days of your youth. Follow the ways of your heart and whatever your eyes see, but know that for all these things God will bring you into judgment. So then, banish anxiety from your heart and cast off the troubles of your body, for youth and vigor are meaningless. (Ecclesiastes 11:8–10)

HOW TO ENJOY YOUR LIFE: PART 1. At the end of the book, the author ends his "thought experiment" and brings God back into the picture. But he continues to remind us about how confused and broken the world is. In these verses he gives a set of practical guidelines for enjoying life despite it all. *However many years anyone may live, let them enjoy them all.* How do we do that? First, be realistic. *Remember the days of darkness, for there will be many.* We should expect not only times of sorrow but also that, even believing in God, life will sometimes feel meaningless. This is an admission that even believers are "subject to futility" (Romans 8:18ff.). We were not created for a world of death, of the loss of love, of violence and loneliness. We must remember that on this side of heaven and Judgment Day, much of life will feel vain and pointless. The first advice: Don't let the times of darkness completely overwhelm you. This world will not last forever.

How do you survive the dark times in your life? Do you use them to grow in faith, or do you merely endure until they are over?

Prayer: Lord, I don't know why I am always surprised by suffering. Both your Word and common sense tell me that, even in good times, it is always on the way. Don't let the dark times darken my heart, but rather let them teach me wisdom. Amen.

However many years anyone may live, let them enjoy them all. But let them remember the days of darkness, for there will be many. Everything to come is meaningless. You who are young, be happy while you are young, and let your heart give you joy in the days of your youth. Follow the ways of your heart and whatever your eyes see, but know that for all these things God will bring you into judgment. So then, banish anxiety from your heart and cast off the troubles of your body, for youth and vigor are meaningless. (Ecclesiastes 11:8–10)

HOW TO ENJOY YOUR LIFE: PART 2. The author is saying more than that we should not be surprised by dark times (March 10) but that we should also *remember* how dark those times were. We should grasp that "all things temporal will disappoint us" to a degree. "We must face the fact or else be crushed by it."[72] The believer's joy must be based in something that can stand up to the inevitable "dark days" that will come because of the fallenness of the world. One of those things is a good conscience. That is, we should remember God's *judgment.* The message: Enjoy yourself, but don't do things you cannot justify before God. Enjoy yourself but keep your conscience clear.

Finally, don't mourn over youth and vigor when they fade. "To idolize the state of youth and to dread the loss of it is disastrous; it spoils the gift even while we have it."[73]

Timor mortis conturbat me is the refrain in many poems. It means "Fear of death disturbs me." Are you afraid of aging, sickness, and death? Will you be facing them alone, or with Jesus at your side?

Prayer: Father, when things go wrong for me, my greatest enemy is self-pity. It whispers to me that, because of my suffering, I deserve pleasures that I know are wrong. Save me from self-pity with a sight of Jesus suffering faithfully for me. Amen.

March 12

"Meaningless! Meaningless!" says the Teacher. "Utterly meaningless!" (Ecclesiastes 1:2) About three in the afternoon Jesus cried out in a loud voice, *"Eli, Eli, lema sabachthani?"* (which means "My God, my God, why have you forsaken me?") (Matthew 27:46)

MORE THAN AN ARGUMENT. The more we take God out of the picture, the more we will feel things are *meaningless*. Genesis 3:16–19 tells us that dissatisfaction and boredom are part of the punishment for sin. And the rest of the Bible tells us that if we die alienated from God, we live forever in eternity experiencing utter meaninglessness and endless, terrible spiritual thirst (Luke 16: 22–25).

What is our hope in the face of this? Ecclesiastes gives us provocative philosophical reasoning, but God does not merely give us an argument. When on the cross Jesus cried out, "My God, my God, why have you forsaken me?" he was experiencing the cosmic meaninglessness of having no God in his life. Jesus was taking our curse for us. He was getting the infinite futility our lives deserve so we could be forgiven and embraced by God. Through faith in Jesus you can lead a God-centered life. You can know that every action is a way to honor him and every event is part of his good plan for you. So everything matters.

Jesus claims to be the good shepherd. What "valleys of shadow" are you facing where you need him to be by your side?

Prayer: Lord, you suffered in the dark for me so that I could live in the light. You experienced cosmic futility so that what I do now counts forever. How can I love and praise you enough? I can't—but help me to start. Amen.

March 13

"Does Job fear God for nothing?" Satan replied. "Have you not put a hedge around him and his household and everything he has? You have blessed the work of his hands, so that his flocks and herds are spread throughout the land. But now stretch out your hand and strike everything he has, and he will surely curse you to your face." The LORD said to Satan, "Very well, then, everything he has is in your power, but on the man himself do not lay a finger." Then Satan went out from the presence of the LORD. (Job 1:9–12)

HIDDENNESS: PART 1. God allows Satan to strike at Job, who, compared with other human beings, does not deserve a life filled with more suffering than is the norm. Modern readers may be appalled at this story, yet it shows, in narrative form, the asymmetrical relationship of the biblical God to suffering. First, notice that all of the bad things happening to Job are Satan's idea. God does not actively generate the evils and suffering. God didn't create a world with disease, disaster, and death in it. The chaotic forces of evil were released when the human race turned from God and the fabric of the world began to unravel (Genesis 3:17–19). But on the other hand, God is still in absolute control. God sovereignly limits and directs the suffering—*"on the man himself do not lay a finger."*

Both of these truths are necessary for us to face and survive the troubles of life with peace. We have to know that God in no way enjoys seeing us in pain, and yet we need to know that there's a plan behind it.

Does suffering ever make you doubt God's goodness? List the reasons.

Prayer: Lord, I have been tempted both to think of you as cruel and to think of life as out of control. Neither idea comforts; rather, they torment. You are loving *and* you are in control. Only those complementary truths will get me through! Help me believe and grasp them. Amen.

March 14

"Does Job fear God for nothing?" Satan replied. "Have you not put a hedge around him and his household and everything he has? You have blessed the work of his hands, so that his flocks and herds are spread throughout the land. But now stretch out your hand and strike everything he has, and he will surely curse you to your face." The Lord said to Satan, "Very well, then, everything he has is in your power, but on the man himself do not lay a finger." Then Satan went out from the presence of the Lord. (Job 1:9–12)

HIDDENNESS: PART 2. God allows Satan only enough room to accomplish the very opposite of what he wanted to accomplish. He gets only enough rope to hang himself. Satan resents Job and wants him discredited and exposed as a fraud. As a result of his assaults, today Job is one of the most famous figures in history. Millions of people have read about his life and been helped by his example.

God hates evil and permits into Job's life only the evil that will completely defeat Satan's intention. Yet at the end Job is never told the plan. He never learns why he suffered. The lesson: God hates evil and suffering and has a plan that will defeat it, but we can hardly see any of the plan. It is hidden too deeply for us to see much of it at all. The people around Jesus' cross also shook their heads and said, "I don't see how God could bring anything good out of this."

If you knew that your suffering was glorifying God before the angels, demons, and powers and principalities of the world, would that change your attitude toward it? How?

Prayer: Lord, my human pride makes me feel that if *I* with *my* reason can't perceive any good reason for this suffering, then there can't be any. Give me the humility that will bring me the peace that comes from trusting you. Amen.

March 15

"Does Job fear God for nothing?" Satan replied. "Have you not put a hedge around him and his household and everything he has? You have blessed the work of his hands, so that his flocks and herds are spread throughout the land. But now stretch out your hand and strike everything he has, and he will surely curse you to your face." The LORD said to Satan, "Very well, then, everything he has is in your power, but on the man himself do not lay a finger." Then Satan went out from the presence of the LORD. (Job 1:9–12)

HIDDENNESS: PART 3. The story of Job conveys the highly nuanced way that godly wisdom should approach suffering. It does not give the pat answers, which are *moralism* and *cynicism.* The moralist says to the sufferer, "Somehow there is unconfessed sin in your life. You need to repent and get right with God. If you live right, your life will go right." The cynic says, "Life is unsatisfying. Then you die. If there is a God, he's out to lunch. You don't owe him anything."

Both of these answers are foolishly simpleminded. The moralist says that the purpose of suffering is simple—it's there to bring you back to God. Sometimes that may be, but not always. (March 16.) The cynic also says the purpose of suffering is simple—there isn't any! Godly wisdom understands that God has purposes but they are deeply hidden. This keeps us from either the smugness of the moralist or the hardness of the cynic—and from the despair that both such approaches can bring to the sufferer.

Have you reached the point in your life where suffering no longer calls God's character into question? Do you trust him, even in your pain and discouragement?

Prayer: Lord, I confess that when I was younger I was much more of a moralist and as I've gotten older I'm too prone to cynicism. And I see so many of my friends moving in the same direction. Save me from that trajectory! Amen.

"Consider now: Who, being innocent, has ever perished? Where were the upright ever destroyed? As I have observed, those who plow evil and those who sow trouble reap it." (Job 4:7–8)

MORALISM. Job loses virtually everything. His "friend" Eliphaz tells him that good people are blessed and wicked people cursed. So it must be Job's fault that he is suffering. His speech sounds remarkably like Proverbs, for it is true that there is a moral order that tends to reward good and punish evil. Yet Eliphaz is a mora*list* who thinks nothing we get is a gift, that everything is earned. He sees the world almost as a machine that you can control with your moral behavior. With that view, every time trouble arrives, it will not just grieve you but destroy you because you will feel it is all your fault.

Instead, we need to know three things. First, that everyone deserves condemnation (Romans 3:10–12,20,23) and so we all live only by the grace of God. Second, that when we suffer it may indeed be in part to correct us or wake us up, but not necessarily. All we know is God has hidden but good purposes. Third, we need to realize that goodness will be rewarded and evil punished, but not fully until "the day when God judges people's secrets through Jesus Christ" (Romans 2:16).

Can you trust God without seeing his purposes?

Prayer: Lord, if my perspective and sense of proportion were right, I would realize that everything I experience that is better than hell is a gift of mercy from you. That truth shocks—then deeply comforts. Heal my perspective with your Spirit. Amen.

March 17

Yet man is born to trouble as surely as sparks fly upward. (Job 5:7)

NO SURPRISE. *Sparks fly upward* from a fire naturally, so human suffering is inevitable. God told us so in Genesis 3:17–19, so we should not be shocked at suffering. Modern Western people are more traumatized by it than others. We have too much faith in our technology and our democratic institutions, and we are conditioned by our secular, materialistic culture to seek most of our happiness in fragile things like good looks, wealth, and pleasure.

It is wise, however, to be ready for suffering. Often most of the painful emotions people experience during adversity are actually the shock and surprise that they are suffering at all. Even many Christians believe that God won't let really bad things happen to them. But Jesus himself disproves that. If God allowed a perfect man to suffer terribly for a greater, wonderful good, why should we think that might not happen to us? "Dear friends, do not be surprised at the fiery ordeal . . . as though something strange were happening to you" (1 Peter 4:12).

How can you have fellowship with Jesus in your suffering?

Prayer: Lord, as I read about your life in the gospels, I see you experiencing pain and rejection on every page. Yet somehow I assume that I deserve a better life than you! My heart's foolishness is so deep when it comes to suffering. Make me ready for it. Amen.

March 18

> "If only you would hide me in the grave and conceal me till your anger has passed! If only you would set me a time and then remember me! If someone dies, will they live again? All the days of my hard service I will wait for my renewal to come. You will call and I will answer you; you will long for the creature your hands have made." (Job 14:13–15)

TRUST. Contrary to what anyone knew up to that time, Job hopes for resurrection. "If someone dies, will they live again?" He asks that after God puts him in the grave, he *remember* him and grant him *renewal*. Why would Job have such hope? The answer is *"You will long for the creature your hands have made."* The word "long" means yearning in love. Job is saying, "I know you love me, and I believe your love is so intense you won't let me stay dead. That's my hope."

Now, if Job knew enough about God's love to trust him in suffering, how much more should we? We have proof that Jesus would not let even death and hell stand between us and him, even if it meant he had to enter into infinite suffering for us. And of course we have the explicit promise of the resurrection. We know he longs for us in love, and he is omnipotent. We can trust him.

Do you trust Jesus, that he will either save you from your suffering in this world or save you on the other side of the grave, by resurrection?

Prayer: Lord, when I hear in your Word that you *long* for me in love, it makes me long for you. You longed for me so much that you were willing to go into the depths and die for me, that I might live. That makes me able to endure what I must for you without complaint. Amen.

March 19

Where then does wisdom come from? Where does understanding dwell? It is hidden from the eyes of every living thing, concealed even from the birds in the sky. Destruction and Death say, "Only a rumor of it has reached our ears." God understands the way to it and he alone knows where it dwells, for he views the ends of the earth and sees everything under the heavens. . . . And he said to the human race, "The fear of the LORD—that is wisdom, and to shun evil is understanding." (Job 28:20–24,28)

REFUSE TRITE ANSWERS. Full wisdom—the ability to truly understand why things happen and what they mean—is unavailable. *It is hidden.* Only God sees all. It is the height of wisdom to see that you can't attain supreme wisdom. Moralists are sure that good people don't suffer, but when they find that they do, the disillusionment is deep. Cynics fortify themselves against suffering by laughing that there is no order or purpose to things.

But it is as foolish to think that there is no order or purpose to things as it is to think you can discern it if you try. The wise approach is not simplistic. "True wisdom . . . refuses all trite answers which suggest either that we know it all or that we can know nothing."[74] Even though supreme wisdom is not available, practical wisdom is, through the *fear of the Lord.* This gives you basic answers about questions of meaning, broad moral principles for guidance, and most of all the presence of God that you will need to get through life.

If you have the loving gaze of Jesus' face, what other circumstances do you think you need in order to be content? List them. Now repent for resting in them too much.

Prayer: Lord, when I visit with a person who is bereaved or suffering, I am tempted to speak in spiritual platitudes. Shut me up, and teach me how to comfort the way Jesus comforts me—not with answers for every question but just with his presence. Amen.

March 20

"People cry out under a load of oppression; they plead for relief from the arm of the powerful. But no one says, 'Where is God my Maker, who gives songs in the night, who teaches us more than he teaches the beasts of the earth and makes us wiser than the birds in the sky?'" (Job 35:9–11)

SONGS IN THE NIGHT. A young man named Elihu gets up and chastises both Job and his friends. Elihu says through suffering God can make us *wiser than the birds in the sky.* It breaks our overconfidence. It shows us we have always been helpless and dependent on God—we just hadn't seen it till now. It brings out the worst in us and can show us personal flaws to which we had been blind. It makes us more tenderhearted and understanding toward others. And it can teach you to love God for himself alone, not just for the things he gives you.

Suffering can do all this—or leave you bitter and broken. What makes the difference? It is *"songs in the night"* to *"God our Maker."* In the dark times, keep singing to God. Sing praise of God himself, of the good things you do have, such as salvation, that cannot be taken from you. Sing and God will be with you "your troubles to bless, and sanctify to you your deepest distress."[75]

Consider the good things that you have and that have happened to you. Why has God given those things to you? Praise him for his love toward you.

Prayer: Father, in difficult times I *will* praise you for your past goodness to me, for your presence with me, and for the tremendous future things you have promised me. As I sing, "let the things of the world grow strangely dim, in the light of your glory and grace."[76] Amen.

March 21

But he knows the way that I take; when he has tested me, I will come forth as gold. (Job 23:10)

GOLD. Job has had times of great darkness, in which his speech is little more than crying in pain. These spiritual valleys are inevitable for people of even the strongest faith. We must also remember that even when Job is saying things he will repent for later, he is still praying. Yes, he is complaining and crying—but to God. So never let your suffering stop you from praying and worshipping.

Why? Because in his best moments, as in Job 23:10, Job comes to see that his suffering was not a punishment but a purification, and that if he holds on to God he'll become pure *gold*. Job is saying, "God knows what he is doing; I don't. But if I simply hold on to him, I will be refined into something great, like gold going through fire." Job earlier had seen the suffering as pointless. Now he realizes it may be the way to become what he's always wanted, before God, to be. "Job is saying that he is precious to God. Only valued metal is put through the fire."[77]

Is your view of God big enough to allow him to purify you as part of his love for you?

Prayer: Lord, even when I don't know what to say to you, I need to tell you *that*. In dark times, prevent me from withdrawing and just talking and thinking to myself. I pray for prayer. Give me a desire to pray and then show me your face. Amen.

March 22

My ears had heard of you but now my eyes have seen you. Therefore I despise myself and repent in dust and ashes. (Job 42:5–6)

SATAN DEFEATED. Finally God appears and speaks. He simply declares that he has created and knows all things—and no one else does. Job expects an explanation, his friends expect a condemnation, but God gives neither. The moralists are thus refuted but so, of course, are the cynics who say God is detached. The very fact that God doesn't denounce Job proves that the suffering wasn't a punishment. And for God even to appear and Job not be struck dead is also proof that his faith has put him in a right relationship with God.

Job *repents*, but not for his sins, which were never the issue. Rather, he abandons his self-justification project, retracting his demand for an explanation. If God had given it, Job might have been tempted to obey God for the sake of all the endless fame he would be getting. Instead, Job says, "I'll serve you just because you are you." Job loves God for himself alone. And Satan is defeated.

When you encounter the living God of the Bible through his Word and his Spirit, every excuse, demand, and complaint dies in your heart. He is God. He loves you. If your view of God is too small, pray for him to enlarge it.

Prayer: Father, what I most need are not reasons and explanations but a clear sight of *you*—you as you are in all your holiness, majesty, and glory. Enlighten the eyes of my heart so I can see your glory by faith. And that will be enough. Amen.

"Who, being innocent, has ever perished? Where were the upright ever destroyed?" (Job 4:7) But he was pierced for our transgressions, he was crushed for our iniquities; the punishment that brought us peace was on him, and by his wounds we are healed. . . . Though he had done no violence, nor was any deceit in his mouth. (Isaiah 53:5,9)

THE ULTIMATE JOB. Like Job, we too get no full explanation for our suffering. Yet we know what Job did not—that God joined us here in our darkness, and that, though truly, perfectly innocent, he perished. Jesus also experienced the absence of God, the betrayal of friends, physical agony, and nakedness. In Gethsemane, Jesus saw that if he obeyed God fully, he'd be absolutely abandoned and destroyed in hell. No one else has ever faced such a situation. Jesus truly "served God for nothing."

The evil that assaulted Jesus, in the end, defeated itself. The death of Jesus for our sins means that someday God can judge and destroy all evil and suffering from the world without destroying us. "This is the final answer to Job and all the Jobs of humanity."[78] When you suffer you can know you are walking the same path Jesus walked—so you are *not* alone—and that path is only taking you to him.

Are you withholding your full trust in God until you get an explanation for some bad thing that happened to you? In light of Jesus' undeserved suffering for you, are you willing to let go of that demand and commit your way to him?

Prayer: Lord, just as Shadrach, Meshach, and Abednego were not alone in their furnace but you walked there with them (Daniel 3:25), now let me know your presence in my times of refining fire. Amen.

KNOWING THE HEART
Understanding the Heart

March 24

> Do not set foot on the path of the wicked or walk in the way of evildoers. Avoid it, do not travel on it; turn from it and go on your way. For they cannot rest until they do evil; they are robbed of sleep till they make someone stumble. (4:14–16)

ACTIONS SHAPE THE HEART. Walking on a *path* always takes you somewhere. Life is likened to a path because every action takes you somewhere. That is, the act changes you, making it easier for you to do it again. Eventually it becomes so natural to be cruel and selfish that you *cannot rest* unless you are doing it. "Sow a thought, reap an action; sow an action, reap a habit; sow a habit, reap a character; sow a character, reap a destiny."[79]

Modern people think feelings determine what we do and that it is hypocritical to act loving if they don't feel loving. Proverbs, however, tells us that our actions shape our feelings. So if you don't feel love for someone, don't let that stop you. Do the actions of love, and often the feelings follow. When Jesus tells us to love our opponents (Matthew 5:43–48), he does not mean to work up warm feelings. He is telling us to seek our opponents' good, even at a sacrifice. So start doing the actions of love—take that path—and you will see your heart changing.

Think of one hard-to-love person in your life. What practical things could you do to begin to love them better?

Prayer: Lord, the feelings of my heart are so unruly, but teach me how to exhort my heart rather than simply listening to it (Psalms 42:5, 103:1–5). And help me in my resolve to also take charge of it by loving and obeying what you command. Amen.

March 25

The path of the righteous is like the morning sun, shining ever brighter till the full light of day. But the way of the wicked is like deep darkness; they do not know what makes them stumble. (4:18–19)

ACTIONS OPEN THE EYES. The paths of love and of selfishness lead to two different end points. But they also differ along the way. One path brightens gradually and the other darkens. The darkness represents increasing self-deception. We say, "I'm not proud, just confident. I'm not abrasive, just direct. I'm not greedy, just sharp in business." The more we follow the path of self, the more we live in denial until, when life breaks down, we do not know what makes us stumble. Self-deception is not the worst thing you can do, but it's the means by which we do the very worst things. The sin that is most distorting your life right now is the one you can't see.

On the other hand, those growing in grace (2 Peter 3:18) take the path *shining ever brighter*. They see more and more things about God and themselves that they were denying. Why? The gospel so assures us of God's love that we are finally capable of admitting the worst about ourselves. In his love, based on Christ's work, not ours, it is finally safe to do so.

Ask two or three good friends, "What is a character flaw of mine that others can see but I can't see as clearly?"

Prayer: Lord, there is no more important petition than this one—show me my hidden faults. Amen.

March 26

Above all else, guard your heart, for everything you do flows from it. Keep your mouth free of perversity; keep corrupt talk far from your lips. Let your eyes look straight ahead; fix your gaze directly before you. Give careful thought to the paths for your feet and be steadfast in all your ways. (4:23–26)

THE HEART SHAPES THE ACTIONS. In the Bible the heart is not primarily the seat of the emotions in contrast to the head as the seat of reason. Rather, the heart is the seat of your deepest trusts, commitments, and loves, from which *everything . . . flows*. What the heart most loves and trusts, the mind finds reasonable, the emotions find desirable, and the will finds doable.

How do you guard your heart? The passage hints that, though ultimately the heart is the central control, our words, eyes, and feet can influence the heart. If we gaze longingly enough at an object, it may capture our heart through the imagination (as when Achan looked, desired, and finally stole the treasure in Joshua 7). If we speak bitterly against someone, we can sour our heart toward them. The best way to *guard your heart* for wisdom is worship, in which the mouth, the mind, the imagination, and even the body are all oriented to God.

Is there some way in which you are failing to guard your heart right now? Are there things you are seeing or doing that may be moving your heart away from God?

Prayer: Lord, help me to guard my heart. Just as I don't want to digest or take bad things into my body, give me the wisdom and self-control not to allow toxic images and beliefs into my heart through my imagination and thoughts. Amen.

March 27

All a person's ways seem pure to them, but motives are weighed by the LORD. (16:2)

GOD AND THE HEART. You don't know yourself unless you know that your motives are never *pure*, and that they always seem better to you than they do to the Lord, who *weighs* them. This has huge implications for decision making and relationships. If you are always sure of your sincerity and purity, you will make impulsive snap judgments. You will be too dismissive of some options and ideas and too doggedly committed to others.

Not trusting your heart prevents two opposite errors. On the one hand, our consciences can be too easy on us. "My conscience is clear, but that does not make me innocent" (1 Corinthians 4:4). Follow God's Word instead of your feelings. If the Scripture says it is wrong, it is. On the other hand, our hearts can be too hard on us. "If our hearts condemn us, . . . God is greater than our hearts" (1 John 3:20). Follow the gospel instead of your feelings. You are loved for Christ's sake, not because your heart and life are perfect. Without God's word of grace to build us up (Acts 20:32), we will fall into false guilt or false innocence.

Into which of these two mistakes are you more likely to fall? What can you do about it?

Prayer: Lord, both an overscrupulous conscience *and* a numb conscience are ways that my heart continues its self-salvation project. They are both ways of refusing to believe I am saved by sheer grace through Jesus. Drill the gospel down into my inmost being by the power of your Spirit. Amen.

March 28

Who can say, "I have kept my heart pure; I am clean and without sin"? (20:9)

NOT EVEN ONE. Proverbs may appear to imply that we can make ourselves good through our efforts. Yet at key places the book reminds us that wisdom is a gift of grace, and here is one of them. No one can make themselves good. Similarly, "there is no one righteous, not even one" (Romans 3:10), and "if you, Lord, kept a record of sins . . . who could stand?" (Psalm 130:3). How does this truth make us wise?

First, it means that everyone is lost. To be *clean* and *pure* is to be acceptable before God, but no one is. Psalm 130:3 says no one can "stand" before God. So the wise do not divide the world into the "good guys" and the "bad guys." Both moral and immoral are alienated from God, though in different ways. Second, it means God must save by grace. So the wise fuel their efforts for right living out of joy and gratitude for the free salvation they have in Christ. They escape the drudgery and crushing motive of seeking righteousness in order to deserve it.

Do you tend to divide the world into the "good" types and "bad" types? How does that contradict a sound doctrine of sin?

Prayer: Lord, I should not be disappointed that people are as bad as they are, so much as amazed that so many of them are as good as they are by your grace. Let me be as gracious to sinners as you are. Amen.

March 29

> Whoever conceals their sins does not prosper, but the one who confesses and renounces them finds mercy. (28:13)

CONFESSION. If we try to cover up our sin, God will expose us. If we expose our sin, God will cover it with his *mercy*. How do we *conceal* sins from others? We lie. We blame-shift and make excuses. We tell people to mind their own business and point to the good things we have done. We rationalize that our motives were good or that our action wasn't technically wrong.

But we also hide our sins from ourselves. We find ways to justify them, as we give lip service and admit a sin but we don't renounce it. Despite the subterfuge, deep down we know we are sinners, that there is something seriously wrong with us. This produces severe imbalances in our psychological life, from which flow many ills: eating disorders, anxiety, substance abuse, overwork, anger. We may find ourselves so needy for affirmation that we stay in the wrong, or even abusive, relationships. The solution? "If we confess our sins . . . we have an advocate with the Father—Jesus Christ, the Righteous One. He is the atoning sacrifice for our sins" (1 John 1:9, 2:1–2).

What is your most typical strategy for concealing your sin—from others or from yourself?

Prayer: Lord, I want and need a clear conscience, but that can't be unless I fully admit where I have a bad one. Unveil to me where I conceal my sin so that I can confess it and let you, and you alone, cover it through your infinite mercy. Amen.

March 30

The discerning heart seeks knowledge, but the mouth of a fool feeds on folly. (15:14)

THE DISCERNING HEART. Fools can be said to be all mouth, always spouting foolishness. The wise, however, are all heart—and every new experience is a way for their hearts to become more *discerning*.

In a TV episode, based on an Agatha Christie story, a retired Scotland Yard inspector explains to an incredulous friend that Miss Marple is the greatest criminologist in England. "There she sits," he says, "an elderly spinster. Sweet, placid, or so you'd think. Yet her mind has plumbed the depths of human iniquity and taken it all in a day's work. She has lived all her life in a little rural village of St. Mary Mead. It's extraordinary! She knows the world only through the prism of that village and its daily life, but by knowing the village so thoroughly, she seems to know the world." Like Jesus, the ultimate wise one, she loves people but she doesn't trust human nature (John 2:23–25). The secrets of wisdom are locked in your ordinary experience if you know how to learn from it. Ask God to help you develop a *discerning heart.*[80]

In what area or way has God enabled you to grow in discernment during the past year?

Prayer: Lord, you are the ultimate teacher of wisdom. You sat with your disciples and taught them in parables. Now help me learn wisdom from my experience. I commit new time to prayer, reading, and solitude, so you can do that for me. Amen.

March 31

As water reflects the face, so one's life reflects the heart. (27:19)

INTROVERT OR EXTROVERT? As water shows us our face, *so one's life reflects the heart.* But whose heart and whose life are being referred to? Is it saying that we should explore our life history to understand what is in our hearts—as did Augustine in his *Confessions*? Or does it mean that by getting to know others, you can learn about your own heart? For example, there is no better way to see what you are doing wrong in your own marriage than to try to counsel and help friends whose marriage is troubled.

There's good reason to think that the ambiguity of the proverb is deliberate. To truly come to wise self-knowledge you must use both methods. Introverts are more naturally inclined to explore their own lives and extroverts to get involved in the lives of others. But both methods for self-knowledge are needed. Introverts should get out more, and extroverts should spend more time in solitary thought.

Are you more of an introvert or extrovert? How can you begin to use the way of wisdom that you are not naturally inclined to use?

Prayer: Lord, "but who can discern their own errors? Forgive my hidden faults. Keep your servant also from willful sins; may they not rule over me" (Psalm 19:12–13). Show me what I must do to cooperate with you in the answering of this prayer. Amen.

April 1

Like a coating of silver dross on earthenware are fervent lips with an evil heart. Enemies disguise themselves with their lips, but in their hearts they harbor deceit. Though their speech is charming, do not believe them, for seven abominations fill their hearts. (26:23–25)

INSIDE AND OUTSIDE. 26:23 introduces the image of a vessel that looks like pure silver but is just valueless clay with a thin *coating of silver dross*. This distinction between the inside and outside is crucial to biblical wisdom. In the fairy tale *The Princess and Curdie*, by George MacDonald, the hero is given a magical ability. He can touch the hand of someone and discern their true inward character. So he might shake the hand of a beautiful woman or man and perceive the claw of a vulture, or he might take the hand of a monster and feel the fingers of a loving child. This ability, of course, enables him to triumph.

The more you grow in godly wisdom, the more you get this same world-beating ability. "Wise folk see through the façade of hypocrisy, withhold trust, and do not take liars at face value."[81] In order to live wisely in our present culture of self-promotion, fake news, alternative facts, and the overthrow of reason, the ability to discern evil disguised as good could not be more important.

Recall a time when you seriously misread someone's character and intentions, perhaps because of attractive superficialities. How likely are you to make the same mistake again?

Prayer: Lord, I live in a culture that puts all the stress on image and beauty. Don't let me be swayed by appearances. Keep me from favoring people based on their looks. Let me remember that the most beautiful soul in history was not beautiful to look at (Isaiah 53:2). Amen.

April 2

The purposes of a person's heart are deep waters, but one who has insight draws them out. (20:5)

DEEP WATERS. If you want to hide something, a good way is to throw it into deep waters. So too our heart motives seem out of sight. However, "wise persons can bring to the surface what others have in mind, even when there are attempts at conceal-ment."[82] This tells us the wise are able to discern motives—both their own and those of others. While we want to think we are telling the truth for noble motives, are we really being driven by insecurity or resentment? While this person assures us he is on our side, is he really just using us for his own purposes?

We must remember it is possible to become overly suspicious or paranoid (28:1), or just uncharitable (1 Corinthians 13:7), which can lead to as many wrong decisions as naïveté. As *insight* is a gift of God (2:6, 9:10), it is better to think of this ability to discern hearts not as a technique but as a spiritual gift from the only one who can see every heart to the very bottom (16:2). Don't look for little signs by which you can "spy the lie." Insight comes through growth in grace and its accompanying self-knowledge. "My own heart"—we need no other—"showeth me the wicked-ness of the ungodly" (Psalm 36:1).[83]

How gullible are you?

Prayer: Lord, I want to be wise but I've often been fooled. Yet I don't want to take an always-skeptical stance either. Both are simplistic. Give me insight into people's hearts so that I trust those I should trust and beware of those of whom I should be wary. Amen.

April 3

> What the wicked dread will overtake them; what the righteous desire will be granted. . . . The righteousness of the upright delivers them, but the unfaithful are trapped by evil desires. . . . Desire without knowledge is not good—how much more will hasty feet miss the way! (10:24, 11:6, 19:2)

TRAPPED BY DESIRE. The "heart" is not mere feeling but rather the seat of our deepest trusts and loves (March 26). Today's society, however, identifies our strongest feelings as the "true self" and insists we express them. But wisdom recognizes that our desires can trap us (11:6). They can also be influenced from outside. Modern consumer capitalism creates the desire to accumulate material goods that, we think, will give us status and identity. Poor parenting can train children to so desire approval and love that they remain in abusive relationships or become workaholics.

Wise people do not simply accept their desires as they are, nor with hasty feet run to fulfill them. Rather, as Augustine counseled, they reorder their desires with the knowledge of the truth. The problem of the workaholic, for example, is not that we love work too much, but that we love God too little, relative to our career. What the righteous desire is ultimately God himself, seeing his face. "I . . . will see your face . . . I will be satisfied with seeing your likeness" (Psalm 17:15). Only if we cultivate our relationship to God and grow the desire for him will our other desires not entrap us.

What loves or desires do you have that are "inordinate," that push God out of the top spot?

Prayer: Lord, I see that I don't really love my job or my comforts or my family too much. I love you too little in proportion to them. Only if I love you supremely will I love everything else well and properly. Capture my heart! Amen.

April 4

A longing fulfilled is sweet to the soul, but fools detest turning from evil. . . . Do not let your heart envy sinners, but always be zealous for the fear of the LORD. There is surely a future hope for you, and your hope will not be cut off. (13:19, 23:17–18)

ORDERING DESIRE. The soul has an appetite. We are drawn to good things that are satisfying, but nothing besides God himself should be a nonnegotiable necessity for life. Every other enjoyment comes with the danger that we make it such. "To set your heart on [any good] thing is to weaken the power to assess it. It must be had, at all costs, not now because of its worth but because you have promised it to yourself."[84]

How, then, can we desire God above all other things? Plato said actions flow from thinking and Aristotle taught that our thinking is shaped by our actions. Proverbs says they are both right. Contemplate 23:17–18. Use the mind to think—what are the only things that finally last? (*There is . . . a future hope.*) Set the heart on God in prayer and worship until you don't just believe but experience awe and wonder (*be zealous . . . fear*) before him. And set the will on obedience. Don't *envy* (or imitate) *sinners*. These things will reorder your desires.

How specifically will you implement any of these strategies this week? See the prayer below for one.

Prayer: Lord, I spend far more time asking for various things than in praise and adoration of your greatness. No wonder, then, that I long for the things more than I long for you. How wonderful that the thing that most honors you will most transform me. I commit myself to giving you that glory every day. Amen.

April 5

Do not envy the wicked, do not desire their company; for their hearts plot violence, and their lips talk about making trouble. (24:1–2)

THE SOCIOLOGY OF DESIRE. Sociologists know that we tend to find most plausible the ideas of the people with whom we spend the most time and to whom our admiration is most directed. If we "sit in the company of mockers" (Psalm 1:1) or of the cruel and violent (verse 2), we will become like them. It is easy to *envy* mockers and cruel people because they are often successful through their ruthlessness.

Today we believe that we can create our own identity through our own free choices. We may think we are being "true to ourselves" when we shed the constraints of traditional values and morality, but in reality we are simply allowing a new community to tell us who we are. "The question of individual identity is always also a question of community, from family and church, school and business, all the way up to nation and state. Communities create the paths we walk."[85]

Why do you hang out with the people you do? Have your choices been influenced by a desire to be like the people you spend time with the most?

Prayer: Lord, because I'm too busy to spend sustained time with other believers, I am being shaped by other communities—through social media, news media, and the stream of advertisements and bulletins that come at me every day. Motivate me to seek friends who believe, and then help me find them. Amen.

Fear of man will prove to be a snare, but whoever trusts in the LORD is kept safe. (29:25)

APPROVAL. The only way to reorder our desires toward God is to identify where our hearts are already committed instead. For the next four days we will look at four typical God substitutes. The first is human approval. The *fear of man* is a *snare*. If we look to human beings more than to God for our worth and value, we will be trapped by anxiety, by an overneed to please, by the inability to withdraw from exploitative relationships, by the inability to take criticism, and by a cowardice that makes us unable to confront others. Our feelings will be easily hurt and we will tend to overcommit out of a desire for acceptance.

The devastation that comes from the fear of man has many forms. It includes parents who are afraid to discipline their children and employees who are unable to call out corruption in their companies. But we must obey God rather than men (Acts 5:29). The only thing that casts out the fear of man is a deep love relationship with God (1 John 4:18). Then we can say, "The Lord is my helper; I will not be afraid. What can mere mortals do to me?" (Hebrews 13:6)

Whose approval is functionally more important to you than God's?

Prayer: Lord Jesus, you said that you were the liberator (John 8:36). Now liberate me from my enslavement to the "fear of man." I am far too concerned about what people think of me. If I have the regard of the King, why should I care about what others say? Never let me forget this. Amen.

Do not love sleep or you will grow poor; stay awake and you will have food to spare. . . . Whoever loves pleasure will become poor; whoever loves wine and olive oil will never be rich. (20:13, 21:17)

COMFORT. A second form of inordinate desire is an inordinate love of physical pleasure and comfort. The *pleasure* described here is the joy that comes from the satisfaction of physical wants. *Wine*, of course, heightens spirits while *oil* was used in cosmetics and indicates beauty and sensual comfort.[86] The Bible isn't against pleasure *per se*. Wine gladdens the heart of man and oil makes the face shine (Psalm 104:15). And the overlove of comfort is no more wrong than the overlove of *dis*comfort. Sleeping when you should work (20:13) and working when you should be resting (Psalm 127:2) are both wrong.

Yet if we become "lovers of pleasure rather than lovers of God" (2 Timothy 3:4), it leads to disaster—not only economic but also emotional and spiritual. At one level, addiction to comfort can make people detached, avoiding entanglements with people in order to protect their own time and convenience. It can also lead to literal addictions to substances and sexual practices. Idolatry takes many forms, and it is the wise man or woman who can locate and destroy anything usurping God's place.

What pleasures are perhaps too important to you—not just giving comfort but giving you a consolation only God should give?

Prayer: Lord Jesus, you left the unimaginable comforts of heaven for a life of hardship on earth for me. Someday I will live in that same unimaginably glorious world. Until then, however, let me not set my heart on thrills, sensations, and comfort but follow in your footsteps. Amen.

April 8

A kindhearted woman gains honor, but ruthless men gain only wealth. . . . The wise prevail through great power and those who have knowledge muster their strength. (11:16, 24:5)

POWER. Another overdesire is the will to power. In 11:16 the word *gains* means to seize or take hold of through sheer power. That is how ruthless men live. By contrast, the kindhearted woman is "someone who is characterized by grace . . . someone who acts for the benefit of others, not expecting a return."[87] While she gives up power to serve others, they serve only their love of power, which can take many forms. Ambition and careerism can be driven by a desire for wealth as a means of gaining power. The overlove of power can also show itself in people who are opinionated, poor listeners, argumentative, highly partisan, unteachable, and afraid to admit when they have been in the wrong.

As the woman gains honor, paradoxically, by *not* seeking honor at all, so Jesus achieved true strength by seeking not power but service. "Who is greater, the one who sits at the table or the one who serves? . . . I am among you as one who serves" (Luke 22:27). 24:5 teaches that wisdom itself—not being wise in your own eyes, loving God, disadvantaging yourself for others—is in the end the greatest *power* and *strength* of all.

When did you last give up significant power in order to serve someone else?

Prayer: Lord, there is nothing more seductive than power. If I am honest, I confess that there are many situations and relationships I enjoy mainly because of the power I exercise in them. Help me to kill the sinful part of my heart that rejoices in that. Amen.

April 9

Do not boast about tomorrow, for you do not know what a day may bring. (27:1)

CONTROL. The greatest nightmare of the approval addict is rejection; of the power addict, humiliation; of the comfort addict, suffering; and of the control addict, uncertainty. Though the sluggard refuses to plan (20:4), the opposite error is to think you can control the future—and your whole life—through planning and management. Those who believe they can eliminate uncertainty *boast about tomorrow*, thinking they have planned for every contingency. People with an overneed for control have trouble sharing power, can't delegate, and tend to manipulate people, using guilt and pressure to get people to do what they want.

But you *do not know what* is to come. The future is wholly in the hands of God (16:1,3,9). Confidence regarding the future is possible for the wise person, but it is not founded on our own abilities. Such confidence must be "realistic, modest, and grounded in the fear of the Lord."[88] This overconfidence in one's ability to control life is always haunted by the nagging sin of worry (Matthew 6:19–34), just as the desire for power is dogged by anger, the fear of man by cowardice, and the lover of pleasure by boredom.

Do you get very anxious when you lose direct control of a relationship or a situation?

Prayer: Lord, you are God, and I will find rest nowhere but in your will, and "that will is infinitely, immeasurably, unspeakably beyond my largest notions of what [you] are up to."[89] Amen.

April 10

> She took hold of him and kissed him and with a brazen face she said: "Today I fulfilled my vows, and I have food from my fellowship offering at home." (7:13–15)

MAGICAL THINKING. Proverbs chapter 7 dramatically depicts an act of adultery. In the process it teaches us how the heart falls into temptation. At the beginning of the tryst the woman says to her would-be lover that she has fulfilled her religious *vows* by making a *fellowship offering* at the temple (cf. Leviticus 3:1–17). This consisted of a meal that many could eat. So, she says, I have prayed and sacrificed to God. Now please come to my home to finish the religious observance. And because my husband is not home (7:19), we can then make love. Put more starkly: "After we finish our prayers and devotions we can commit adultery!"

The disconnect between her public profession of faith and the conduct of her private life is startling but all too common. She has exchanged wholehearted discipleship for a magical view in which God is more like an idol who can be placated by various observances. We need to learn that unconditional obedience *is* the only sacrifice that is reasonable, in light of all God has done for us through creation and redemption (Romans 12:1–2).

Is there any place that you see a disconnect between your public profession of faith and your private life?

Prayer: Lord, I have come to realize—or perhaps just to finally admit—that there are parts of my life I simply disconnect from my belief in you. I act as if you don't exist in that area of my life. I repent and ask your help to change that. Amen.

April 11

> "So I came out to meet you; I looked for you and have found you! I have covered my bed with colored linens from Egypt. I have perfumed my bed with myrrh, aloes and cinnamon. Come, let's drink deeply of love till morning; let's enjoy ourselves with love!" (7:15–18)

ENTERING IN. Temptation has stages. First comes rationalization (7:14). In this case the lovers share a fellowship sacrifice meal. They must find a way to reconcile the adultery with their self-image as still-being-good people. There are many ways to do this. The self-pitying, overworking man might look with desire at a woman who is not his wife and say, "After all I've sacrificed, I deserve this."

Second, we believe an overpromise. The woman says, literally, "I looked for you *only*" (verse 15), meaning "You are the one I've been looking for all my life." What is promised is a kind of cosmic fulfillment that no sexual encounter can ever deliver. Third comes the titillation of the senses—the aromas, the sights, the physical arousal (*"I have perfumed my bed . . . let's drink deeply of love"*). By now, applying the brakes and saying no is nearly impossible. Temptation is impossible to completely avoid. But as Martin Luther is reputed to have said, "While you can't stop the birds from flying over your head, you can stop them from making nests in your hair." That is, stop things before they get away from you.

Have you seen these stages of temptation play out in any area of your life?

Prayer: Lord, you asked your disciples in Gethsemane to watch and pray against temptation, but they did not. Oh, how I want to be different. Help me discern the very first stages of temptation to lust, pride, anger, or greed—so I can turn from sin before I lose control. Amen.

April 12

"My husband is not at home; he has gone on a long journey. He took his purse filled with money and will not be home till full moon." With persuasive words she led him astray; she seduced him with her smooth talk. All at once he followed her like an ox going to the slaughter, like a deer stepping into a noose till an arrow pierces his liver, like a bird darting into a snare, little knowing it will cost him his life. (7:19–23)

TOO EASY—TOO HARD. Sometimes there is another stage to temptation (see April 11 for the others). It is reassurance that there will be no real consequences. *"My husband is not at home . . . and will not be home till full moon"* (7:19–20). Temptation is extremely powerful if you believe "no one will ever know!" But in reality there will always be a heavy cost (verse 23) for transgressing the givenness of God's spiritual and moral order. In the case of adultery, it could mean inward and outward shame or the financial and physical danger that comes from a wronged husband's wrath (6:33–35). And God will always know.

The seventeenth-century writer Thomas Brooks, in his book *Precious Remedies Against Satan's Devices*, argued that Satan tempts you by assuring you that you can always repent later. "But he who now tempts you to sin upon the account that repentance is easy, will, ere long, bring you to despair, and forever destroy your soul, [and] represent repentance as the most difficult and hardest work in the world."[90]

Have you experienced this satanic device? When and how?

Prayer: Lord, I know this demonic lie—that I can sin now and later ask forgiveness. But when I've gone that route I've discovered that my heart becomes too hard and despondent to repent. Thank you for today's reminder of this device of Satan, and call it to mind the next time he uses it on me. Amen.

April 13

> Now then, my sons, listen to me; pay attention to what I say. Do not let your heart turn to her ways or stray into her paths. Many are the victims she has brought down; her slain are a mighty throng. Her house is a highway to the grave, leading down to the chambers of death. (7:24–27)

DEFENSE. How then can we defend ourselves against the many temptations that face us, whether they are in the arena of sex, money, power, or something else? First, watch your *heart* (7:25a). Temptation always starts in the inward thoughts. We can't stop ideas from occurring to us, but we must not entertain them. Fondling the secret thoughts, thinking out rationalizations, exploring the possible consequences—all of these trains of thought are allowing the temptation to make its case to us. Second, we must not *stray into her paths* (verse 25b). That is, we should literally stay away from places, situations, and persons that make it easy for our minds to go down the wrong trail.

Third, we should assure ourselves of the inevitable damage and spiritual destruction that always come (*a highway to the grave . . . down to the chambers of death*—verse 27). Look down that highway and see the ultimate tragedy and wrongfulness of sin: It grieves God and spurns the sacrifice he made to save you in Jesus Christ.

Have you seen in your own life how these three strategies have helped you in exercising self-control and defense against temptation?

Prayer: Lord, my ultimate defense against the enticements of sin is to remember that it was sin that led you to the cross. You died—you lost everything—to free me from sin. How can I trample on your costly love by giving in to it? Never let this thought leave me. Amen.

April 14

> A heart at peace gives life to the body, but envy rots the bones. . . . A cheerful heart is good medicine, but a crushed spirit dries up the bones. (14:30, 17:22)

THE WHOLE PERSON. Long before modern medicine and psychology, Proverbs taught that emotional well-being was connected to physical health and well-being. *Envy rots the bones* but *a cheerful heart is good medicine.* Yet today specialization and bureaucratization mean that physician, psychiatrist, social worker, and minister often end up treating only one isolated aspect of the person, without consulting one another or looking at the person as a whole.

English minister Richard Baxter, even in the seventeenth century, knew that depression could be rooted in a physiological cause, emotional trauma, moral guilt, or spiritual warfare with evil forces.[91] Baxter was not trained in modern science. He knew this from the Scripture in general and the book of Proverbs in particular. Godly wisdom refuses to reduce depression, for example, to any one cause. It does not have simply a chemical or simply a moral or simply a spiritual cause. All the dimensions of our nature are usually involved. It is foolish to reduce the solution to just "take a pill" or to just "repent."

Have you ever taken a too-simplistic or reductionistic approach to a problem that turned out to be complex—physical, emotional, and spiritual all at once?

Prayer: Lord, as a modern person I love quick solutions for problems that you can access on a short YouTube video. But the world you've made has far more dimensions than anyone can imagine. Help me to be patient, to seek much advice, and to depend on you in order to make progress with my problems. Amen.

April 15

Anxiety weighs down the heart, but a kind word cheers it up. (12:25)

ANXIETY. The Hebrew word translated as *anxiety* means the emotional distress caused when something vital to your life is threatened.[92] The key to dealing with anxiety is to look at our heart attitude toward the thing threatened. There are many things that are considered important for a high quality of life in this world. Yet as we have seen, if we rely on God the most, that makes everything else less vital and thus our lives less fragile.

Anxiety cannot be completely eliminated. Because Paul loved his young churches, he was anxious for them (2 Corinthians 11:28), and yet he counsels us to avoid debilitating anxiety by deliberately resting our hearts in God rather than anything else (Philippians 4:6–9). In this proverb, however, we are told we should not try to deal with anxiety on our own. We need *a kind word* from others. We need people to affirm us, to relate their own experience, to point us to God, or even just to be there so we don't feel so alone.

What helps you the most when you are anxious? Have you used all the spiritual resources you have for anxiety?

Prayer: Lord, you have instructed that I deal with anxiety through, among other things, thanksgiving (Philippians 4:6–9). So I thank you for all the ways in the past you took care of me. And I thank you ahead of time, knowing it will be wise and good, for whatever you do with my future. Amen.

April 16

Hope deferred makes the heart sick, but a longing fulfilled is a tree of life. (13:12)

HOPE. At the core of the human heart are not just emotions but hopes—things we look to and trust in to make us happy. When something we long for is *deferred* or delayed, we become heart-sick.

It is wisdom to recognize that the condition of deferred hopes is one that can never be fully remedied in this life. The book of Hebrews likens the whole Christian life to the period when the Israelites had been delivered from slavery but were not yet in the Promised Land (Hebrews 11:13–14). The second clause of 13:12 is saying that when our longings are fulfilled, life flourishes briefly, as it did back in paradise, where we had access to the Tree of Life (Genesis 2:9). But the New Testament tells us we will know full satisfaction only in the new heavens and new earth (Revelation 22:2), which will be ours not through our efforts but through the work of Jesus Christ. As we have seen, his cross became a tree of death for him so that we could have the tree of life by faith. We face disappointment now by reminding ourselves of what is to come, guaranteed by Christ's sacrifice.

Do an honest assessment—what are your greatest hopes? Are they being "deferred"? How can you use the spiritual resources you have to help your heartsickness?

Prayer: Lord, I often am indeed heartsick because of deferred hopes. Help me strengthen my heart in two ways. Remind me through your Word that we are in the wilderness, not in the Promised Land. And make yourself my most cherished hope—because I can have you now! Amen.

April 17

Each heart knows its own bitterness, and no one else can share its joy. (14:10)

ALONE. No one can fully share the joys and know the sorrows of another human being. No one has experienced your life exactly as you have. The implications for wisdom are many. From the outside, never be completely assured that you can absolutely predict or understand the behavior of another person. You may guess wrongly what a person is thinking, what things motivate him or her, and why certain feelings are so strong.

From the inside, remember that no one can read your mind. If you don't want to be terribly lonely, you will have to open your heart and reveal yourself. Finally, in the end, only the Lord can know all the thoughts of the heart (1 Corinthians 2:11), and he knows them better than you do (Jeremiah 17:9–10; Proverbs 21:2). Jesus walked through death for you, and now only he can take you by the hand when you walk through the ultimate dark place, the door of death (Psalm 23:4).

Though we all need human friendship, it will not replace true friendship with God. Can you say that you enjoy friendship with God? Why or why not?

Prayer: Lord, I have great friends and a great family, but only you are truly, always with me. The only way, then, that I can avoid terrible loneliness is to spend more and more time with you. Don't let the world squeeze out my time with you. Amen.

April 18

Even in laughter the heart may ache, and rejoicing may end in grief.
(14:13)

LOOK DEEPER. Experienced counselors know well the truths behind this proverb, but anyone who wants to live wisely must know them too.

First, it means there is a tragedy and a sadness to life from which no amount of celebration or rejoicing can provide a full escape. Some wounds never really heal. The festal joy that Jesus brings is always partial in this life, never full. Jesus himself did a lot of weeping, not because of anything wrong with him but because his perfect, loving heart was necessarily affected by the sadness of human life. So will ours be. Second, "our moods are seldom untinged with their opposites, and are none of them permanent."[93] Perhaps the simplest lesson is that we should look past the surface statements of "I'm fine, thanks" and even "life of the party" behavior and listen more carefully if we are to discern how a person is really doing.

Do you tend to turn everything into a joke or carry on in a lighthearted way? That can be pleasant to some, but might it not be a denial of or insensitivity to the genuine sadness of life?

Prayer: Lord, in this world even the happiest times are tinged with sadness. But that is offset with a knowledge of your promises, so even the saddest times can be tinged with happiness. Trouble makes us depend more on you and in prayer seek more your love. Indeed, you make "my griefs to sing."[94] Amen.

April 19

Light in a messenger's eyes brings joy to the heart, and good news gives health to the bones. (15:30)

JOY. If the verse of April 18 exhorted us to look more carefully to see how a person is doing, this proverb suggests looking at the *eyes*, especially at their *light*. We speak of eyes shining, gleaming, brightening, and we don't mean any literal light coming through them. Observant people know that even if a person's words are positive, a lack of light in the eyes can reveal sadness. If the messenger here is the radiant face of a friend who brings some encouraging news, we learn how important relationships are for a life of joy.

So for joy in our hearts we need people with light in their eyes. But where do they get it? Paul tells Christians that they can have a joy not based on circumstances at all, which requires thoughtfulness and meditation on what God has done for us and will do for us (Philippians 4:4,11–13). There is, then, a joy that comes only through the ultimate message—the gospel, which literally means "the news that brings joy." If you believe in Jesus, then you have truly seen "a great light" (Matthew 4:16), and it is inevitable that your eyes will reflect it to others.

Would anyone say that your joy and happiness lifts up their hearts?

Prayer: Lord, give me the joy that I need to live the day. I lack joy because I don't spend sustained time in detailed thanksgiving for both temporal and spiritual gifts and blessings. And I don't simply rejoice enough just in being in your presence. Provoke me to do the things that bring your joy into my life. Amen.

April 20

The wicked flee though no one pursues, but the righteous are as bold as a lion. (28:1)

GUILT. Behind the insecurity that many experience is a guilty conscience. The more we lie and betray, the more we fear being betrayed until we *flee though no one pursues*. This goes beyond just remorse for past misdeeds. Even in our modern relativistic culture, we see "The Strange Persistence of Guilt."[95] We struggle mightily with a sense that there is something wrong with us, that we are not who we should be. The Bible tells us this is a repressed knowledge that we are sinners (Romans 1:18).

Those whose consciences are clear toward God do not have to be looking back over their shoulders. They can be *bold as a lion*. Why? If your sins are covered by God's grace (Psalm 32:1), then your past will not be pursuing you (Numbers 32:23) but only God's goodness and mercy (Psalm 23:6).[96] Lady Macbeth could not rid herself of the stain of guilt on her hands, but Jesus is the messenger of the covenant (Malachi 3:1–4) who can cleanse us of any stain and guilt (1 John 1:7).

Do you have a guilty conscience about anything?

Prayer: Father, when I don't confess the things I know I've done wrong, I overwork and overcommit. I see now that this is because I am trying to atone for my own sins. But I can't. Let me rest in your Son's sacrifice, and rest content. Amen.

April 21

A person may think their own ways are right, but the LORD weighs the heart. (21:2)

GOD'S SCALES. 16:2 said we think our motives are pure when they are not (March 27). Here 21:2 says something a bit different. We think we can determine what is right, just and true, but humans do not define what is right or wrong—God does.[97] We live in an era when we are told, "No one has the right to tell anyone else how to live," that we can define right and wrong for ourselves. Yet this cultural assumption is riddled with contradictions. We hold it but in the next breath criticize people for bigotry or greed or cruelty. Justice has one set of scales—God's. He alone *weighs* every *heart*.

So don't overly trust your moral instincts and motives. We say we confront people "for their own good," but really are we just trying to punish them? We tell ourselves we are attracted to someone out of love, but really is it because their looks and beauty build up our ego? Let God's Word search and sift your instincts and motives through study and prayer.

Are you too quick to ascribe good motives to yourself? Recall a time when you fooled yourself about the real reasons you pursued something.

Prayer: Lord, I whiplash back and forth between too much introspection and too little. Cure this in me with the gospel. Your unconditional love for me in Christ keeps me from either trying to earn your love through self-examination or fearing to do it at all. Amen.

April 22

The human spirit can endure in sickness, but a crushed spirit who can bear? (18:14)

THE CRUSHED SPIRIT. As we have seen, Proverbs sees that the emotional and physical health are integral and both important. But this text adds nuance to that. It teaches that without physical well-being, life is hard, and without any joy, it is unbearable.[98]

What is the implication? There's nothing more important than maintaining your inward, spiritual life. A broken body can be sustained with difficulty by a strong spirit, but a broken spirit cannot be sustained by even the physically strongest person in the world. We are taught that our happiness is based on external things such as beauty, health, money, and status. Here we are being told, "No, it has nothing to do with your outward circumstances. Happiness is determined by how you deal with your circumstances from inside, how you process, how you address, and how you view them."

Is there anything that is crushing your spirit?

Prayer: Lord, I do blame my circumstances for my unhappiness, and that makes me secretly resentful toward you. But my joy is largely determined by where I rest my heart. Free me from enslavement to circumstance. Let me rest my hope and heart in you. Amen.

April 23

A happy heart makes the face cheerful, but heartache crushes the spirit. The discerning heart seeks knowledge, but the mouth of a fool feeds on folly. (15:13–14)

HAPPINESS IS A CHOICE. Remember that the "heart" in the Bible is not the emotions but our trusts and attitudes. The *happy heart*, we are told here, is the *discerning heart*, filled with wise convictions and commitments. 15:13–14, then, is telling us that the wise heart leads to cheerful emotions, and the foolish heart to crushed emotions. The principle is a subtle one but important. It means, ultimately, that happiness is a choice. Our "thoughts and attitudes . . . not the circumstances, are decisive.[99]

We have gone far enough in the book of Proverbs to see, however, that we are not talking about mere stoicism, a simple clamping down of emotions through willpower. The heart consists of the attitudes and stances toward life. We can choose to reflect with our mind and to fire our imagination through art, singing, and worship—all so that the truths and realities of God and of his grace and promises fill our view.

What is making you unhappy? How can the insights of these proverbs help you today?

Prayer: Lord, I am so, so spiritually weak, that in order to live the life I should, I need *both* a mind convinced by solid arguments *and* an imagination fired with the beauty of your character and story. Show me how to bring both into my life. Amen.

April 24

Better a patient person than a warrior, one with self-control than one who takes a city. (16:32)

SELF-CONTROL: THE IMPORTANCE. *A warrior* knew how to conquer and master a whole city. But these proverbs argue that even *better* is the patient, self-controlled person who knows how to conquer and master himself. This means that is it harder to master yourself than to master others, or even a whole nation. There are too many examples of world beaters who won prizes or literally conquered nations but who could not control their tempers, their tongues, or their emotions.

In ancient times people with *self-control* and prudence were highly admired over those who followed whim and passion. Today self-control is often seen as unhealthy. Following one's passion, feeling one's anger, and being spontaneous are all valued in the world of the creative and sophisticated. Yet so many of our most famous celebrities, following this pattern, have made a shipwreck of their lives. As we have seen, biblical wisdom is all about the goodness of emotion, yet it is God's Word, not our intuitions and feelings, that must be sovereign.

Where has a lack of self-control brought trouble into your life?

Prayer: Lord, the last of the "fruit of the Spirit" (Galatians 5: 22–23), self-control, seems to be also the slowest to grow in me. I can be loving and even humble before I can get control of my tongue and behavior. I repent and ask you to show me the way forward. Amen.

April 25

Like a city whose walls are broken through is a person who lacks self-control. (25:28)

SELF-CONTROL: THE PROBLEM. Without a wall the residents of ancient cities were vulnerable to attacks by bands of robbers, other nations' armies, and even animals. A person who *lacks self-control* is just as defenseless. If you can't control your appetite for food, you will ruin your body. If you can't control your tongue or temper, you will say things that can't be unsaid or taken back. If you can't control your sexual desires, you will ruin relationships. If you are impulsive and imprudent, not thinking things out, you will make rash decisions. If you can't say no to people, you will overpromise and either be exhausted and overextended or have a life filled with disillusioned people and broken relationships.

A city doesn't have to be completely without a wall in order to be sacked. The wall just needs to be *broken through* at one point to let the enemy in. So a lack of self-control—even in just one area of life—is a life-threatening problem.

Where is your "wall" broken or most vulnerable? In what area of life do you most need self-control?

Prayer: Lord, help me to do a survey of my life the way ancient soldiers examined their city wall. Show me where I most need fortification in my self-control. I have an idea, but I want to take time to examine myself with your help. Amen.

April 26

The name of the LORD is a fortified tower; the righteous run to it and are safe. The wealth of the rich is their fortified city; they imagine it a wall too high to scale. (18:10–11)

SELF-CONTROL: THE SOLUTION. In ancient times a wall was a safe place in an attack, but *a fortified tower* was even better. These two proverbs indicate that everyone has a place of ultimate security, a "fortification," something about which they say, "If I have that, I'll be safe." The wealthy, the powerful, the beautiful all think that these things are their "towers."

But the wise person runs into *the name of the Lord*. In the Bible, God's name is a way of speaking of his nature and attributes. To run into God's name is to deliberately rehearse and tell yourself who he is. Jesus asked his fearful disciples in the storm, "Where is your faith?" He chastised them for failing to remember all that they had seen him do (Luke 8:25). If you panic, you are failing to remember (to "run into") his power, his wisdom, his love for you. Self-control in any situation is the critical ability to both recognize and choose the important thing over the urgent thing. To honor, trust in, and please God is always the most important thing.

What are you facing right now that is difficult? What attribute of God might you be forgetting—and might help greatly if you remembered it?

Prayer: Lord, the more you are on the periphery of my thoughts and feelings, the less self-control I have. The more you are in the center, vividly before the eyes of my heart and attention, the more I can control myself. Lord, grab and hold my attention, moment by moment, so I can live as I should. Amen.

April 27

Evildoers are snared by their own sin, but the righteous shout for joy and are glad. (29:6)

SHOUT FOR JOY. Because God's creation has an order within it, evildoers are *snared by their own sin*. But, as we have seen, the arcs of sin and righteousness toward their destinies can be very long. For the time being, sin may bring prosperity and righteousness may lead to suffering. In fact, it is only in eternity that sin receives its full retribution and goodness its complete reward.

So evildoers may not be "snared" for a long time. But there is no reason for believers to wait until the end to *shout for joy* and be glad. Indeed, anyone leading a wise life, regardless of the inevitable difficulties, will have times of shout-out-loud joy and laughter. In his very first miraculous sign, Jesus revealed himself to be Lord of the feast, who comes to bring us festal joy (John 2:1–11). Every time we participate in the Lord's supper, we are literally getting a foretaste of that final, endless, incomparable feast that has been guaranteed to us by his death and resurrection (Isaiah 25:6–8; Revelation 19:6–8). Here is the joy that we can access anytime.

When was the last time you experienced shout-out-loud joy in God? Has it been too long?

Prayer: Lord, at the wedding feast of Cana (John 2) you sat among the joyous, thinking of your coming sorrow. But you went to the cross so we can sit here surrounded by sorrows, sipping the coming joy. How I praise you for your great salvation. Amen.

April 28

> Whoever is patient has great understanding, but one who is quick-tempered displays folly. . . . A hot-tempered person stirs up conflict, but the one who is patient calms a quarrel. . . . Fools give full vent to their rage but the wise bring calm in the end. . . . An angry person stirs up conflict, and a hot-tempered person commits many sins. (14:29, 15:18, 29:11,22)

THE DANGER OF ANGER. These texts give us an extensive list of the dangers of anger. A wise person is patient with people, seeing extenuating circumstances and legitimate reasons that people misbehave. By contrast, the *quick-tempered* responds in rage rather than understanding, reducing everything to a simplistic black-and-white analysis (14:29). Anger creates greater conflict and destroys the good that cooperation and compromise can bring (15:18). While anger is not a sin in and of itself, it should be a passing thing, directed without excess to solve a problem, resulting in calm at the end (29:11). In the same way, God's anger is for a moment, but his favor lasts a lifetime (Psalm 30:5). Remember, uncontrolled anger is a "gateway drug" for many other sins (29:22). No other sinful emotion has led to so much violence and, literally, to so many dead bodies.

Think of the actions and words you most regret. How many of them were done in anger?

Prayer: Father, I have seen relationships and lives ruined irreparably by anger. Yet denied, pent-up anger can be destructive. I confess that I deny my anger even to myself. Your anger against me was never wrong, and yet you put it aside through Jesus. Teach me how to heal my anger through Jesus as well. Amen.

April 29

A hot-tempered person must pay the penalty; rescue them, and you will have to do it again. (19:19)

ONE'S OWN WORST ENEMY. The first clause literally says in the Hebrew, that the characteristically angry person "carries around punishment." This means that no one has to slap some kind of penalty or fine on the angry man or woman. Their loss of temper always entails natural consequences that they can't escape. For example, it leads the people who see the blowup to not trust the person as much as they did before.

But we should not imagine that a *hot-tempered* person is necessarily always someone who is melting down in rage. There is a kind of Christian who is habitually abrasive, critical, and ungenerous in dealing with people. They are seldom affirming and usually undiplomatic. They are prone to harsh language and cutting humor and they bristle easily when contradicted. What is behind all this unattractive behavior? It is an undercurrent of anger, like a hidden underground stream rather than a visible one on the surface that noisily rushes over stones.

The second clause tells us that people prone to anger are constantly getting themselves into new trouble. They are their own worst enemies.

How have any of these various forms of anger brought its consequences into your life in the past?

Prayer: Lord, I know anger is not always wrong, but it is seldom righteous when it appears in my life. Help me detect where it is flowing in my life. I will need both your humbling grace and your assuring love if my anger is going to subside. Please supply them. Amen.

April 30

Wealth is worthless in the day of wrath, but righteousness delivers from death.... The mouth of an adulterous woman is a deep pit; a man who is under the LORD's wrath falls into it. (11:4, 22:14)

THE GOODNESS OF ANGER. God himself is a God of wrath. St. Paul tells us not to sin in our anger (Ephesians 4:26), meaning that there is a proper place for it. So anger is not itself something bad but very quickly goes bad in us.

Anger is energy released to defend something you love. God is angry toward the evil that dishonors him and ruins that which he loves. But the problem with human anger is this—we tend to overlove the wrong things. It is not wrong to value your name and reputation, but if you love them too much, there will be inordinate anger that essentially is just a defending of your ego. Parents may get inordinately angry at children mainly because the children embarassed them before others. Because our loves are confused and out of order, our anger—basically a good thing—so often does evil. We need to look to the one whose anger was always guided by love not for himself but for us (Mark 3:5; John 2:14–17).

Think of the last time you got really angry. What were you defending?

Prayer: Lord, it is a sin for me to *not* get angry at the wrongs done to others. But I don't do that. Instead I get angry when my will is crossed. Help me learn to get angry at sin, not at sinners— at the problems, not the persons. Amen.

May 1

A gentle answer turns away wrath, but a harsh word stirs up anger. (15:1)

HELPING THE ANGRY. The first way to help an angry person is to surround them with nonangry speech. Abrasive words create more anger. In fact, a single *harsh word* can be a spark to stir up a blazing fire or rage. The word *harsh* means painful. When we argue, our words can have two quite different purposes. We can speak to simply make the truth clear (which may be painful to hear), or we can speak specifically to inflict pain, to make the other person feel foolish or bad. Of course we tell ourselves and others that the former motive is what drives us, but usually it is the latter. And one zinger word can destroy a relationship and put up a wall of bitterness that lasts years or a lifetime.

In contrast, the *gentle answer* means speaking patiently, tenderly, as affirmatively as possible, and always calmly. One of the best ways to help an angry person learn patience is to surround him with patient people. A gentle answer must still be truthful (Ephesians 4:15) but filled with evident concern and no ill will.

When was the last time you had an argument? What were your motives? Were your words gentle?

Prayer: Lord, when your disciples let you down in your hour of greatest need in Gethsemane, your words were so gentle (Matthew 26:41) and without any rancor. Even when you are stern with me, you overwhelm me with love. Let me be the same with everyone. Amen.

May 2

> Do not say, "I'll pay you back for this wrong!" Wait for the LORD, and he will avenge you. (20:22)

PERSPECTIVE. The second way to help the angry person is to give him a new perspective on vengeance. An angry person seeks to pay someone back for something—done either to him or to someone else. This requires a sense of having the high moral ground; the angry person tells himself that he would never do what that other person did. He feels that this gives him a warrant to inflict insult or pain on the other.

Instead, 20:22 tells the angry person that only God occupies high enough moral ground for vengeance. God knows all that was in the person's heart and what they deserve. You don't. God alone is holy—he alone "would never do what they did"—and so has the right to inflict judgment. You don't. God also has the power to do so in the time and manner that might lead them to repentance (Romans 2:4). You don't. If a true wrong has been done to you, *he will avenge you*. You don't have to.

Is there someone in your life whom you are having trouble forgiving? Is it because you feel you have the high moral ground?

Prayer: Lord, I now see that I cannot stay angry at someone unless I feel superior to them. Why should a saved sinner like me feel like that? If you paid me back for all I've done to you, where would I be? Help me remember these gospel truths when I'm tempted to be angry. Amen.

May 3

Do not gloat when your enemy falls; when they stumble, do not let your heart rejoice, or the LORD will see and disapprove and turn his wrath away from them. (24:17–18)

GLOATING. We have a German word that has come over into English usage—*schadenfreude*. It means to have joy because of someone else's sorrow or shame. When someone who has opposed our views and beliefs falls into scandal or turns out to be a hypocrite, we may clap our hands and say, "Ha! That shows I was right." When someone who we feel has done us wrong falls into trouble, we fist-pump "Yes!" Gloating is nothing but anger waiting for its moment and enjoying it.

But 24:17 tells us we are never to *gloat* when an opponent falls. And verse 18 shows that verse 17 is not just a suggestion. "Your glee may well be [in God's sight] a more punishable sin than all the guilt of your enemy."[100] Instead, when your opponent falls, examine yourself for your own flaws. "So, if you think you are standing firm, be careful that you don't fall" (1 Corinthians 10:12). And look to the one who did not get his joy out of our sorrow but, through his death on the cross, gave us joy through *his* sorrow (Isaiah 53:4).

Have you learned of something bad that happened to someone—and found it satisfying to you? Why?

Prayer: Lord Jesus, when you prophesied the destruction of the city that would put you to death, there was not a hint of gloating or pleasure. You just wept for them (Luke 19:41–44). Reproduce this temper of yours in me. Amen.

May 4

Hatred stirs up conflict, but love covers over all wrongs. . . . Fools show their annoyance at once, but the prudent overlook an insult. (10:12, 12:16)

ANNOYANCE. *Conflict* (Hebrew *madon*) in Proverbs does not refer to principled disagreements or respectful arguments. It is something God hates (6:19) and at the heart of conflict is *annoyance*, a word that means contempt and disdain between people. Everything said in conflict is to belittle rather than convince.

The solution is *love* (verse 12), and this doesn't primarily mean feelings. Nor does it mean to refrain from correction if it is necessary (27:5,6). When 10:12 says that love *covers* wrongs, it does not mean "cover up." Anger tries to expose and strip the other person, to make them look terrible. Love refuses to pay back and deliberately seeks to put the other person in the best light. It seeks to put their needs ahead of your own, all in the interest of helping the person change, if possible. Keep in mind that anger is energy released to defend something you love. When you are in a dispute, stop releasing your anger against the other person in order to defend your ego. Instead release your energy against the problem (not the person) that is dividing you.

Do you show annoyance in your face-to-face or online speech? If you argue, do you do it to strip or to cover the other person in love?

Prayer: Father, you pour out your anger against sin and evil, and you put away your anger through Jesus Christ. I, however, am constantly annoyed by and disdainful of so many people. Give me a far more gracious spirit that overlooks slights and puts opponents in the best possible light. Amen.

May 5

LOVING YOUR ENEMY. The final defeat of inordinate anger is not to merely refrain from payback but to positively love and do good to people who have wronged you. We are not merely to not curse but to bless (Romans 12:14). We are not merely to refuse to repay evil with evil (Romans 12:17) but to overcome evil with good (Romans 12:21).

Why is such behavior called *burning coals on the head*? Our opponents may find our kindness toward them to be painful, as Javert finds Valjean's forgiveness unbearable in *Les Misérables*. They want confirmation that their contempt for us is justified, and kind behavior robs them of it. But our motives are never to make them uncomfortable. Beware of being kind out of a desire to appear "more noble than thou." That isn't love—it's a subtle revenge. Do good to them. They may not want you to do it, but as far as it depends on you, you are to try (Romans 12:18).

Is there someone whom, while you are not trying to harm them, you are simply staying away from? How could you do good to them?

Prayer: Lord, I confess that this is one of the most radical and hard directives in your Word for me. I congratulate myself that I am not paying them back—and now you say to do them positive good! Lord, let me start by praying for them. Amen.

May 6

A heart at peace gives life to the body, but envy rots the bones. (14:30)

THE POWER OF ENVY. In the Bible we are told that God is a jealous God (Exodus 34:14). But in God it is jealousy *for* something. Jealousy is "the proper intolerance of disruptive intrusion and is thereby a mark of love (as the opposite of indifference.)"[101] Jealousy in its essence is a commitment to a relationship. It is stirred up when it moves us to maintain a threatened relationship or restore a broken one. Paul speaks of his jealousy that the Corinthians would be exclusively devoted to God. This moves him to use some strong language to wake the readers up (2 Corinthians 11:2ff.).[102]

Sinful jealousy is not jealousy *for* but *of* someone. *Envy* is wanting someone else's life. You see they have something better than you do, and instead of rejoicing in the good they have, you weep over the fact that you don't have it. So envy is wanting aspects of somebody else's life. As the second clause tells us, this *rots the bones*. It can literally eat you up—physically and spiritually.

Be honest and admit whose life you wish you had. How can your belief in the gospel—in what you have in Christ—undermine envy?

Prayer: Lord, I confess I envy other people's bodies, bank accounts, relationships, and many other things. I keep this envy a secret, even from myself, because it is so embarrassing. But it robs me of joy and you of your rightful glory. Help me root it out of my heart. Amen.

May 7

Anger is cruel and fury overwhelming, but who can stand before jealousy? (27:4)

THE EVIL OF ENVY. This says *jealousy* can be more harmful than anger. Why? Envy is wanting someone else's life (May 6). But it is not just that. In envy we don't just want other people's lives; we resent and begrudge them their lives. In praise you recognize people who are better than you and you rejoice in it. But in envy you recognize people who are better off and you burn with bitterness. John Gielgud, the great British actor, in his autobiography said, "When Sir Laurence Olivier played Hamlet in 1948 and the critics raved, I wept."[103]

Envy is being unhappy at other people's happiness. Envy weeps because of those who are rejoicing and rejoices if they are weeping. It is the exact opposite of the godly state of mind (Romans 12:5). And the best way to stop it is to look at Jesus, about whom it could be truly said, "In all their distress he too was distressed" (Isaiah 63:9).

Is there someone you feel has the life you deserve more? Is that belief and feeling diminishing your happiness to any degree? What can you do about it?

Prayer: Father, I need the ability to be happy for people who have what I badly want. That is a love of which I am not capable but one that I can't really live without. I do not want to live in resentment. Help me, Lord! Amen.

May 8

Do not let your heart envy sinners, but always be zealous for the fear of the Lord. There is surely a future hope for you, and your hope will not be cut off. . . . Do not fret because of evildoers or be envious of the wicked, for the evildoer has no future hope, and the lamp of the wicked will be snuffed out. (23:17–18; 24:19–20)

THE ANTIDOTE TO ENVY. *Envy* stems from two preoccupations. First, we are obsessed with what we deserve. Our hearts refuse to remember grace and instead think only of what we have earned. Second, we are preoccupied with the present. The solution is to look up to the Lord (23:17b) and look ahead in *hope* (23:18). That is, we should realize that our true reward is based on God's grace. Also we should remember that in the end, believers will not lack anything (Psalm 17:15).

Christians have a way of "looking up" that Proverbs could not provide. Jesus did not complain about experiencing death when he deserved life—all so we could have life when we deserved death. Jesus was the most unenvious human being who ever lived. When you realize what he did for you, it will begin to erode your envy. If he didn't complain when he received a life infinitely worse than he deserved, why should we complain when all of us get a life infinitely better than we deserve?

Can you see how much less you enjoy life because you think so much about what you deserve? How can you use the gospel—the example of Jesus—to help you stop that?

Prayer: Lord Jesus, you did not deserve the death you got—but you did not begrudge it. And I do not deserve the salvation I got through your suffering, but you do not begrudge that either. I praise you for your generous spirit and ask that you reproduce it in me. Amen.

May 9

"There are those who curse their fathers and do not bless their mothers; those who are pure in their own eyes and yet are not cleansed of their filth; those whose eyes are ever so haughty, whose glances are so disdainful; those whose teeth are swords and whose jaws are set with knives to devour the poor from the earth and the needy from among mankind." (30:11–14)

FACETS OF PRIDE. Each verse begins with a description of a different type of person. People who turn on their parents (30:11) are not the same as people who oppress the poor (verse 14). Yet in another sense, all these verses are speaking about facets of pride, which here is seen as corrupting and distorting all relationships.

First, pride makes us hate authority (verse 11) and so resist our parents, the first authority figures in our lives. Next, it blinds us to our flaws (verse 12), distorting our relationship to ourselves, so we cannot change what is wrong with us (our *filth*). It also makes us *haughty* and *disdainful* toward others (verse 13). Finally, it moves us to be ruthless and unjust to those with less social power than us (verse 14). Pride is an all-around evil. "Unchastity, anger, greed, drunkenness, and all that, are mere fleabites in comparison: it was through Pride that the devil became the devil: Pride leads to every other vice: it is the complete anti-God state of mind."[104] How diametrically opposed this is to the "mind-set" of Christ (Philippians 2:1–5), who said, "I am not seeking glory for myself" (John 8:50).

How does pride distort your relationships?

Prayer: Lord, I confess that I am too proud to admit how proud I am. It is only as I read of your great humility in the gospels that I begin to see my lack of it. Show me more of this painful truth so that I can be more free from the poisonous effects of pride. Amen.

May 10

Whoever derides their neighbor has no sense, but the one who has understanding holds their tongue. (11:12)

LOOKING DOWN. Proverbs forbids deriding, meaning to belittle, to treat as unimportant. The Bible links the impulse to despise or look down on someone to pride (Psalm 123:4). What is the sin of pride? It is one thing to take pride in one's work or possessions. But sinful pride takes no pleasure in having something—only in having more of it than the next person. So proud people are not really proud of being successful or intelligent or good-looking; they are proud of being richer, smarter, or better-looking than the people around them. It's the comparison and pleasure of being above the rest, the deriding and despising in the heart, that is the essence of pride.[105]

Jesus forbade speaking contemptuously or treating anyone disrespectfully (Matthew 5:22). And though Jesus' claims of divinity were so lofty, his actual demeanor and behavior were kind and lowly. He associated with people whom respectable society considered outcasts. And he looked down on no one. So how can we?

What person or kind of person do you, frankly, despise? What can you do about that?

Prayer: Lord, you ate with the tax collectors—collaborators with the Romans—as well as the prostitutes and sinners. When you were here on earth, you despised no one. You even ate with Pharisees—you were not bigoted toward bigots. Change my heart so I can walk in your footsteps. Amen.

May 11

The LORD tears down the house of the proud, but he sets the widow's boundary stones in place. (15:25)

FALSE MAJESTY. Pride not only looks down on others; it also fails to look upward. It refuses to let God take his proper role in our lives. The Hebrew word for *proud* (15:25) is *ge'eh*. Applied to God it means supreme majesty, so to use it for a human being is ironic but also very telling. We want to be our own saviors and lords. We want to run our own lives, to earn our own self-worth, to decide what is right and wrong for us.

Lewis Smedes writes: "Pride in the religious sense is refusal to let God be God. It's to grab God's status for one's self. . . . Pride is turning down God's invitation to [be] a creature in his garden and wishing instead to be the Creator, independent, reliant on your own resources. . . . Pride is the grand delusion, the fantasy of all fantasies, the cosmic put-on."[106] Because pride makes us overconfident and out of touch with reality, it makes us foolish. It also, according to this verse, leads to social injustice. But when the proud try to trample on the helpless, they find themselves opposing God himself.

What are some of the ways that we can refuse to "let God be God" in our lives?

Prayer: Lord, I don't like some of the things I find taught in the Bible. I don't like some of the ways you arrange the circumstances of my life. I confess I don't even like the doctrine of grace—I'd rather earn my salvation so you owe me. In all these ways I refuse to let you be God. Forgive me. Amen.

May 12

"Those who are pure in their own eyes and yet are not cleansed of their filth; those whose eyes are ever so haughty, whose glances are so disdainful." (30:12–13)

UNSYMPATHETIC. The eyes of the proud are *haughty*, literally, they "lift up their pupils." They don't look people in the eye to understand and engage them as equals. They look past them to the goals they have for themselves, for which others are mere instruments, objects.[107] They see others as a means to an end, as dispensers of acclaim, admiration, and other ways to bolster their self-image. Pride makes sympathy nearly impossible. Pride keeps us from really noticing people, from putting ourselves in their shoes, from recognizing when they are hurting or unhappy. It keeps us absorbed with our own agenda and needs. If the proud see someone suffering, they think they are too smart to let that happen to them, or they feel too sorry for themselves about their own problems to care about someone else's.

By contrast, look at Jesus sighing deeply over the deaf-mute (Mark 7:34), weeping at the tomb of Lazarus (John 11:35), and being our sympathetic high priest (Hebrews 4:14–16). Here is one who looks us in the eye with a full ability to enter into our troubles.

Do people seek you out to talk to you about their problems? If not, is it because you are not very sympathetic?

Prayer: Lord, I confess that my own self-pity and self-absorption make me impatient with people who have problems. I want to surround myself with "low-maintenance" people. But if you had done that, where would I be? Reproduce your sympathetic heart in me. Amen.

May 13

A person's wisdom yields patience; it is to one's glory to overlook an offense. (19:11)

TOUCHINESS. A body part that is injured or inflamed responds with instant recoil when touched. The Hebrew word for *patience* here means a relaxed face rather than one that instantly snarls when provoked. When people say something you don't like, do you shoot right back? Or do you slow your response and act rather than react? What is so touchy about us? We feel we must defend our glory or honor. It is our ego that is so sensitive.

This should tell us something. We don't notice body parts unless there is something wrong with them. We don't say, "My elbows are working great today!" But the ego calls attention to itself every minute. Sin has distorted our identity, the very basis of our sense of self. We need saving, repairing grace. If our ego was working properly, we would know that true glory is to let a slight or irritation go without paying back. Jesus said, "Father, forgive them, for they do not know what they are doing" (Luke 23:34). That is real glory.

Do you fairly easily feel hurt, slighted, and put down, and do you take criticism very hard?

Prayer: Lord, today I was very touchy with someone. Yes, I was tired and stressed out over many things. But so what? You were under far greater stress and never shot back an angry word. Let me wonder and praise you for your patience until it begins to grow in me. Amen.

The LORD detests all the proud of heart. Be sure of this: They will not go unpunished. . . . Pride goes before destruction, a haughty spirit before a fall. (16:5,18)

THE BLINDNESS OF PRIDE. The Bible does not say that pride might lead to *destruction*—it says it *will*. Why? The practical reason is that pride makes it difficult to receive advice or criticism. You can't learn from your mistakes or admit your own weaknesses. Everything has to be blamed on other people. You have to maintain the image of yourself as a competent person, as someone who is better than other people. Pride distorts your view of reality, and therefore you're going to make terrible decisions.

In *Troilus and Cressida*, when the great warrior Ajax says, "I do hate a proud man," a character says to the audience, "Yet he loves himself: is't not strange?" Ajax is completely blind to what all others can see—he is a man of enormous pride. It led him to kill himself in his humiliation when the armor of Achilles was awarded to Ulysses rather than to him. As another character says about Ajax, "He that is proud eats up himself."[108] Indeed.

What negative practical results of pride have you seen recently worked out in your own life or the lives of others you know?

Prayer: Lord, my pride makes me sometimes feel inferior and sometimes superior. It sometimes makes me too afraid and sometimes not cautious enough. It seems to be at the root of so many other things wrong with me. Do whatever it takes, Lord, to diminish its power in my life. Amen.

May 15

Where there is strife, there is pride, but wisdom is found in those who take advice. . . . A fool's mouth lashes out with pride, but the lips of the wise protect them. (13:10, 14:3)

THE STRIFE OF PRIDE. There is another practical reason that pride leads inevitably to a fall, namely, because it stirs up interpersonal *strife*. 14:3 says the *pride* of one's mouth *lashes out*, but comparison with the second clause of the verse, where wise speech protects the speaker, reveals that the pride of a man's mouth lashes *him*.

Bruce Waltke writes that the image in this verse is of a man or woman beating themselves with a rod or whip. How does arrogant speech do that? It is because "the indiscreet, insulting speech" that always marks the braggart and the thin-skinned "prompts others to react with anger, derision, disdain, and revenge."[109] Pride means you are constantly getting into arguments, and it is only a matter of time before you pick a fight with someone who can really hurt you. Humble, careful, discreet speech, on the other hand, disarms people and protects you from the great cost of interpersonal strife. The ultimate example of this is Jesus himself, who, unlike fools who turn friends into enemies, made a career out of making enemies into friends (Romans 5:10).

Identify someone who is opposing or criticizing you. How could you at least try to disarm the animosity and make the person a friend?

Prayer: Lord, I need help with my tongue. I can speak intemperately and later regret what I've said. And I see some relationships that have been hurt by my ill-advised words. Teach me how to reach out in peace and make friends where I have potential enemies. Amen.

May 16

Better to be lowly in spirit along with the oppressed than to share plunder with the proud. (16:19)

GOD HATES THE PROUD. There are practical reasons that pride leads to destruction, but there are also what we could call cosmic reasons. The Lord loves *the oppressed*—the widow, the fatherless, and those without power. But why?

Within one being of the triune God there are three persons loving and glorifying one another through eternity (John 17:1–6), an "*other*-orientation" of love.[110] Therefore, if you are scrambling for glory and recognition for yourself rather than giving it and serving others, you are going against the grain of the universe. The servant life of Jesus Christ is a revelation of the nature of God, the very heart of things. You are also on a collision course with God's future, because the Bible says that, eventually, God is going to lift up the humble and put down the proud. If God wants us to identify with the oppressed by being lowly in spirit, why should we hate it so much when we don't get recognized and treated as we feel we deserve?

Do you take it hard when you are snubbed or ignored?

Prayer: Lord Jesus, I still covet glory and honor, but I know I should serve without thought of getting credit. So hard! Make your selfless love for me so palpable and affecting that I don't care what others think. Amen.

> Wisdom's instruction is to fear the LORD, and humility comes before honor. (15:33)

THE PARADOX. Those with humility do not seek their own honor. Yet they are the ones who receive it. (*Humility comes before*—leads to—*honor.*) This paradox is at the core of the biblical message. The Old Testament shows us God bringing his salvation into the world through Sarah rather than Hagar, through Leah rather than Rachel, through Jacob rather than Esau, through David and not his older, more presentable brothers. God ordinarily works through the girl nobody wanted and the boy everybody has forgotten, in every generation.

And when God came into the world, he came into the world as a poor man—not a general or an aristocrat. At the end he did not take power but lost it and died, yet by his sacrifice he brought salvation to the world. The dishonor of the cross led to our being given glory and honor. And now the humility of repentance and simple faith in Christ bring the unimaginable honor of being in Christ, adopted and accepted. The ultimate power in the universe showed that it was strong enough to become weak (Philippians 2:5–8). Humility is the only way out of foolishness and into honor.

When was the last time you saw this biblical paradox played out in your life or in the life of someone you know?

Prayer: Lord, I am swayed by people's credentials and appearance, but you aren't. If you judged me like that I'd be lost! Keep my vision clear so I am not dazzled by sheen and glitz. Amen.

May 18

Do not exalt yourself in the king's presence, and do not claim a place among his great men. It is better for him to say to you, "Come up here," than for him to humiliate you before his nobles. (25:6–7)

MODESTY: TRUE AND FALSE. How does humility show itself in daily life and interactions? One way is through the trait of modesty, or its lack. Immodest people exalt themselves in numerable ways. They do it in conversations—interrupting routinely, always assuming their thoughts are more penetrating and important. They do it in the workplace, always taking credit for what others have done, never taking the blame. They can do it online, "playing to the crowd" by loudly promoting themselves. Self-promotion can also take more harmful forms, such as unwarranted litigation, ruthless power plays, and other ways to manipulate people and climb the ladder of success. 25:7, however, shows that there is nothing wrong with receiving honor in itself. That means there is such a thing as false modesty, which is a not-so-subtle way of promoting oneself as particularly humble.

Jesus turns Proverbs' advice against social climbing into an attitude toward all of life (Luke 14:7–11). True modesty is not thinking less of yourself but thinking of yourself less. We should not even notice where we are in the pecking order but should simply be looking to serve those around us.

Prayer: Lord, the whole subject of humility is difficult to even approach. Even when I pray for it, I sense a secret self-satisfaction growing over my modest demeanor. All I can say is that, Lord God, be merciful to me a sinner, and never let me forget I am only that—a loved sinner. Amen.

May 19

> "I am weary, God, but I can prevail. Surely I am only a brute, not a man; I do not have human understanding. I have not learned wisdom, nor have I attained to the knowledge of the Holy One." (30:1–3)

LONGING FOR GOD. The speaker says he has no more understanding of life and God than an animal (*a brute*). Exaggeration? Yes, but a healthy, paradoxical one. He says he doesn't know God, but that very statement is a mark of spiritual awakening. Those who are confident they know God well don't. Those who cry that they don't know him at all have begun to do so. Sometimes a keen sense of God's absence is a sign that he is actually drawing us closer to him.

The man who cried, "I do believe; help me overcome my unbelief!" was actually putting faith in Jesus at that moment (Mark 9:24). The first step to remedying ignorance is to know the full extent of your ignorance. "If anyone would like to acquire humility I can, I think, tell him the first step. . . . If you think you are not conceited, you are very conceited indeed."[111] The sage in 30: 1–3 took that first step by admitting the infinite gap in knowledge between God and human beings, and therefore the need for God's revelation. The next step is to listen to the Word of God and admit we are sinners in need of grace.

Can you honestly say you have a hunger to know God?

Prayer: Lord, teach me the absolutely essential spiritual skill of repentant self-examination, but help me to avoid the self-absorption of morbid introspection. Amen.

May 20

It is to one's honor to avoid strife, but every fool is quick to quarrel. . . . Pride brings a person low, but the lowly in spirit gain honor. (20:3, 29:23)

SELF-RENUNCIATION. In 2006 a gunman killed a number of Amish schoolchildren before killing himself. Unlike in other U.S. communities, where the surviving families of shooters have received death threats and had their homes vandalized, the Amish community forgave and loved the gunman's family. Some expressed hope that others could emulate this example.

But forgiveness, as socially and emotionally healthy as it is, is a form of self-renunciation, and we live in a culture that counsels self-assertion. If we are not being treated with the honor we think is our due, we are trained to protest loudly, and our anger is considered a sign of self-respect. Our society, then, does not produce forgiving people, but rather those who are *quick to quarrel* and who assert their honor. So our culture will continue to grow in *strife*.[112] "Most of us have been formed by a culture that nourishes revenge and mocks grace."[113] Again we see that it is the height of dignity not to always be standing on one's dignity. Ironically, the person most quick to defend himself comes off looking weak.

When was the last time you felt you had to defend yourself? Were you too quick?

Prayer: Father, your Son is now my great advocate (1 John 2:1). His shed blood defends me against the penalty of the eternal moral law. In him I am pardoned and accepted. Why, then, do I feel the need to defend myself all the time? Take away my need to do so by reminding me of my wonderful high priest. Amen.

May 21

CORRECTION. The irony is that pride, which hates *correction*, inevitably leads to public failures that bring *shame*, a translation of a Hebrew word that means to be taken lightly. So human arrogance brings about its own greatest nightmare. What, then, can remedy pride?

Here is one way: Deliberately submit yourself systematically to correction from others. The only path to become not a lightweight but a person of honor is the formative discipline of submitting one's ego to another self.[114] You must lose your pride to find it rightfully. This can happen inside the church, if we take vows to submit to the counsel and instruction of wise leaders. This can happen in a marriage if we make it safe for our spouse to correct us. This can happen when we give Christian friends the right to speak to us regularly about our flaws and sins (Hebrews 3:13). It can happen, but only if you choose for correction to be a part of your life.

Do you live in a Christian community with genuinely close, accountable relationships so this can happen? Have you experienced correction recently?

Prayer: Lord, I don't have enough people in my life I trust to correct me. I will need the patience and commitment to cultivate them and then the courage to open up to them. Give me both! Amen.

May 22

A person is praised according to their prudence, and one with a warped mind is despised. . . . Let someone else praise you, and not your own mouth; an outsider, and not your own lips. (12:8, 27:2)

PRAISE. Self-praise from *your own mouth* almost always backfires. It makes others less willing to give you credit. "Pride . . . is his own trumpet," writes Shakespeare, "and whatever praised itself but in the deed, devours the deed in the praise."[115] And yet, as 27:2 implies and as 12:8 states, faith communities should find ways of regularly praising and appreciating one another, since we do need genuine, truthful *praise*. 31:10–31 gives us the words of a husband delighting to praise his wife in detail for her virtues.

The church should be the place where people praise one another and not ourselves. The honor we have in Christ (Ephesians 1:19; John 17:23, cf. John 12:43) means that we cease to worry about how much attention we are getting from others and can devote ourselves to building up those around us (Romans 12:10). "Only God's praise [in Christ] cannot be angled for and cannot corrupt."[116] If we are assured in the gospel that we have the acclaim and delight of God through Christ, then we won't be constantly hungry for praise, we won't resent when it is not there, and we won't be puffed up by it when it comes. And we can be generous with it—the humblest people praise others the most.[117]

Are you quick to praise and affirm others? Ask someone you know well if you are good at it.

Prayer: Lord, it is astounding that while I myself am a sinner, in Christ I actually receive your praise and delight (Romans 2:29; Zephaniah 3:17). Let that be sufficient to my soul, so that I readily thank and praise others. Amen.

May 23

> When justice is done, it brings joy to the righteous but terror to evildoers. . . . Whoever loves pleasure will become poor; whoever loves wine and olive oil will never be rich. . . . The wise store up choice food and olive oil, but fools gulp theirs down. (21:15,17,20)

PLEASURE LOVING. *Wine and olive oil* were consumed at feasts and were a great good (Psalm 104:15). But when the love of pleasurable physical sensation dominates, it is the deadly sin of "gluttony." Today this word means only overeating, but traditionally it meant the inability to live a life of delayed gratification. "Gluttony offers a whirl of dancing, dining, sports, and dashing very fast from place to place to gape at beauty-spots."[118] Gluttony may lead to literal addictions to food, drink, or drugs, to *gulping them down*, but even if it does not, the spirit of gluttony is always to take the easy way out.

The wise find their joy in *justice* rather than in sensual pleasure (21:15). Indeed, doing justice often involves the sacrifice of one's comforts and pleasure. For example, to give generously to the poor deprives you of wealth, which can bring physical comforts. But there is a deeper joy that is the by-product of deprivations for the sake of God and neighbor. The great mistake of gluttony is to seek happiness directly rather than as a by-product of living responsibly. "The pleasure-lover strikes out towards joy *itself*, and finds poverty (17)."[119]

Give examples of how the sacrifice of immediate pleasure leads to a greater satisfaction and happiness.

Prayer: Lord, there has never been a society like mine, where the powerful forces of the media, marketing, and culture urge me to gratify my desires for comfort and pleasure. You died with only one possession—your robe. Oh, make me wise here, neither legalistically enjoying hardship for its own sake nor avoiding it. Amen.

May 24

Honor the LORD with your wealth, with the firstfruits of all your crops; then your barns will be filled to overflowing, and your vats will brim over with new wine. . . . Wine is a mocker and beer a brawler; whoever is led astray by them is not wise. (3:9–10, 20:1)

DRINKING. Proverbs calls wine *a mocker*. Intoxication humiliates and ruins. Proverbs warns against inebriation, a state in which the safeguards of self-control are removed. An overdependence on alcohol for facing the stresses of life can lead to economic insecurity (21:17, 23:19–21) or to acts of abuse and injustice (31:4–5). And yet, as 3:9–10 shows, Proverbs does not necessarily counsel abstinence, for wine is also seen as a good gift (Genesis 27:28; Deuteronomy 14:26). Jesus himself made wine one of the two elements in the Lord's Supper (Matthew 26:27–29).

Yet when leaders are making crucial decisions (31:4–5) or believers are taking specific vows to God (Numbers 6:3), wine and beer are prohibited. The wise person recognizes that "these two aspects of wine . . . its benefits and its curse, its acceptance in God's sight and its abhorrence, are interwoven into the fabric of the Old Testament, so that it may gladden the heart of man (Psalm 104:15) and [also] cause his mind to err (Proverbs 28:7)."[120]

Do you have the "appreciative ambivalence" of Proverbs toward alcoholic drinks? What measures are you taking to avoid their dangers?

Prayer: Lord, so many things are neither bad nor good but to be used with discretion. It is wisdom to know what they are and how to use them wisely. Failure to discern has ruined many lives. Protect me and my loved ones from foolishness in regard to food and drink. Amen.

May 25

Who has woe? Who has sorrow? Who has strife? Who has complaints? Who has needless bruises? Who has bloodshot eyes? Those who linger over wine, who go to sample bowls of mixed wine. Do not gaze at wine when it is red, when it sparkles in the cup, when it goes down smoothly! In the end it bites like a snake and poisons like a viper. Your eyes will see strange sights, and your mind will imagine confusing things. You will be like one sleeping on the high seas, lying on top of the rigging. "They hit me," you will say, "but I'm not hurt! They beat me, but I don't feel it! When will I wake up so I can find another drink?" (23:29–35)

ROCK BOTTOM. The drunk is a staple of comedies. "*They hit me . . . but I'm not hurt! They beat me, but I don't feel it!*" But addiction is a tragedy. The delirium tremens (23:33), the injuries from falls and fights (23:29) are depicted here in sad detail. All addicts start with just one drink, so how can any drinker avoid the trap?

When wine becomes more than a good food but something one gazes at and lingers over for its qualities, it has become almost sexual in its allure. Drink (or any other food) can become a deep consolation, a way to find relief from anxiety. The insatiable need sharpens over time, but the addict is helpless. "*When will I wake up so I can find another drink?*" Overcoming addiction is never simple and takes a lifetime. But St. Paul was right when he pointed to the ultimate consolation we need. "Do not get drunk on wine. . . . Instead be filled with the Spirit" (Ephesians 5:18). Being filled with the Spirit means seeing Christ vividly and joyfully (John 15:26, 16:14). That is the joy that makes it possible to cast other consolations aside.

Addiction can take many forms. What do you do to handle stress, anxiety, and unhappiness?

Prayer: Lord, let me take my woes and sorrows to you—not to food and drink, not to sexual release, not to video games, not to late-night viewing. "Here of life the fountain flows; here is balm for all our woes."[121] Amen.

May 26

> The craving of a sluggard will be the death of him, because his hands refuse to work. All day long he craves for more, but the righteous give without sparing. (21:25–26)

SLOTH DOESN'T LOVE THINGS. Lazy people have inordinate cravings for ease, rest, and comfort.[122] Ironically, lazy people live dissatisfied lives because they are not dissatisfied with their lives enough. Dorothy Sayers defines "sloth" as "the sin which believes in nothing, cares for nothing, seeks to know nothing, interferes with nothing, enjoys nothing, loves nothing, hates nothing, finds purpose in nothing, lives for nothing, and only remains alive because there is nothing it would die for."[123]

Lazy people do not love life enough to work hard to enjoy more of it, and they don't love people enough to work hard so they can—as the righteous can—*give without sparing* (21:26). To remedy sloth, look to "Jesus, the pioneer and perfecter of faith. For the joy set before him he endured the cross, scorning its shame, and sat down at the right hand of the throne of God" (Hebrews 12:2). He endured crushing burdens with joy, because he loved us enough to save us. Now love him enough to do the work before you.

Do you work only out of a sense of duty or in order to gain and serve things you love? How could a change in your motives change the way you work?

Prayer: Lord, give me the right motives to ask for what I am about to ask. Let me make enough and have enough to "give without sparing" to many people. Amen.

May 27

The lazy do not roast any game, but the diligent feed on the riches of the hunt. . . . A sluggard buries his hand in the dish; he will not even bring it back to his mouth! (12:27, 19:24)

SLOTH DOESN'T FINISH THINGS. When we think of a lazy person, we think of someone who doesn't start things. But there is also a kind of person who is always making plans and always starting but never finishing any project. They don't stay at jobs long, and they always blame the job itself rather than their own lack of stick-to-it-iveness. Either they lose interest because of a lack of inner passion for anything (May 26) or they have failed to count the cost and so find themselves overwhelmed.

And so the sluggard fails to bag his quarry (12:27). His meal goes cold on him before he can get to it (19:24). If you are someone who doesn't finish things, remember the one who loved you to the very end (John 13:1) and did not give up until he was able to say, "It is finished" (John 19:30).

Is there a project you have not been able to finish? Stir up your love for the people who would benefit from it, look to the "finisher" of our faith (Hebrews 12:2 KJV), and finish it.

Prayer: Lord, indeed, "having loved [your] own . . . [you] loved them to the end" (John 13:1). Now make me like you, Lord Jesus. Make me someone who does what I promise and finishes what I start. Amen.

A sluggard says, "There's a lion in the road, a fierce lion roaming the streets!" As a door turns on its hinges, so a sluggard turns on his bed. A sluggard buries his hand in the dish; he is lazy to bring it back to his mouth. A sluggard is wiser in his own eyes than seven people who answer discreetly. (26:13–16)

SLOTH DOESN'T FACE THINGS. This portrait of the slothful is a satire. They exaggerate the danger of doing things—*"There may be a lion in the road!"* They are as tightly attached to their leisure as a door to its hinges. The effort of eating exhausts them too much to finish.

But the theme running through all this is a tragic blindness. These verses paint the sluggard's features in such broad strokes in order to make the point that he is completely unable to see them. "He is not a shirker but a 'realist' ([Proverbs 26:]13); not self-indulgent but 'below his best in the morning' (14); his inertia is 'an objection to being hustled' (15); his mental indolence a fine 'sticking to his guns' (16)."[124] His excuses look ridiculous to everyone else (verse 13) but not to him (verse 16). As with all other kinds of fools, there is the problem of denial, because sluggards are wise in their own eyes. They cannot face things and, especially, they cannot face what they have become.

What are your "go-to" excuses when you really simply don't want to tackle a difficult task?

Prayer: Lord, this proverb exaggerates the excuses of the lazy person, but I detect milder forms in me when I am avoiding hard things. I think of them now and they are embarrassing, but they won't be easy to give up because they feel like protection. Give me the courage to put them aside. Amen.

May 29

> Sluggards do not plow in season; so at harvest time they look but find nothing. (20:4)

SLOTH DOESN'T NOTICE THINGS. In ancient agriculture you had to observe the weather closely and go to work in season—at the opportune time. One of the marks of a lazy character is that he demands his own schedule. He is too self-absorbed to notice windows of opportunity that, once closed, are gone forever.

In Ecclesiastes we are told that there is "a time to search and a time to give up; a time to keep and a time to throw away; a time to tear and a time to mend" (Ecclesiastes 3:6–7). There is nothing comforting about the fact that everything in this world changes and passes away. Because God has "set eternity in the human heart" (Ecclesiastes 3:11), constant changes are a grief to us. But the lazy heart will not come to grips with this and work hard (or rest) at the right moment. The sluggard needs to learn that only in God's ultimate future will we experience perfect *shalom* and rest through the Prince of Shalom, Jesus Christ (Isaiah 9:6). Until then, there is work to do.

Think of opportunities you have missed. Why did you miss them? How can you become wiser so as not to miss them in the future?

Prayer: Lord, "when the set time had fully come," you came (Galatians 4:4). Even you were attentive to opportunity and timing! I confess that I try to make the world fit my schedule rather than adapting to how things are. Give me a godly flexibility that trusts your plan more than mine! Amen.

May 30

One who is slack in his work is brother to one who destroys. (18:9)

SLOTH DESTROYS. Laziness *destroys*. As we have seen, laziness hurts you, but it also ruins the good of those around you. How? One obvious way the lazy do that is by not "pulling their weight" in the family or society and thereby increasing the burden on others. But also, the slothful think of themselves first, even in the work they choose to do. They select work for their own comfort or benefit rather than for how it helps others, the community, and society.

Dorothy Sayers observed that during World War II many people in the military found themselves doing work that was vastly more satisfying than their ordinary careers. Why? "For the first time in their lives, they found themselves doing something not for the pay"—army pay was miserable—"and not for the status"—everyone was just thrown in together—"but for the sake of getting something done for us all."[125] The social fabric strengthened and psychological health improved. This is wisdom—working for others rather than for one's own advancement. So both laziness and work chosen just for one's own selfish benefit destroy community.

Be blunt with yourself—are you *"slack in your work"*?

Prayer: Lord, the whole book of Proverbs works against my individualist spirit. I don't like to think that people around me have any claim on my money, my time, and even the selection of my career. Give me the mind of Christ (Philippians 2:3–5). Impart it to me with your Word and Spirit. Amen.

May 31

Laziness brings on deep sleep, and the shiftless go hungry. (19:15)

SLOTH IS PROGRESSIVE. Sloth first brings on deep sleep and then hunger. In other words, sloth brings a progressive decline of one's ability to work hard. Just as a person who has lost physical conditioning cannot suddenly run a marathon, so the slothful finds him- or herself less and less able to endure sustained periods of mental exertion or labor. There can be a slow, perhaps irretrievable loss of the basic attitudes and habits necessary for good work. Those include keeping commitments, getting work done on time, not being controlled by outside circumstances, being a self-starter who does not need reminders and coercion, and taking pride in the high quality of one's work. Once these habits are lost—or if they are never formed—it is extraordinarily hard to recapture them.

While the progress of sloth is natural, there is another gradual process, the progress of "sanctification," that is supernatural and can overcome the natural decline of sin. It is never complete in this life (Philippians 3:12), but it entails gradual conformity, step by step, to the likeness of Christ (Ephesians 4:23–24).

Ask a friend or someone who knows you well: Am I more unselfish, more at peace, and more disciplined than I was?

Prayer: Lord, I could ask for no greater thing than sanctification. By your free grace, renew me in my whole person after Christ's image, that I might die more and more unto sin and live more and more unto righteousness.[126] Amen.

June 1

The way of the sluggard is blocked with thorns, but the path of the upright is a highway. (15:19)

SLOTH GIVES NO REAL REST. The slothful person here is contrasted not with the hardworking but with the upright (cf. Matthew 25:26). Laziness is not just a temperament but a moral failing. Sloth is self-centered rather than loving. It is dishonest, "trying to sidestep the facts and one's share of the load."[127] And it is extremely foolish. *The way of the sluggard is blocked with thorns* means laziness leads ultimately to more work. If you don't brush your teeth every day, it will lead to costly and painful dental surgery or to infections that can threaten the health of the whole body.

But the image of thorns reminds us that, in a fallen world, all work is laborious and difficult. "Thorns and thistles" (Genesis 3:18) result when human beings turn from God. Now, all work is to a degree frustrating and difficult, even for the upright. But on the cross Jesus took our curse, and the crown of thorns, so that those who believe in him will someday have a renewed, perfect world. He got the thorns so we could have the highway.

How have you seen in your life that laziness leads to more work overall?

Prayer: Lord, I am anxious about the hardness of life. It makes me want to give up. But you promised to speak peace to your people (Psalm 85:8). So help me say to my heart: "Be still my soul: thy best, thy heav'nly Friend; through thorny ways leads to a joyful end."[128] Amen.

June 2

The one who guards a fig tree will eat its fruit, and whoever protects their master will be honored. (27:18)

THE DIGNITY OF WORK. The paradox in the final clause is that even the most menial tasks of a servant who *protects their master*, if they are done well, are cause for *honor*. *All* work done well has a dignity in the eyes of God (cf. Ephesians 6:5–8).

In the Babylonian creation myth, the *Enûma Eliš*, humans were created to do the work considered beneath the gods. Yet in Genesis you see God literally with his hands in the dirt (Genesis 2:7) doing manual labor and not considering it beneath him. Even now the Holy Spirit renews the face of the earth (Psalm 104:30). When God created a paradise for humanity, he put work into it (Genesis 2:15). And when Jesus came to earth, he came not as a man of leisure but as a carpenter. If you're not doing work, and work in which you can take pride, you're being cut off from part of your humanity. There will be an atrophy of your soul, because the Bible says work is not a necessary evil; work is a good. Yet it doesn't have to be a great world-changing career. Any work that is useful to others and done with excellence is deserving of honor.

Do you undervalue so-called blue collar work? Do you mistrust or despise people who have careers that take more skill and education than you have?

Prayer: Lord Jesus, I live in a society that, in some places, overly values high-paying jobs that require years of education and, in others, deeply distrusts these same people. But these distinctions of class and status don't matter to you. Let them not matter to me either. Amen.

The Seven Deadly Sins: Greed

June 3

> The greedy bring ruin to their households, but the one who hates bribes will live. (15:27)

GREED KILLS. *The one who hates bribes* refuses to compromise integrity, even when it means the loss of a big payday. But for *the greedy*, the means justify the ends. Greed says, "If I could make huge money, even if it requires that I lie or bribe, then why not?" The greedy find ways to justify dishonest financial dealings to themselves, and there is no better way than to say that it will benefit your family or your household.

But this is an illusion. When their misrepresentations, bribes, and lies are made public, the greedy have brought ruin to their households. Indeed, when 15:27 says that those marked by honesty and prudence in financial matters will live, it hints that exposed corruption can lead not only to economic disaster but even to suicide. Jesus and Paul add that greed threatens your soul (Mark 8:37; Ephesians 5:5). So even if the bribe or lies are not exposed, if your heart is set on money in a greedy way, it will poison your character and weaken your family. But the one who puts integrity and service ahead of profit will live.

What kinds of justifications have you used or seen others use to cut ethical corners in financial dealings?

Prayer: Lord, there are scores of smaller and larger ways to cheat and misrepresent in financial dealings with employers, customers, buyers, and sellers. Make me a person of absolute integrity with regard to money. Amen.

June 4

Those who trust in their riches will fall, but the righteous will thrive like a green leaf. (11:28)

GREED DESTABILIZES. As we will see later, the Bible is not against wealth creation or profit. What, then, is greed? We saw yesterday that one sign of a greedy heart is that it puts wealth before moral principle. Another mark of a greedy heart is that it does not merely enjoy wealth but has come to *trust* in it. Job claims that to say to money, "You are my security," is a grave sin (Job 31:24–28).

Some trust wealth for safety in this world. Others trust it for a sense of significance and worth. But these are things only God can give us. What is the result? The greedy *will fall*, a Hebrew word that means to fall to one's death. Why? If God's love is the basis of your self-image, then when the inevitable financial downturn or business failure occurs, you will be grieved. But these ups and downs will be far more devastating if your very self is tied to the level of your prosperity. Greed destabilizes your life. Only God is completely reliable (22:19). And only Jesus— and his salvation—is true treasure (Colossians 2:3).

What do you tend to trust money for—security, power, acceptance by others, control?

Prayer: Lord, I see people who are trusting in money but blind to it. How, then, do I know that *I* am not doing this too? Help me to dare to look at my heart and talk to my closest friends in order to discern my real spiritual attitude toward money. Amen.

June 5

Better a little with the fear of the LORD than great wealth with turmoil. Better a small serving of vegetables with love than a fattened calf with hatred. (15:16–17)

GREED STARVES. The *fattened calf* was valuable (1 Kings 4:23) and a sign of celebration (Luke 15:23). But when *love* is life's main dish, it doesn't matter if the rest of the meal is just a bit of *vegetables*. And *if hatred* is the main course, even a fattened calf cannot redeem it. The greed that can pay for the richest food will still starve the human soul of that for which it most hungers, because greed is self-serving and the opposite of self-giving love.

These texts correct simplistic views that see wealth as always a sign of God's favor and hard work. That is how Job's friends read things. Even Jesus' disciples were shocked by his teaching that wealth could be a hindrance to spiritual growth and salvation, not a help (Luke 18:25–27). Yet this text is not so much about the problem of wealth as the greatness of love. "In a broken world where injustice and the absurd can prevail . . . faith (represented here by '*love*' and '*the fear of the Lord*') can transform a meal of vegetables into a continual feast (15:15)."[129]

In your own life experience have you seen a person or family become more unhappy and unsatisfied as they became more prosperous?

Prayer: Lord Jesus, sometimes a lucrative job or deal will give us less time for family and friends. Sometimes we see we could make more money if we disadvantaged someone else. Lord, you lost power in order to fulfill your loving purpose for us. Let me never choose money over love. Amen.

June 6

> For this command is a lamp, this teaching is a light, and correction and instruction are the way to life, keeping you from your neighbor's wife, from the smooth talk of a wayward woman. Do not lust in your heart after her beauty or let her captivate you with her eyes. (6:23–25)

WHAT IS LUST? 6:25 warns against *lusting* after someone's *beauty*. It is one thing to recognize and appreciate someone's physical attractiveness. It is another thing to be intensely driven to possess someone's beautiful body for your own. We often say that a lust-driven man "wants a woman'" But, as C. S. Lewis points out, "strictly speaking, a woman is just what he does not want. He wants a pleasure for which a [beautiful] woman is a necessary piece of apparatus."[130]

Real love moves you to give yourself fully to a particular man or woman. Lust works in the opposite direction. It wants to get a fulfilling, self-maximizing experience from the person. In the biblical view, the purpose of sex is not personal self-expression (in order to be happy) but personal self-donation that brings permanent unity and life (in imitation of Christ, Ephesians 5:22ff.). Sex without the giving of oneself is a monstrosity, akin to a body walking around without a head. Lust and sex without marriage is like tasting food without swallowing and digesting it.[131]

Why is pornography so widespread? In light of this reflection, what are the great dangers of it?

Prayer: Lord, Achan lusted after the beauty of the gold, so he stole it (Joshua 7:21). If I allow myself to gaze at and lust after someone's physical beauty, I too might be inflamed and steal it, taking it wrongly. Help me redirect my desire for intimacy and beauty into communion with you, fairest Lord Jesus. Amen.

June 7

For the lips of the adulterous woman drip honey, and her speech is smoother than oil; but in the end she is bitter as gall, sharp as a double-edged sword. Her feet go down to death; her steps lead straight to the grave. (5:3–5)

SEX AS HONEY. Sin is always sweet in the mouth and poisonously bitter in the stomach. Sin always "shows us the bait but hides the hook,"[132] as a good fisherman does to the fish he wants to catch and fry. Anything contrary to the Word and will of God, even if it leads initially to pleasure and prosperity, will disappoint.

Using *honey* as a metaphor for sexual sin is apt, because honey can be electrifyingly sweet and pleasurable but cannot provide even the nourishment of a single square meal. And too much honey can make you ill. According to the Bible, then, sex outside of a lifelong covenant of marriage is like trying to live on honey alone. Sex without a promise of mutual whole-life commitment can lead one party to make a far greater emotional investment than the other, with agonizing results. Or it can teach both parties to use sex for pleasure and not for radical self-giving. Either way, it's honey followed by hunger.

Think of the ways that sex outside of a lifelong covenant of marriage is like eating honey rather than enjoying a full meal.

Prayer: Lord, keep me from falling for the false promise of sexual joy and intimacy apart from marriage. That lie has destroyed so many. Help me learn how to defeat sexual temptation. Amen.

June 8

Drink water from your own cistern, running water from your own well. Should your springs overflow in the streets, your streams of water in the public squares? Let them be yours alone, never to be shared with strangers. (5:15–17)

STRANGENESS. The Hebrew word for the "adulterous" woman (5:3) literally means the *strange* woman. Married sex is likened to the refreshment and joy of well water; but why have sex with *strangers*? This is not saying you should have sex only with someone you know. Rather, it is a claim that sex outside of marriage is alien to your true nature. Imagine going by rocket to Venus. If you got out and inhaled the atmosphere, you would die. Why? Because the clouds of sulfuric acid are alien to the nature of your lungs.

"In the end, humans can no more live outside God's moral order than can the . . . fish . . . live outside God's biotic order. Outside the ordinances of God we find not life but, ultimately, death."[133] When God says, "You must give yourself sexually only to someone to whom you've given yourself wholly, legally, and permanently in marriage," he is saying, "This fits who you are, who I made you to be." Sin leads to alienation from your own nature and God's created order, and that leads to destruction.

Why is the Christian sex ethic criticized today? Can you give answers to those objections, or do you believe some of them yourself?

Prayer: Lord, when the church was new, its sex ethic was considered crazy, narrow, and offensive. Two thousand years later we are in the same place. Help me to be as faithful and confident in what your Word says about sex as that great cloud of witnesses. Help me to understand, defend, and practice it. Amen.

June 9

May your fountain be blessed, and may you rejoice in the wife of your youth. A loving doe, a graceful deer—may her breasts satisfy you always, may you ever be intoxicated with her love. (5:18–19)

COMMODITY. In a time when marriage was most often contracted to secure social standing, we are told that being *intoxicated with . . . love* should be the mark of a marital relationship (September 5 and 24). Spouses are to give themselves to each other in joyful abandon. When people have sex outside marriage, maintaining their independence and right to walk away at any time, it turns sex into just a dispensed commodity, with both persons remaining detached and in control. Instead, sexual union should always and only take place between a husband and a wife who share every other kind of union—legal, social, financial, personal—in marriage. Then sex becomes both a sign of the union and a way to deepen it. When two people are committed to be with each other—through plenty and want, joy and sorrow, sickness and health, repentance and forgiveness—sexual intimacy becomes richer and richer. All your spouse has done for you and means to you can somehow pass into your lovemaking, and the two truly become one.

In what ways does sex outside marriage differ from sex within it?

Prayer: Lord, you were willing to die for me. And no one can have your love shed abroad in their hearts unless they give their whole lives to you. So protect your people from the tragic mistake of thinking sex outside a marriage covenant is somehow, sometimes all right in your eyes. It isn't. Amen.

June 10

May your fountain be blessed, and may you rejoice in the wife of your youth. A loving doe, a graceful deer—may her breasts satisfy you always, may you ever be intoxicated with her love. Why, my son, be intoxicated with another man's wife? Why embrace the bosom of a wayward woman? (5:18–20)

COUNTERFEIT INTIMACY. Marital joy includes sexual pleasure (5:18–19) but much more. In the Bible no one is called your *blessing* (verse 18) unless they have the power to produce well-being in you and are deeply connected to you in faith and social bond.[134] Marriage brings growth that is impossible outside of the security of the bonded union. Because you cannot just walk away when things get difficult, it brings increased self-knowledge, emotional and spiritual growth, deep mutual affirmation and support, and the distinct joy you can have only in the presence of someone with whom you have been through thick and thin.

Sex outside marriage is "to exchange true intimacy for its parody."[135] A parody is a cartoonish imitation. When you have given yourself wholly to another in marriage, and the other person has also made a solemn commitment that would be hard to break, there is a new level of trust and thus freedom from fear, and so you can, literally, *lose yourself* in their love (verse 19).[136] If you have not done so, you may only lose yourself.

In what ways does the trust that a solemn vow and a legal bond bring enhance love and spiritual growth?

Prayer: Lord, I see that true intimacy between human beings depends not on fleeting "chemistry," sexual or otherwise, but on long-term commitment and faithfulness to helping the other person be all they should be before you. Let all my relationships—and not just marriage—reflect this insight from you. Amen.

June 11

Can a man scoop fire into his lap without his clothes being burned? Can a man walk on hot coals without his feet being scorched? So is he who sleeps with another man's wife; no one who touches her will go unpunished. (6:27–29)

THE FREEDOM OF LIMITS. In likening sexual infidelity to *fire [in one's] lap*, we return to the familiar theme of God's created order. Limiting sex to marriage is analogous to limiting ourselves through diet and exercise, which leads to the freedom of health. Honoring God's design leads to liberation. "Self-limitation . . . and deliberate acceptance of inter-personal and cosmic limits are basic to biblical wisdom. When humans practice self-discipline in relation to . . . sex, food, sleep, exercise, work, play, speech it promotes self-knowledge, self-mastery, and paradoxically, freedom."[137] Dietrich Bonhoeffer wrote, "None learns the secret of freedom save only by way of control."[138]

How do we accept the freedom of God-ordained limits? The one way is to remember the benefits to us. So we pray: "O God, who art the author of peace and lover of concord, in knowledge of whom standeth our eternal life, whose service is perfect freedom . . ."[139] But in the end we are best motivated by looking at our Savior limiting himself for us. "Our God contracted to a span—incomprehensibly made man."[140]

Think of all the ways you accept the loss of smaller freedoms in order to get greater ones.

Prayer: Lord Jesus, indeed you not only limited yourself for me but you enslaved yourself, "taking the very nature of a servant" (Philippians 2:7). How, then, can I view your commands to me about sex, money, and power as burdensome? Keep me from ever resenting your wonderful precepts. Amen.

June 12

My son, give me your heart and let your eyes delight in my ways, for an adulterous woman is a deep pit, and a wayward wife is a narrow well. Like a bandit she lies in wait and multiplies the unfaithful among men. (23:26–28)

SEX AND FAITH. When the text calls an adulterous partner a *deep pit*, it means a trap. But the term also has the connotation of *the* pit, Sheol, the underworld. So adultery not only creates this-world practical problems but also jeopardizes the state of your soul. How? It is true that our beliefs shape our behavior, but behavior also influences our thinking and belief. Many believers have testified that when they violated their conscience, God became less real to them. I have talked to college students from church backgrounds who started having sex because they lost their faith, but I met just as many who lost their faith because they started having sex.

So sexual sin can multiply the unfaithful. "Those who think to explore life this way are flirting with death. It is no mere detour from the best path but, in the fullest sense, a dead-end."[141] The father who is exhorting his son here asks him to give him his heart. Even better, we should ask the Lord, "Give me an undivided heart, that I may fear your name" (Psalm 86:11).

Where have you seen in your life or someone else's life that behavior affects and shapes beliefs?

Prayer: Father, it is true that as I believe, so will I live. But it is also true that as I live, so will I believe. If I act in love and faithfulness toward you, I sense love from and to you growing in my heart. So provoke me, by your Spirit, to ever obey and serve you regardless of my state of mind or emotions. Amen.

KNOWING OTHERS
Friendship

June 13

> One who has unreliable friends soon comes to ruin, but there is a friend who sticks closer than a brother. (18:24)

INTENTIONALITY. This says that a friend can be better than a sibling—quite a statement in a culture that was far more family oriented than ours. But how so? Your family may be there for you but they may not really like you or understand you. And there can be long stretches of life in which you have no romantic partner or spouse. A friend, however, may *stick* with you over the years *closer than a brother.*

In the early stage of your life, you were shaped most by your family. But for the rest of your life you will be shaped largely by your friends. You become like the people with whom you spend the most time. As we will see, you can't live without friendship. But remember how deliberate friendship must be. Erotic attraction and family relationships push themselves on you in various ways, but friendship will not. It must be carefully, intentionally cultivated through face-to-face time spent together. And in a busy culture like ours, it is one thing that is often squeezed out.

How have your best friends over the years shaped and influenced you? Who are your best friends now?

Prayer: Lord Jesus, you befriended a handful of disciples and through those friendships you changed the world. Help me choose my friends wisely, cultivate them carefully, and learn all I should learn from them so I can grow into the person you've called me to be. Amen.

June 14

A friend loves at all times, and a brother is born for a time of adversity.... Many curry favor with a ruler, and everyone is the friend of one who gives gifts. The poor are shunned by all their relatives—how much more do their friends avoid them! ... Many claim to have unfailing love, but a faithful person who can find? (17:17, 19:6–7, 20:6)

CONSTANCY. What are the marks of a friend? The first we can call constancy. *A friend loves at all times*, through good times and ill. 19:6–7 reminds us of the painful truth that most relationships are transactional. That is, people seek out other people to get economic, social, or emotional benefits from their relationship. When someone becomes poor and loses their social utility, they are shunned and avoided by their so-called friends. "One who has unreliable friends soon comes to ruin" (18:24). And, we see, they were never really friends.

Friends will be there for you when the chips are down, when you have very little to give to them. For a friend, you are not a means to some end but cherished for yourself. And constancy entails availability. Even when it's inconvenient, you can get a friend at all times. However, this means that the best friendships take time, and everyone's time is limited. So while in theory you could have many friends, 20:6 is realistic. Good friends don't grow on trees, nor can you have a large number of them. Give more time to the ones you have.

How can you be more intentional about deepening the friendships you have and giving more time to them?

Prayer: Lord Jesus, you set your face to go up to Jerusalem to die. When you got there all hell was let loose upon you, and still you did not shrink but stood your ground—all for me. How can I, then, not be there for my friends in their times of need? Make me a great friend for others as you were for me. Amen.

June 15

Better is open rebuke than hidden love. Wounds from a friend can be trusted, but an enemy multiplies kisses. (27:5–6)

TRANSPARENCY. A second requirement for friendship is transparency. The King James Version renders the first part of Proverbs 27:6 as "faithful are the wounds of a friend." What are "faithful wounds"? The phrase means that real friends do open rebuke, they tell each other things they need to hear even if they are painful. If you are too afraid to say what needs to be said, you are really an enemy of your friend's soul.

Have you ever listened to a recording of yourself and thought, "I don't sound like that"? But yes, you do—you can't hear from within your body what your voice really sounds like outside. And without the perspective of others, we will never know our strengths and weaknesses. If you have a measure of status in the world, or if you have chosen friends poorly, you may be just be surrounded by flatterers (29:5). Transparency is scary, but we need it. And to get courage, look to the one who became so vulnerable for you that he died on the cross. How faithful were the wounds of this friend for you!

How many real friends do you have—friends who will speak the truth in love to you?

Prayer: Lord Jesus, you became a vulnerable human being to show us the truth about ourselves. You were faithful and constant even to death on the cross. Now, Lord, reproduce in me that same character and let me be a friend to others as you have been a friend to me. Amen.

June 16

Like one who takes away a garment on a cold day, or like vinegar poured on a wound, is one who sings songs to a heavy heart. . . . If anyone loudly blesses their neighbor early in the morning, it will be taken as a curse. (25:20, 27:14)

SENSITIVITY. A third mark of friendship is sensitivity and tact. Why does someone show inappropriate heartiness when others are just waking up (27:14)? Why do they use humor inappropriately (26:19) or speak lightheartedly to grieving people with a *heavy heart* (25:20)? It is because they are emotionally disconnected and therefore clumsy. They don't know the other person's inner topography well enough to know what hurts or helps, what inspires or bores, what stimulates or irritates.

If I can be content when you are sad, I'm not your friend (25:20). Friends voluntarily tie their hearts to one another. They put their happiness *into* their friends' happiness, so they can't emotionally flourish unless their friends are flourishing too. Jesus tied his heart to us so that even in his suffering he knew joy because of the salvation he was bringing to us (Hebrews 12:2; cf. Isaiah 53:11). The friendship connection may not be as emotionally intense as that which comes in romance, nor always as enduring as family ties (though remember 18:24 on June 13). All the more reason friendship is so valuable, because such a link is both deliberate and voluntary.

Are you putting in the effort to be a friend?

Prayer: Lord, our sin causes you pain (Genesis 6:6) and our broken hearts draw you to our side (Psalm 34:18). You love us more tenderly and sensitively than a nursing mother does her child (Isaiah 49:15). Let me be so moved by your love for me that it makes me highly sensitive to the needs of those around me. Amen.

June 17

As iron sharpens iron, so one person sharpens another. (27:17)

COUNSEL. The fourth mark of a true friend is counsel. Friends give "heartfelt advice" (27:9). Friends *sharpen* and challenge one another, being vulnerable and sensitive to one another but also making proposals for how the other should change. Friends regularly have constructive clashes that sharpen each party's understanding of the world and of themselves.

Therapists give you advice, but you don't do it back. A supervisor may offer criticism, but it would not be appropriate to give equal criticism back. The mutuality of the deep counsel that friends can give is rare and something everyone needs. Sometimes it is sweet and pleasant (27:9 on June 18) and sometimes sharp and perhaps painful (27:17). True friendship is both "reassuring and bracing."[142] If you have this kind of exchange and growth in a romantic relationship or in a family relationship, it is because you have incorporated this aspect of friendship into those connections. But you're never going to become the person you need to be, or that you can be, without it. It sharpens you the way nothing else does.

With how many people do you share a relationship in which there is mutual counsel and critique?

Prayer: Lord, today to "friend" something is to "like" rather than dislike. I have not been conditioned to have friends who dislike things about me and tell me so! But my heart knows—and your Word says—that I need them. Lead them to me and give me the willingness to be open to them. Amen.

June 18

Perfume and incense bring joy to the heart, and the pleasantness of a friend springs from their heartfelt advice. (27:9)

DISCOVERY. Friendship is *pleasantness* that means, literally, sweetness. At the time of Proverbs, people could not create sweetness in food, only discover it. Friendship is like that. We can work at it, enhancing constancy, transparency, sensitivity, and counsel. Yet friendship begins with a discovery. We must find persons with common loves and vision. C. S. Lewis wrote, "Where the truthful answer to the question, 'Do you see the same truth?' would be, 'I see nothing and I don't care about the truth; I only want a friend,' no friendship can arise. . . . There would be nothing for the friendship to be about. . . . Those who have nothing can share nothing; those who are going nowhere can have no fellow travelers."[143]

Christian faith can create a deep affinity between people who are different in every other way. That is why friendship between believers from diverse racial backgrounds can be so powerfully formative. They are empowered by faith in the ultimate friend of our souls (John 15:13–15), whose constancy, vulnerability, and love cannot be surpassed.

Do you have Christian friendships across racial and national barriers? How could you cultivate new ones and deepen the ones you may have?

Prayer: Lord, your gospel brings down barriers between people of different ethnicities and cultures (Galatians 3:26–28), yet I associate and hang out with my own (racial and social) kind too much. Enrich me and show the world the power of the gospel by helping me grow in cross-racial Christian friendships. Amen.

June 19

> The words of the reckless pierce like swords, but the tongue of the wise brings healing. . . . The tongue has the power of life and death, and those who love it will eat its fruit. (12:18, 18:21)

WORDS KILL. You are not wise unless you fully grasp the power of *words*. Words *pierce like swords*—they get into your heart and soul. When you say a hurtful word, you can never make things as if it had never been uttered. It's like the wound from a sword. The wound may heal, but your body will never be the same as if the sword had never cut you. The scar remains.

Words of the reckless can wound your reputation, making it hard for people to ever fully trust you again. 18:21 goes further and says that words can even kill. Words have been triggers for murders, suicides, and actual wars. Also, words kill psychologically. Call a child "stupid" or "not worth anything" and that person may spend all his or her life trying to rid him- or herself of the self-doubts it has planted in them. Words designed to hurt are like toxic chemicals. Once they get into the ground, they just pollute everything. Sticks and stones can only break our bones, but words can be soul destroying.

Have you seen the toxic power of rash words in your life or the lives of others?

Prayer: Father, help me to guard my lips so that I don't wound someone deeply with rash words. And also, let me so immerse myself in *your* Word and what it tells me of who I am in Christ, so that other people's hurtful words won't wound me. Amen.

June 20

> From the fruit of their lips people are filled with good things, and the work of their hands brings them reward. . . . The soothing tongue is a tree of life, but a perverse tongue crushes the spirit. (12:14, 15:4)

WORDS MAKE ALIVE. Words can wound but also heal. The tongue can be soothing and *a tree of life*. Words are like fruit or food for us; we need them to live. Most of us can remember, years later, the words from a passage in a book, or said by a friend or teacher, that "turned on a light," or that implanted new ideas that we never forgot.

We also need words coming from the outside to affirm and validate us. Imagine an artist who does a painting. Does she say, "I don't care that everyone else says it's trash; I like it"? If she is going to truly take pride in her work, someone else will need to offer words of praise for the art. Supremely, the Word of God has a living power to relate us to God and change our minds and hearts (Hebrews 4:12; 1 Peter 1:23). We do not live by bread alone but by good words, especially those in line with God's.

Are you aware of the great power even your offhand words have to bless others? When was a time you have seen this power in your life or someone else's?

Prayer: Lord, each of us has a host of people around us who are eager for, and desirous of, words of blessing and affirmation from us. I am often too distracted to deliberately praise and appreciate people every day. Find me ways to say to others, "Well done, good and faithful servant" (Matthew 25:23). Amen.

June 21

A perverse person stirs up conflict, and a gossip separates close friends. (16:28)

WORDS DIVIDE. Friendships, as we have seen, are all about words. But malicious and hurtful, dishonest and deceptive, and even just clumsy and inappropriate words can deliver a blow to a friendship from which the relationship may never recover.

Here speakers with two kinds of relationship-destroying speech are mentioned. The first is the person who *stirs up conflict*. As we have seen, candor is good, even when the truth telling is painful. But there is also a kind of person who loves debate, who gives criticism too readily, and who always seems to be in the middle of an argument with someone. The other kind is a *gossip*, someone who criticizes people behind their backs, putting them in the worst light. (About gossip more comes later in the year.) Bruce Waltke says that both kinds of speakers have a need to always put others down as a way of building themselves up.[144] This makes close friendship impossible. Instead we should look to the one who does not quarrel or shout at people (Matthew 12:19–20) but speaks kindly to his friends even when they let him down (Matthew 26:41).

Where have you last seen either of these behaviors do damage to relationships?

Prayer: Lord, help me to be honest with myself about the divisiveness of my words. I tell myself that I'm just speaking up for the truth, but lay bare my motives so I can see when I am really only trying to make myself look good. That happens far more often than I dare to think. Amen.

June 22

Evildoers are trapped by their sinful talk, and so the innocent escape trouble. From the fruit of their lips people are filled with good things, and the work of their hands brings them reward. (12:13–14)

WORDS FILL. The parallelism here is revealing. In verse 14 good words *fill* us inwardly *with good things*. The implication is that evil speech's harm is also inward (verse 13). How? Words embody and strengthen thoughts. When you say, "I hate you. I wish you were dead," you say it because you feel it. But afterward you feel it more because you said it. What you say fills your heart.

This does not mean you should not be honest about your feelings (cf. 10:18). But when you have hate, you should use words to confess it, not to ventilate it. Talk about it to God or to friends and say, "I have this anger, this discouragement, this temptation." Your words will, as it were, make the thoughts visible. You can sift them and get perspective on them and throw out the foolish and sinful ones much more easily because you've talked about them. Managing our speech is a way to get our whole self under control (James 3:2). Jesus was perfect and so his speech was perfect (John 7:46).

Where have you seen this idea about the inwardly shaping power of words illustrated in your own life?

Prayer: Lord, I can truly pray, "Set a guard over my mouth, Lord; keep watch over the door of my lips" (Psalm 141:3). I beg you to do that, mainly for the sake of your name but also because my heart cannot survive my evil words. Amen.

June 23

Those who guard their lips preserve their lives, but those who speak rashly will come to ruin. (13:3)

WORDS EXPOSE. This saying warns against speaking *rashly*, but that is more than just a lack of carefulness. The Hebrew word is often used for sexual promiscuity, for exposing things that should be kept covered. Impulsive, imprudent talk refers to how our words can reveal the deepest recesses of the heart. So while foolish speech can harm us inwardly (June 22) it can also harm us outwardly, exposing us to the world. There are innumerable examples of people who spoke rashly and were discredited and shamed for their speech forever after.

According to Jesus, all words—good and bad—are indicators of our heart. "The mouth speaks what the heart is full of" (Matthew 12:34). The tongue reveals what is at the core of our being (James 1:26). An abrasive tongue, a lying tongue, a foolish tongue—all of these are signs of a person who has resentment, dishonesty, and pride in his or her own heart. But the irony is this: Others will be able to see (through your words) more of your heart than you will.

Recall a time when your rash words brought you trouble. What in your heart led to it?

Prayer: Lord, I know I must change my heart, putting to death its sinful impulses (Romans 8:13). But I take my good time, because I think no one can see the selfishness, pride, and anxiety of my heart except you and me. But my tongue shows it to the world. No more procrastination. Help me change. Amen.

June 24

The words of a gossip are like choice morsels; they go down to the inmost parts. (18:8)

WORDS INTERPRET. Gossip makes the speaker look good and the object of the gossip look bad. We will look in more detail at gossip later in the year. For now the more general lesson is that words have the power to define reality. Words do not just report facts—they explain their meaning, and that determines how the listeners see the world and live in it.

Negative words about someone *go down to the inmost parts*, meaning, in this case, they control how we see the person. Though God wants us to have truth in our inward parts (Psalm 51:6), there are many things we would more readily believe about ourselves and the world, and so words that distort reality are *choice*—they have enormous appeal. Words create and sustain prejudices, biases, fears, and anxieties that are virtually impossible to uproot.

Jeremiah sets a better model: He ate God's word and delighted in it (Jeremiah 15:16; cf. Colossians 3:12–20). If we do that, then distorting words will not take hold of our inward parts and create a false worldview.

How do common phrases like "You have to always be true to yourself" create false worldviews that seem completely self-evident to people?

Prayer: Lord Jesus, the words I read and hear daily try to redefine all reality by leaving you out of the center of it. Move me to be immersed in your Word so I can be like the man you touched twice so that he could see the world clearly (Mark 8:25). Amen.

> Those who flatter their neighbors are spreading nets for their feet. (29:5)

WORDS INFLATE. Our words should be kind and affirming, but here we are warned about *flattery*. It is a word that means to compliment someone not to simply praise something good for its own sake or to build the person up in love, but in order to gain some advantage for yourself (Jude 1:16). With that as a motive, the claims of flattery are often not tied to reality. They exaggerate in an effort to appeal to the ego and gain benefits from the grateful recipient.

But how is flattery a *net* for the one who listens? Instead of helping the listener get an accurate picture of their strengths and weaknesses, the flatterer deliberately gives them an inflated, unrealistic self-view. The essence of foolishness and its destructiveness is to not see yourself as you really are. Like all well-laid traps, flattery hides itself, but when the trap springs and the net comes up, the victim is helpless. Christians must never use flattery, not in business to get customers or investors, and not even in evangelism (1 Thessalonians 2:4–6).

Is there any part of your life—family life, business, or other—in which you engage in flattery to get things for yourself?

Prayer: Lord, I admit that there are times when I engage in flattery as ways to manage difficult people or to maintain other important relationships. I am sobered at how you hate this kind of untruthful speech (Psalm 12:2–3). I repent for it and ask that you would give me the courage to change. Amen.

June 26

A scoundrel plots evil, and on their lips it is like a scorching fire. (16:27)

WORDS SPREAD. Proverbs explores the many aspects of the power of words. Long before the Internet, words had a remarkable power to "go viral." Technology now enables false rumors and fake news to spread instantly. But in another sense it has always been so. People in fire-prone areas of the country know how fast an untended little campfire can devour a whole forest. False reports (or even true but unkindly meant words) have always had the power to spread *like a scorching fire* to ruin reputations and alienate people from one another.

James may have had this proverb in mind when he wrote: "Consider what a great forest is set on fire by a small spark. The tongue also is a fire" (James 3:5–6a). James adds, however, that false and unkind words also spread *within* and "the tongue . . . sets the whole course of one's life on fire" (James 3:6).[145] By contrast, the word of Jesus' kingdom, the gospel, "is like a yeast that . . . worked all through the dough" (Matthew 13:33). The gospel also has the power to go viral, to work its way through a life, a community, or a whole society to bring reconciliation with God and man.

Where have you last seen the damage that false and unkind words can do through their spread?

Prayer: Lord Jesus, protect me from the spreading power of harmful words. Prevent me from producing them and hurting people. Also, protect me from their power to poison my relationships and hurt my good name. "Vindicate me . . . and plead my case" (Psalm 43:1). Be my advocate. Amen.

June 27

An honest witness tells the truth, but a false witness tells lies. . . . An honest answer is like a kiss on the lips. (12:17, 24:26)

TRUTHFUL WORDS. What are the marks of good words? The first is *truth*. 12:17 speaks of testimony in a courtroom that corresponds to reality, without shading or hiding facts. Jesus insisted that his disciples speak every word as truthfully as if they were under oath and had just sworn on a stack of Bibles (Matthew 5:33–37).

A kiss on the lips (24:26) was and is an act of special intimacy. This verse means that lying is fundamentally a lack of love. Joy Davidman wrote: "There are the lies of gossip . . . which make haters out of us; the lies of advertising and salesmanship, which make money out of us; the lies of politicians, who make power out of us."[146]

Every lie uses rather than loves a person. By keeping the truth from them, you put them in a dependent posture and exploit them. There is no such thing as a harmless lie. And God's Spirit will never work through dishonest words, however you lie to yourself about your motives.

When was the last time you lied to someone? What are the kinds of situations in which you have a tendency to shade the truth?

Prayer: Father, Jesus told the truth even though it got him tortured and killed. And he did it for me. How, then, can I shrink from telling the truth, the whole truth, and nothing but the truth—even when it costs me? Lord, increase my faith in you so I can be truthful regardless of the consequences. Amen.

June 28

An honest witness does not deceive, but a false witness pours out lies. . . . A truthful witness saves lives, but a false witness is deceitful. . . . Do not testify against your neighbor without cause—would you use your lips to mislead? (14:5,25, 24:28)

NOT DECEIVING. Truthfulness is contrasted with *deceit*. Statements should not be evaluated only by what they say but also by what they intend to do. If words are technically factual but stated in such a way as to mislead, then they are still dishonest—perhaps even more powerfully so. Effective lies are those that include the greatest possible amount of truth and yet still deceive. It's not enough simply to give factually accurate statements so you can say to yourself, "Well, I didn't really lie." You must never use facts in a misleading way to advantage yourself.

Tell the truth, the whole truth, and nothing but the truth. Don't exaggerate and spin. Don't leave out crucial parts of the truth that might make you look bad. "Speak truthfully to your neighbor" (Ephesians 4:25), looking to the one whose very reason for coming was to testify to the truth (John 18:37).

When you indulge in political speech, when you do advertising or marketing, when you report to your investors, when you give customers information about your products, when you report to superiors, do you ever use selective, factually accurate but misrepresenting speech?

Prayer: Father, I confess that I often twist the truth in order to look good, usually avoiding outright lies. I do it before I even know what I'm doing. Help me stop this. Help me remember that you will judge me for every idle word. Make me a person of truth. Amen.

June 29

The integrity of the upright guides them, but the unfaithful are destroyed by their duplicity. (11:3)

INTEGRITY. *Integrity* means being one and whole, not marked by duplicity. People of integrity are not one way in one setting and completely different in another. Are you a churchgoer on Sunday but ruthless in business during the week? Do you say conservative-sounding things to traditional people but liberal-sounding things to younger adults? Do you present yourself as one kind of person online but live as a very different kind of person in real life? We have the technology to brand ourselves, creating the image we want to project. We pad résumés, add facts to bios, falsify academic research, do whatever it takes to sell ourselves.

But the wise and upright are driven by integrity, consistency of character. They don't have multiple selves, a real self, and a host of pseudoselves. They have one real self and it is not hidden. It is on display in every setting, in every role. With them, what you see is what you get.

Have you seen this behavior in yourself in any area—that you speak and act one way in one setting or with one crowd but very differently in another? Where do you lack integrity?

Prayer: Lord, I confess that I sometimes "play to the crowd." But *you* always see me; you are always there. You have the only set of eyes and opinion I should care about. Let me always live consciously before your face. That will heal my lack of integrity. Amen.

June 30

A false witness will not go unpunished, and whoever pours out lies will not go free. (19:5)

POURING OUT LIES. The image of literally lying with every breath, reminds us of how pervasive and diverse lying can be.[147] There are all kinds of lies, and it is possible to lie constantly through the day. There are polite lies. You say, "I would love to go, but I already have an appointment." There are euphemisms. You say, "I think your writing is too sophisticated for our readers," when you mean, "You are a bad writer." There are exaggerations. Spouses constantly say, "You *always* . . ." or "You *never* . . ."—statements that are not only factually untrue but designed to bludgeon.

There is word inflation. Christians are especially bad about this. "It's such a blessing. The Lord was there. It was just incredible." Sometimes the Lord is indeed there, sometimes the event really *is* a blessing, but when events always are, that creates cynicism. Then there are so-called benevolent lies, like when you continually lie to cover up for friends when you actually ought to be confronting them about how they're living. There are routine business lies. You say, "We are for quality," when privately you make unreasonable demands on your employees. We *pour out lies.*

Watch yourself for a day. How often you shade, twist, hide, or obscure the truth?

Prayer: Lord, the sins of my tongue are so many! Because of pride I talk too much or harshly, because of fear, too little or dishonestly. Forgive me, and cure me of the false motives that make my speech so unlike yours. Amen.

July 1

It is a trap to dedicate something rashly and only later to consider one's vows. (20:25)

KEEPING PROMISES. A major part of truth telling is keeping one's *vows* or promises (Psalm 15:4; Matthew 5:33–37). Lewis Smedes wrote: "My wife has lived with at least five different men since we were married—and each of the five has been me. The connecting link with my old self has always been the memory of the name I took on back there: 'I am he who will be there with you.'"

How can we keep our promises? Look at Jesus. To fulfill God's promise to save us (Hebrews 8:6), he came and died. He truly was the one who said, "I am he who will be there with you." A Christian's whole life, then, is based on a promise kept at great cost. "When I make a promise I bear witness that . . . I am not fated. I am not determined. When I make a promise to anyone I rise above all the conditioning that limits me. . . . No home computer ever promised to be my loyal help. Only a person can make a promise, and when he does, he is most free."[148]

When was the last time you failed to keep a commitment you made? Are there any promises you ought to make but are afraid to make?

Prayer: Lord, I receive life (2 Timothy 1:1), the Spirit (Galatians 3:14), and union with you, all through your "great and precious promises" (2 Peter 1:4). Since I live only by promise, make me a person of my word, not afraid to make and not too weak to keep commitments. Amen.

July 2

Honest scales and balances belong to the LORD; all the weights in the bag are of his making. . . . "Every word of God is flawless; he is a shield to those who take refuge in him." (16:11, 30:5)

THE GOD OF TRUTH. Concern for truthfulness is not merely practical but right. Business schools' ethics classes advise honesty as the most profitable business policy. But God desires honesty in business even when, as here, dishonesty in *scales and balances* could make you a lot of money and never be found out. The reason? God is truth by nature—all his words are flawless and true. The Lord is the real in contrast to the fictitious; he is the absolute in contrast to the relative; he is the substantial in contrast to the ephemeral.

We are to "put on the new self, created to be like God" (Ephesians 4:24) and "therefore . . . speak truthfully to [our] neighbor" (Ephesians 4:25). We must be truthful if we are to be like God, for he cannot lie (Titus 1:2; Hebrews 6:18), he always keeps his promises (2 Corinthians 1:20). He always means exactly what he says and says exactly what he means—he cannot be inconsistent with himself. Above all, Jesus is Truth itself (John 14:6). He reveals God, the ultimate truth, perfectly (John 1:18; Hebrews 1:3).

What are the problems with the ethical reasoning that we should be honest because it is the most practical policy?

Prayer: Father, as I read in your Word about what a God of truth you are, I want to be far more careful about speaking before I know what is true. How often I've passed on falsehood inadvertently just because I was too unconcerned about truthfulness to check things out. Let me walk in truth so I don't dishonor you. Amen.

July 3

Anxiety weighs down the heart, but a kind word cheers it up. (12:25)

KIND WORDS. The second mark of good speech is kindness. It is not enough for words to be truthful. The word translated as *kind* means "personal and kind, pleasant and sweet, timely and thoughtful."[149] Because our words must be life-giving (15:4), we must never use truth as a weapon. You must ask yourself why you are telling the truth. Is it to win an argument? To punish or pay back by embarrassing the other person? To undermine something true that the person is saying but you don't want to hear? To defend your pride? To complain? To make yourself look good to others?

St. Paul says every word must pass this test—"that it may benefit those who listen . . . according to their needs" (Ephesians 4:29). When you tell the truth, you should always have a "ministry motive." You should only confront to help another person achieve illumination and understanding or to remove distance and barriers between you and the other person. Speak the truth, but in love (Ephesians 4:15). If you do so, it can lift up even someone sinking in anxiety and fear.

Think of the last time you had to challenge someone. Did you have a ministry motive? Were your words kind?

Prayer: Father, "in lovingkindness Jesus came, my soul in mercy to reclaim."[150] If I live only by the kindness of Jesus, how can I be unkind? With your Spirit, make your love so real it keeps me from being irritable, impatient, or indifferent to anyone else at all. Amen.

July 4

A gentle answer turns away wrath, but a harsh word stirs up anger. (15:1)

GENTLE WORDS. When Proverbs talks of kind words, it speaks of our speech's motives. When it speaks of *gentle* words, it is speaking of speech's form—its tone and demeanor. Being gentle does not mean agreeing (August 6), but it does mean being respectful and friendly. We are called to speak gently even (or especially) in an angry confrontation, rather than answering with *harsh*, hard words in kind. Speaking gently in such moments is difficult, not least because of the fear of appearing weak. So Rehoboam, afraid of looking unkingly, gave a harsh answer that actually destroyed his kingdom (1 Kings 12:1–16).

If you do not curse back when cursed (Romans 12:14), it disarms and de-escalates the argument. If you respond gently, there's a chance the angry listener may say, "I don't want to hear this, but it's very obvious this person cares." Ironically, gentle speech is ultimately more persuasive than "so take *that*!" arguments. Harsh words play well with people who already agree with you, but they won't persuade or help the truth to spread. Follow the one who, when he was reviled, did not revile in return (1 Peter 2:23).

When was the last time you saw someone de-escalate an angry situation with gentle words?

Prayer: Lord Jesus, you are meek and gentle (Matthew 21:5) and yet threw out the money changers from the temple (Matthew 21:12). Lord, conform me to your image, make me like yourself—assertive but not self-assertive. Amen.

July 5

The tongue of the righteous is choice silver, but the heart of the wicked is of little value. . . . The lips of the righteous know what finds favor, but the mouth of the wicked only what is perverse. . . . The words of the reckless pierce like swords, but the tongue of the wise brings healing. (10:20,32, 12:18)

APT WORDS. 12:18 warns that our words must be *choice* (well crafted), not *reckless* (thoughtless and impulsive). 10:32 directs that we *know what finds favor*, what appeals and persuades, in our words. Of course, because our words are to be truthful, they can sting, and we might be moved to confront a friend out of love (27:6). So to find pleasing words cannot mean that you never say anything to make people unhappy. Rather, it means we are to fit our words to the listener's circumstances, capacity, sensibility, temperament, and culture so they are as persuasive, moving, and attractive as possible.

"A truth that makes no impression as a generalization may be indelibly fixed in the mind when it is matched to its occasion and shaped to its task."[151] Don't just say, "Well, I told the truth." If you truly care about the truth, you will want people to believe it. Say it, then, in a way that makes it as hearable as possible. Words take craftsmanship. You need truthful words. You need kind and gentle words. And you need apt, appropriate, beautiful words.

Are you careful with your words or are you impulsive, speaking without a lot of thought?

Prayer: Father, my words are often half-baked, poorly thought out. I am no prophet, but could you purify my words so they are far more attractive and persuasive to listeners than they are now? I ask that not for my honor but for yours. Amen.

July 6

The prudent keep their knowledge to themselves, but a fool's heart blurts out folly. . . . A person finds joy in giving an apt reply—and how good is a timely word! . . . Like apples of gold in settings of silver is a ruling rightly given. (12:23, 15:23, 25:11)

TIMELY WORDS. Closely related to words being apt is that they also be *timely*. Sometimes the best wisdom is to not speak much at all (12:23). There are situations such that nearly any words will make conditions worse. When you meet with a grieving person who just lost a loved one, words should be sparing.

Another kind of untimely word is being too familiar before the person feels you have the right to speak to them in that way. A third kind of untimely word is when something is said publicly that should have been saved for a private time. Finally, words are untimely if they assume knowledge or experience the listener does not have. Sometimes the thing we say first to someone should have come third, or fifth, or later. Timeliness is difficult to achieve, because our natural temperaments usually incline us toward being too quick or too slow to speak. So pray for wisdom (James 1:5)! And look to the one who never spoke an untimely word. "No one ever spoke the way this man does" (John 7:46).

When was the last time you (or someone else you know) said something that was true but untimely?

Prayer: Lord, my words are either too early or too late—early because I get impatient, late because I get scared. Help me to trust you so much that I rest more content and confident in life. That will make my words more timely. Amen.

July 7

Fools find no pleasure in understanding but delight in airing their own opinions. . . . To answer before listening—that is folly and shame. (18:2,13)

PREJUDICE. To *answer before listening* is both a practice and an attitude. At the most practical level, this describes someone who habitually interrupts. Interrupters see no real need to let the other person finish. They aren't really engaged in a genuine conversation. They aren't responding to what you actually said. Rather, they see the interaction as one more opportunity for airing their own opinions (18:2).

At a deeper level, however, speaking before listening means to be prejudiced, to literally "prejudge" someone before you know the full truth about them. Prejudice assumes somebody is the way "all those kinds of people are" instead of caring enough about the truth to find out what this particular person is like, what this particular person is really saying. We habitually assume that all people of different gender, races, classes, vocations, and cultures are basically the same. But when someone treats us that way, we feel dehumanized. Prejudice is a form of answering before listening. Remember Jesus, who constantly challenged racial (Luke 10:30–37), class (Luke 17:11–19, 18:22), and gender (John 4:1–42) prejudice.

Is there a kind or class of person that, frankly, you don't like, and that therefore you tend to stereotype rather than listen to?

Prayer: Lord Jesus, if you were prejudiced, you not only would not have died for people from every tongue, tribe, and nation, but you wouldn't have come to human beings at all! When I am tempted to look down at "that type," help me to remember your unprejudiced, free grace for me. Amen.

July 8

The one who has knowledge uses words with restraint, and whoever has understanding is even-tempered. (17:27)

CALM WORDS. An *even-tempered* person is cool spirited. A hot-spirited person is excitable, impatient, and insistent on having their say *now*. A cool-spirited person is calm and patient. The wise know what they have to say may be true and crucial, but they also know God is in charge and only he can open hearts (cf. Acts 16:14; John 6:44).

"Three reasons can be found for this praise of calmness. First, it allows time for a fair hearing (Proverbs 18:13; cf. verse 17); second, it allows tempers to cool (15:1: "A gentle answer"); and third, its influence is potent: "A gentle tongue can break a bone" (25:15).[152] Jesus never gave way to unrestrained or inflamed speech even when under the greatest affliction (Isaiah 53:7) or the greatest provocation (1 Peter 2:23). Keep in mind, though, Jesus is not merely an example to live up to. As your Savior he can send you his Holy Spirit, which gives us an inner love for him and changes us into his likeness.

Are your words always even tempered and calm? When was the last time they were not? What was the result?

Prayer: Father, when Elijah listened for you, you were not in the earthquake, wind, or fire but in the "still, small voice." Though my sin should provoke you, you do not respond to me in wrath but in grace. Make my words calm and gracious, too. Amen.

Sin is not ended by multiplying words, but the prudent hold their tongues. . . . The one who has knowledge uses words with restraint, and whoever has understanding is even-tempered. Even fools are thought wise if they keep silent, and discerning if they hold their tongues. (10:19, 17:27–28)

ECONOMY OF WORDS. The wise *hold their tongues* rather than *multiplying words.* "Proverbs consistently teaches that fewer words are better than many words."[153] Why? The more you say, the more can be used against you (10:14, 13:3). The more you say, the less you get to listen to others and so the less well informed your words will be when you do speak them (18:13). Also, the more you say, the less people will listen to you—they simply won't wade through it all. Then too, people who talk too much appear to be more interested in themselves than in you, and often it is the case.

Another reason for keeping words few is that the wiser you are about a subject, the simpler and clearer your explanation. Simplicity lies on the far side of complexity, after we have worked through the issues. If you can't be brief, you may not know enough about the subject to speak about it. Finally, controlling our tongue is a way to gain self-control in general (James 3:1–2). If we can master the difficult task of controlling our speech and our desire to pontificate about every subject, then self-control in other areas will be much easier.

Do you talk too much? Ask a couple of people who know you well to be frank with you.

Prayer: Lord, I often love to hear myself talk. I can ramble and hold forth but, while occasionally entertaining, that doesn't build people up. Your words are perfect—never a wasted one. I will never be able to imitate that, but give me the self-control and wisdom to make each of my words count. Amen.

Like an earring of gold or an ornament of fine gold is the rebuke of a wise judge to a listening ear. . . . Whoever rebukes a person will in the end gain favor rather than one who has a flattering tongue. (25:12, 28:23)

FORTHRIGHT WORDS. We are to be truth tellers, not only in being reliable witnesses but also in being forthright in confrontation. 25:12 tells us that a forthright, well-crafted *rebuke* is like an ornament of *fine gold*—a thing of beauty, a work of art! And 28:23 reminds us that the straight talker will in the end get more respect and favor than the person who only compliments and flatters out of a fear of disapproval.

Despite his meekness and gentleness, Jesus speaks frankly to the woman at the well about the wreckage of her sex life (John 4:9,27). He tells Zacchaeus to stop his government-backed extortion racket (Luke 19:1–9). He's the one who says, "Neither do I condemn you" and "Go now and leave your life of sin," in the same breath (John 8:11).[154]

So, yes, we need to be kind, gentle, and careful, but also transparent, forthright, and direct. We die without both kinds of words.

Most of us have more trouble with one set of traits than the other. Are you better at forthright and true words or gentle and kind words?

Prayer: Lord Jesus, when Paul stood before the emperor, though no one else came to his defense, you stood by him and enabled him to speak forthrightly (2 Timothy 4:16–17). Oh, please, stand by me and with me, that I can tell people the truth. Amen.

July 11

Gracious words are a honeycomb, sweet to the soul and healing to the bones. (16:24)

HEALING WITH WORDS. Here the *honeycomb* is a positive metaphor. Jonathan, in the midst of battle and faint with hunger, ate honey and it revived him. "His eyes brightened" (1 Samuel 14:27). So too there are words that are "sweet to the soul" and healing to the whole person.

All aspects of good speech have distinct capacities to heal various ills. Kind speech can heal anxiety (12:25); gentle speech can extinguish anger and resentment (15:1); forthright words can heal ignorance and self-deception (19:25, 27:5). If you can approximate speech that maintains the balance of wise words—honest, nondeceptive, kind, gentle, apt, timely, unprejudiced, calm, forthright, and few—then you will be in a position to help any listener.

When Jacob asked God for the blessing he had been seeking all his life, God gave it to him (Genesis 32:29). When we believe in Christ, we get this blessing and more (Ephesians 1:3). From this inner fullness our words can bless and build up because we know the one who is the living Word.

Look back over marks of wise words—honest, nondeceptive, kind, gentle, apt, timely, unprejudiced, calm, forthright, and few. On which one (choose only one) do you need the most work?

Prayer: Lord, I see people around me who are in great need of things I can give them with my words. But I'm too busy, too afraid, too indifferent, too self-absorbed to even notice the opportunities. Clear my vision and anoint my lips so that my words can be sweet to the souls of others. Amen.

July 12

The hearts of the wise make their mouths prudent, and their lips promote instruction. . . . One who loves a pure heart and who speaks with
grace will have the king for a friend. (16:23, 22:11)

THE HEALING OF WORDS. Our words can heal—but what
will heal our words? It is *the hearts of the wise* that make their
speech *prudent* and with grace. Jesus said that "the mouth speaks
what the heart is full of" (Matthew 12:34), so "make a tree good
and its fruit will be good" (verse 33).

Willpower is not enough to do that. A *pure heart* means one
"who does not trust in an idol" (Psalm 24:4). So the more our
heart is fixed on the Lord and nothing else for our joy, hope, salvation, worth, and safety, the more our words will resemble wise
speech. The builders of the Tower of Babel, whose hearts were
set on "mak[ing] a name for [them]selves" (Genesis 11:4), had
their speech so corrupted that society broke down. At Pentecost
the curse of Babel was reversed. Hearts were filled with the
beauty of Jesus and his saving works, and when they spoke their
speech was compelling to everyone who heard. As from Jesus
himself (John 7:46), there were no unnecessary, untruthful,
inapt, unkind, ungracious words. The quality of our speech, our
prayer life, and our walk with God improve together.

Do you see evidence of your words being slowly healed?

Prayer: Lord, you answered Jacob's desperate request for the
blessing, though secretly, because the Bible doesn't provide your
words to him (Genesis 32:29). I also need you to bless me in my
most secret, inward being and fill it with your love (Ephesians
3:16–19) so my words will become like yours. Amen.

July 13

> A gossip betrays a confidence, but a trustworthy person keeps a secret.
> (11:13)

GOSSIP. To be *gossip* a statement does not have to be false. 11:13 speaks of true information about someone that should have been kept in *confidence*. Gossip, then, is negative information that may or may not be true, designed to make the speaker and the hearer feel superior to the object of the gossip. James 4:11 says, "Brothers and sisters, do not slander one another." The verb "slander" here simply means to "speak against" (Greek *katalalein*). It is not necessarily a false report, just an "against-report"—one that undermines the listener's respect and love for the person being spoken about. Proper evaluation is gentle, guarded, well meant, and always reveals the speakers' belief that they share the frailty, humanity, and sinful nature of the one being critiqued. It always shows a profound awareness of your own sin. It is never "against-speaking."

Because the human heart is driven by self-justification, gossip is almost irresistible (18:8). Because it is highly contagious, the wise quarantine it by not repeating it (17:9, 16:28, and 26:20) and by avoiding the company of tale bearers (20:19). Gossip is listed in Romans 1:29 as one of the sins of a people or a person who has chosen to worship idols rather than God. It is no minor thing.

Are you able to distinguish gossip from a nonslanderous evaluation? Do you engage in gossip?

Prayer: Lord, I know that if I think more carefully about what gossip is, I will find I engage in it and encourage it. I have wronged many people over the years through it. Help me to be far more attentive and sensitive to it in myself and others. And forgive me for the sinful talk I have done. Amen.

July 14

A perverse person stirs up conflict, and a gossip separates close friends. . . . A gossip betrays a confidence; so avoid anyone who talks too much. (20:19) Without wood a fire goes out; without a gossip a quarrel dies down. (16:28, 26:20)

GOSSIP'S EFFECTS. *Gossip* is devastating to relationships. It *separates close friends* when the kind of intimate information that close friends know about one another is shared with others (16:28). This often is inadvertent, simply the inevitable carelessness that comes from talking too much (20:19). But it may also come from a more deliberate habit of mind, someone who cannot resist the power that comes from being able to share juicy tidbits and so command the attention of others (16:28).

Gossip also keeps *quarrels* going within communities (26:20). When two people are at odds, they can speak to each other directly and make things right. Gossip complicates that. John might be trying to reconcile with Tom, but he won't be able to do it if John's friends also keep gossiping against Tom, thereby inflaming Tom's friends, who in turn slander John. It is much harder to reconcile large groups of people to one another when they are talking about something in which they are not directly involved (July 28). Gossip is like cancer to the body of Christ.

When was the last time you saw a community weakened by gossip?

Prayer: Lord, how deceptive gossip is—to the gossiper! I want to warn, I want sympathy and to sympathize, I want a good laugh, and yet these are all excuses I use to hurt other people's reputations. Help me recognize gossip when I am doing it (or hearing it) so I can turn from it. Amen.

Like a north wind that brings unexpected rain is a sly tongue—which provokes a horrified look. (25:23)

GOSSIP'S SUBTLETY. 25:23 talks about a *sly tongue*, reminding us that gossip and slander are subtle and elusive. Gossip comes in many disguises. It can be a heads-up about "something you should know." It can masquerade as an expression of false compassion for "poor so-and-so." It can even come in the form of a request for prayer. Gossip is also not always conveyed by words themselves. James 5:9 says, "Don't grumble against one another," and the word "grumble" here means literally to groan and roll the eyes at someone. Body language is as important for conveying a disdainful attitude as actual words. When everyone exchanges exasperated, horrified looks, shakes of the head, eye rolls, sighs, and ironic laughter, the damage is done even with little said.

How can you assess if your statement about someone is gossip or not? Ask: Is this something I should be talking to the person about directly? Is this information something the person wouldn't mind my sharing? Is this the kind of thing I would want someone sharing about me?

Have you heard anyone tell you something recently that you knew qualified as gossip? How did you respond to the speaker? How should you have responded?

Prayer: Lord, I can harm someone's reputation not just with my tongue but also with my body language. Lord Jesus, you never grumbled, complained, or derided people. Do what it takes to keep me from doing these things. Amen.

July 16

> Whoever loves discipline loves knowledge, but whoever hates correction is stupid. . . . The way of fools seems right to them, but the wise listen to advice. (12:1,15)

OPEN TO CORRECTION. As we have seen, it is of the essence of wisdom to be open to *correction* and criticism. We show ourselves to be people of reason only when we listen to *advice* and when we constantly "test ourselves for prejudice."[155] Ancient people were steeped in prejudice—stereotypes about other classes, races, and cultures—while modern people think of themselves as very open-minded.

But no one is objective, and we can start with the modern person's prejudice against anything that is not modern and "enlightened." Every culture has deep "background beliefs" about life that are so taken for granted that they are invisible to us *as* beliefs. We think of them as "just the way things are." No one becomes wise unless they allow these beliefs to be examined and challenged, supremely by God's Word but also by teachers, colleagues, family members, and friends. If you always know best, you are *stupid* (12:1,15).

Name a belief you got from your culture or community that you have rejected because of what you learned in God's Word.

Prayer: Lord Jesus, we are not to be conformed to this world in our minds (Romans 12:2). The world and society I live in press upon me as "common sense" many beliefs that are simply not true. Let your Word dwell in me so richly (Colossians 3:16) that I can discern and resist these errors. Amen.

July 17

Whoever heeds life-giving correction will be at home among the wise. Those who disregard discipline despise themselves, but the one who heeds correction gains understanding. Wisdom's instruction is to fear the LORD, and humility comes before honor. (15:31–33)

BE TEACHABLE. We must not merely *heed . . . correction* episodically, when it comes to us unbidden. We should also seek *discipline* in the form of *instruction* and learning (15:32–33). That is, we should habitually seek out others who know more than we do about a subject and learn from them. We should have an entire life marked by being teachable rather than opinionated.

Verse 32 tells proud, unteachable people that they are only despising themselves. Only through deep reverence for God and openness to being instructed (verse 33) will we get a "proper sense of self, of realistic humility"[156] This reminds us also that, at the most fundamental level, it is only through repentance, the ultimate teachability, that we can be saved at all (Acts 11:18; Matthew 4:17; Luke 13:3). To humble yourself in repentance and believe in Jesus as Savior brings you the ultimate honor and glory—the eternal love of God (John 17:20–26). "Paradoxically, the one who grants himself no glory before the glorious God in the end is crowned with the glory and wealth that give him social esteem (see 3:16; 8:18; 11:16)."[157]

Are you teachable, or do people see you as opinionated? Ask two or three people who know you well.

Prayer: Lord, I am not teachable because I'm too proud to want advice and too scared that I might hear something I don't want to hear. So remind me of your greatness to humble me, and remind me that the gospel itself, my very joy and life, was something I didn't want to hear. Amen.

July 18

A rebuke impresses a discerning person more than a hundred lashes a fool. . . . Flog a mocker, and the simple will learn prudence; rebuke the discerning, and they will gain knowledge. . . . When a mocker is punished, the simple gain wisdom; by paying attention to the wise they get knowledge. (17:10, 19:25, 21:11)

DEGREES OF TEACHABILITY. In ancient times forty lashes was the punishment for the worst crimes. *A hundred lashes*, then, is hyperbole to make a point. Even the worst possible consequences cannot change the character of some people (17:10). The more often they lose jobs, are expelled from school, are fined or punished, the more they blame others and become entrenched in their ways. At the other end of the teachability spectrum is *a discerning person* who learns from a single *rebuke* what others must suffer devastating losses to understand.

In the middle of the spectrum of teachability are the *simple* (19:25)—a group we have met before. They are not as quick to learn as the discerning, and yet they are not as set in their ways either. They will have to see some disaster or punishment hitting someone—as when a mocker is punished—but then they may *learn prudence* and change their ways.

The point of these sayings is that there are degrees of teachability. You must learn to assess how teachable people are before you hire, join, or in some other way throw your lot in with them. And you must assess yourself.

When have you learned something important from watching someone else's life? Where are you on the teachability spectrum?

Prayer: Lord, between the discerning person who learns through a single, wise rebuke and the fool who never learns from anything, I am firmly in the middle. I confess you must send me messages multiple times before I read them. Forgive me and work on my heart until I hear you the first time. Amen.

July 19

For lack of guidance a nation falls, but victory is won through many advisers. . . . The wise prevail through great power, and those who have knowledge muster their strength. Surely you need guidance to wage war, and victory is won through many advisers. (11:14, 24:5–6)

GET ALL THE ADVICE YOU CAN. We must not be indecisive (James 1:8), but too many people are impulsive. Proverbs urges you not to merely "get a second opinion" before making a decision, nor even to just consult with a few intimate friends. It calls us to have *many advisers*, literally, a "multitude" of them.

Why? The first reason is because if you consult only a couple, you are likely to choose people from your own party or point of view. These proverbs, then, "counter the danger of caucus-dominated political practices."[158] They call us to transcend partisanship. The second reason is for thinking "outside the box." To devise creative solutions you have to foresee all the problems and generate all possible options. No two or three people will be able to do that, and the resulting plan will find no new way forward. Jesus, all by himself, brought a plan for salvation that shocked both liberal Sadducees and conservative Pharisees (cf. Mark 3:6). But we will not be wise without *many* advisers.

Do you have advisers from across a spectrum of opinions and backgrounds?

Prayer: Lord, I find it difficult just to ask where an item is at a grocery store. Yet even you, as Father, Son, and Holy Spirit, take counsel together. Give me friends who can be counselors, and then give me the humility to listen to them. Amen.

July 20

Though you grind a fool in a mortar, grinding them like grain with a pestle, you will not remove their folly from them. (27:22)

LET EXPERIENCE CORRECT YOU. Wisdom is listening to advice from others. But it also includes listening to what life itself tells you through experience. Suffering can grow us (Hebrews 12:7–11)—breaking us of overconfidence, making us more sympathetic, showing us our weaknesses, and helping us to become more resilient and dependent on God. But none of this is automatic. Some people can be ground to dust, *like grain with a pestle*—an image of excruciating pain—but they learn nothing.

Adversity drives some people deeply into God's love but convinces others that a God of love cannot exist. What will make the difference? The essence of foolishness is to be "wise in your own eyes." The temptation for those who suffer is to assume that because we can't think of any good purposes God may have for our suffering, there can't be any. If you can't imagine a God infinitely wiser and more loving than you, then you won't be able to trust him and grow in grace. The most basic wisdom is to trust the character of God, who has suffered and died in Jesus Christ for you and who will not withhold anything necessary for your ultimate joy.

Think of a time of great trial or suffering in your life. What things did you learn and what ways did you grow through it?

Prayer: Lord, in times of trouble I just grit my teeth and hold on stoically until the storm passes. But that is no way to learn from you. Oh, the next time, draw me into prayer, real prayer, until your presence and love reach new levels in my heart. Amen.

July 21

Whoever remains stiff-necked after many rebukes will suddenly be destroyed—without remedy. (29:1)

TOO LATE. A *stiff-necked* ox or horse, which would not bend its neck at the direction of the driver, would be useless and even dangerous, and might be destroyed. The metaphor is applied to those who are wise in their own eyes and who resist God's Word and rule. Is there any hope for them?

Because salvation is by faith and repentance, not our good works and performance (Romans 3:28), in one sense anyone can at any time turn to God (Isaiah 45:22). "There is no sin so great that it can bring damnation on those who truly repent."[159] But a person can spiritually drift until they are too hardened to consider real repentance (28:14). While God's door to hear contrition is never shut, our window of opportunity to produce it can be.[160] If we ever sense the impulse to repent, we should respond immediately and not presume in our pride that we will be capable of it at any time and place we choose (2 Timothy 2:25). To not do so is to be stiff-necked.

Have you ignored open windows of opportunity for spiritual growth that now seem closed? If this question convicts you, is this not a new opportunity for change?

Prayer: Father, make me a chief repenter. Let me be the first to admit my fault, and to repent quickly, without grudging, without excuses, without bitterness, knowing that repentance is a path through grief to greater joy. Amen.

July 22

A wicked person listens to deceitful lips; a liar pays attention to a destructive tongue. . . . A false witness will perish, but a careful listener will testify successfully. (17:4, 21:28)

WHAT *NOT* TO LISTEN TO. The more a liar you are, the more you become willing to *listen to deceitful lips*. It is easy to fool a person who thinks he's clever. The heart that nurtures pride and envy wants to justify its own flaws and hidden sins. That means, first, being highly vulnerable to liars who tell you untrue things that flatter you and hide unpleasant facts from you. Also, it means being gullible and too ready to believe gossip or bad reports, because you want to believe the worst about others. In the end, both those who lie and those who listen to the lies *will perish*. Liars get exposed, and those who base practice and policy on lies will experience disaster.

Only the one who listens well is worth listening to (21:28). Jesus, the suffering servant, listened perfectly to his Father and so speaks the truth perfectly to us (Isaiah 50:4–5). We must be like him, something that can happen only if we spend time in his company. If we do so, through worship and prayer, we will speak well and boldly and it will be evident to others that we have been with Jesus (Acts 4:13).

Are you too gullible, too willing to believe reports that confirm your prejudices? Or, on the other hand, are you too skeptical, too unwilling to believe people?

Prayer: Lord, there are so many things I want to believe, because they will justify me. Help me live each day on a platform of your justification, Jesus, and that will make me a far better judge of truth. Amen.

July 23

A whip for the horse, a bridle for the donkey, and a rod for the backs of fools! (26:3)

DON'T BE A MULE. Animals are tamed through carrots and sticks, because we can't sit down and explain to them why they should behave this or that way. A fool is someone who can be dealt with only in the same way. Psalm 32:9 exhorts, "Do not be like the horse or the mule, which have no understanding but must be controlled by bit and bridle or they will not come to you." Instead, the Lord says to us, "I will counsel you with my loving eye on you" (Psalm 32:8).

The contrast is between obeying God only because we must and knowing God personally, out of a desire for his loving glance. Commenting on Psalm 32:8–9, Kidner writes, "Those who invite the rod are those who contrive to ignore the glance."[161] Sometimes, of course, we all need God to bring us up short, to use some hard circumstance to show us we have been complacent or stupid. But as soon as possible we should return to fellowship with him through prayer and his Word. Let him guide you rather than the hard knocks of life.

Can you think of something you had to learn from the "hard knocks of life" that you could have and should have learned from God's Word?

Prayer: Father, isn't this my worst sin against you? I obey because I have to, not because I want to. I repent because of the consequences of sin, not just because it grieves you, the God I love. Show me again the suffering love of your Son for me, until I obey, not like a donkey but out of grateful joy. Amen.

July 24

Blows and wounds scrub away evil, and beatings purge the inmost being. (20:30)

STRIPES THAT HEAL. We should not require God to use adversity as the only way to shape us (July 23). Nevertheless, there is seldom real growth without life's difficulties, its *blows and wounds.* People who have led completely charmed lives are often superficial and unable to sympathize with others, and usually have an unrealistically high estimation of their own endurance, patience, and strength.

20:30 points out that the external discipline of the body can strengthen *the inmost being.* Military experience testifies to the inner discipline that painful basic training can bring. But in the context of the whole Bible, a larger principle is in view. Paul said his outward nature, through afflictions and difficulties, aging and illness, was "wasting away," yet "inwardly" he was being renewed day by day. "For our light and momentary troubles are achieving for us an eternal glory that far outweighs them all" (2 Corinthians 4:16–17).

In the end, however, it is not our wounds but Jesus' wounds that purify us. With his stripes and wounds we are healed.[162] His suffering for us means we can trust him in our difficulties and, when we do that, our afflictions can make us like him.

Recount a time in which adversity pushed you toward Jesus, and spend some time today thanking him for working in your life.

Prayer: Lord Jesus Christ, only to you, of all the deities in all the religions of the world, can we say, "To our wounds, only God's wounds can speak, and not a god has wounds, but Thou alone."[163] Seeing your wounds for me enables me to bear my wounds with patience. Amen.

July 25

> It is a sin to despise one's neighbor, but blessed is the one who is kind to the needy. (14:21)

RESIST SUPERIORITY. Human relationships constantly break down. Like a house, they regularly need both minor repairs (which we call "maintenance") as well as major restorations. The wise person has the skill set to do both.

One way to do minor "maintenance" is by resisting the natural tendency to feel superior or to *despise*, those around you. 14:21 shows us this is one of the reasons that people are not *kind to the needy*—but the consequences are broader. Unless you resist this natural urge to justify yourself by comparing and looking down at others, your relationships will not survive their normal bumps and turns. How can we avoid this?

Meditate on this. Indwelling sin guarantees that we are never as holy as our beliefs should lead us to be, and God's graciousness to his creation guarantees that others are never as wicked as their unbelief might otherwise lead them to be. So remember, you may have things to learn from people who are very flawed but through whom God may be accomplishing his purposes.

When was the last time you despised your neighbor in your heart? It is an important spiritual exercise to learn to catch yourself doing this and repent on the spot.

Prayer: Lord, whenever I meet someone, I instinctively look for faults—or just posit them—so I can feel superior. That sins grievously against your command to "value others above yourselves" (Philippians 2:3). I am so unlike you. I repent. Conform me to your image. Amen.

July 26

All a person's ways seem pure to them, but motives are weighed by the LORD. (16:2)

BE SELF-CRITICAL. Another way to resist the natural tendency to feel superior to others (July 25) is to be self-critical. Our *motives* seem *pure* to us—without guilt or sin. However, the Lord knows better. "The disciple should evaluate his motives and conduct against God's revealed standards and not absolutize his own estimation of them."[164] One way to do this is to remember Satan's accusation against Job—that he did not love God for himself alone, but rather he obeyed because of the benefits he received (cf. Job 1:8–10). That is a profound criticism and is always partly true of us.

For Christians, new views of our sin can be accompanied by deeper discoveries of how righteous in Christ and perfectly loved we are (Philippians 3:9). So conviction of sin can lead to both greater humility and greater gratitude and joy at the same time. This humility about the impurity of our motives should prevent us from being too sure of our position and from speaking too strongly against people on the other side of a conflict (August 1).

How have you seen that your motives are impure even for the many good things you do? How does knowing that make you kinder in relationships?

Prayer: Lord, I have a heart that continually inclines me to sin, and I'm spiritually powerless to change one bit of it without your supernatural help. How can I feel superior to anyone at all? Remind me of that—and of your amazing love for me—every time I meet someone new. Amen.

July 27

If a wise person goes to court with a fool, the fool rages and scoffs, and there is no peace. (29:9)

CHOOSE YOUR BATTLES. *Fools rage* or, we would say, "rant." They *scoff* and mock their opponents, rather than making an argument or a case. Ranters and scoffers do not persuade or build bridges They merely "energize the base"—that is, they preach to those who already agree with them and confirm the views and biases people already have. Today this is the main form of public discourse.

The realism of this proverb shows that sometimes engaging a ranter is unavoidable. We are told to expect a long and painful process. But we must enter it maintaining other commitments, such as not despising the ranter (July 25) and always treating people respectfully (May 10). We are never to do to the ranter what the ranter is trying to do to us—to marginalize and demonize rather than convince. In the New Testament we are directed to, as much as it is within our control, live at peace with the people around us (Romans 12:18), even those who rage and scoff.

Do you rant? Do you enjoy reading or listening to ranters?

Prayer: Lord Jesus, you answered your opponents wisely and brilliantly but patiently and constantly. How I want to give back to my critics—with verve—the same disdain they show me. But I want to be like *you*, not *them*. Change my heart to make it so. Amen.

July 28

Like one who grabs a stray dog by the ears is someone who rushes into a quarrel not their own. (26:17)

DON'T BE A BUSYBODY. When two people are having a conflict with each other, it can wreak havoc on those around them. There is a strong temptation to take sides. It is hard not to sympathize with the party you know best. It is also hard for that person not to share his or her hurt with you in a way that does not vilify the other party in the conflict. As a result we can have second- and third-order unreconciled relationships. The enemy of your friend, and the friends of your friend's enemy, all become your enemies. It's a mess—but it happens all the time.

If you *grab a stray dog by the ears* you will be bitten. And if you quarrel with someone whose issue is not with you but with someone else, there is no way to resolve it. A wise person should suspend judgment (you can't know all the facts) and encourage the parties toward reconciliation. Beyond that, a wise person "should walk away from a dispute in which he has no interest," a *quarrel not their own.*[165]

When was the last time you saw a larger community divided by a conflict between two individuals? Have you yourself been drawn into such a division?

Prayer: Lord Jesus, technology makes it so easy to be caught up in a quarrel not my own. But you refused to become "a judge or an arbiter" (Luke 12:14) in disputes that were not crucial to your mission. Give me the humility and singleness of mind to not take sides or fuel these wildfires of the tongue. Amen.

July 29

Like a maniac shooting flaming arrows of death is one who deceives their neighbor and says, "I was only joking!" (26:18–19)

BE CAREFUL ABOUT HUMOR. Since July 25 we have been listing skills for "relational maintenance"—things we need to do to keep relationships in good repair. Another one is in this proverb. Proverbs counsels care in the area of humor.

The great danger is that our joke may cross the line into cruelty. Humor is often spontaneous, and we have to assess in a split second whether the funny thought we have just had should be expressed. It is too late afterward to see the hurt and say, "Oh, I'm so sorry! I never meant . . ." The wise person makes quick assessment and refrains if there is any danger. Humor is culturally variable; what is acceptable in one time, place, or situation may cause hurt or anger in another. In general, it is wiser to make yourself the object of your humorous observations, rather than someone else. That makes you less likely to give offense, but even self-deprecating jokes can make people uncomfortable. Take special care with humor.

When was the last time you saw a joke (by you yourself or someone else) go wrong? Why did the humor misfire?

Prayer: Lord, I have painful memories of thoughtless words that were like knives that cut. You are so exquisitely careful with words and with hearts. Help me to remember the infinite worth of every human soul as I speak. Amen.

July 30

Whoever loves a quarrel loves sin; whoever builds a high gate invites destruction. . . . Without wood a fire goes out; without a gossip a quarrel dies down. As charcoal to embers and as wood to fire, so is a quarrelsome person for kindling strife. (17:19, 26:20–21)

DON'T LOVE AN ARGUMENT. Some people enjoy debating. This may stem from the kind of genuine intellectual curiosity represented by the Socratic dialogue. But 17:19 literally says *Love quarrel—love sin.* 26:20–21 confirms that the community can never have peace when there's *a quarrelsome person* present.

Some people are argumentative because they cannot distinguish between essential truths worth contending for and secondary or nonessential issues. Others are argumentative because their pride makes it hard for them to admit when they are in the wrong. A simple "I'm sorry" is beyond them and they need to save face. Some others simply are irritable, lack impulse control, and can't resist making caustic remarks that inflame things. 17:19 says the person who *loves a quarrel* is like the status seeker who builds *a high gate* in order to look as if he lives in a mansion. Perhaps the main reason for loving an argument is that being proved right can be an exercise in power rather than in truth. Instead, look to the one who does not "wrangle or cry aloud" (Matthew 12:19 RSV).

Are you quarrelsome? Which of these reasons for argumentativeness might be true of you? How could you change?

Prayer: Lord, I love an argument if I think I can win it, and I hate it if I think I can't—which shows I am valiant not for truth but for myself. Reproduce in me your spirit of goodwill and gentleness so I won't "love a quarrel." Amen.

July 31

Drive out the mocker, and out goes strife; quarrels and insults are ended. (22:10)

DON'T ENJOY INSULTS. Because their cynicism appears as sophistication, mockers often are ringleaders like Lampwick in *Pinocchio* or Regina in *Mean Girls*. Mockers' main currency is the *insult*, the often hilarious and even brilliant put-down. An insult is a kind of verbal cartoon. As cartoonists exaggerate some feature of a person to make him or her look ridiculous, so the insult exaggerates or plays up some feature of a person's looks or character to make them appear foolish.

Humility and love can certainly motivate us to confront a person if it is best for him or her. But insults are produced by wise-in-their-own-eyes arrogance. If you have a propensity for insults, you will always be undermining relationships. Strong medicine is prescribed here. A community that cares about the nurture of loving relationships should ask the insulter to change—or leave. (*Drive out the mocker.*) To humble and heal the spirit of the mocker, remember that the insults and curses that we deserve have fallen on Jesus (Romans 15:3).

Do you enjoy witty put-downs too much? Do you hand them out yourself? Is there a member of your community or circle who does this and should be spoken to about it?

Prayer: Lord Jesus, brilliant put-downs draw me so swiftly into laughing and despising people—calling them "Racas," inferior idiots (Matthew 5:22), in my heart. If anyone had the right to mock and jeer, you did. But you didn't. Burn away my pride and make me like you. Amen.

August 1

All a person's ways seem pure to them, but motives are weighed by the LORD. (16:2)

DON'T IMPUTE MOTIVES. We looked at this proverb before, but there is one implication of the saying that we have not yet addressed. Because only God can truly assess the *motives* of the heart, we should not think we can judge other people's motives perfectly either. Matthew 7:1 condemns "judging" people, and that cannot mean we should not evaluate them. Rather, to "judge" someone means to make a final condemnation (not just a critique of something about them), which entails the kind of final knowledge of heart motives that only God has.

1 Corinthians 13:7 says love "always trusts, always hopes." This does not mean that we should be naive, but it certainly means we should not be constantly, habitually suspicious of people, nor be quick to assign motives of envy, pride, resentment, or greed to someone's action when we cannot really see into the heart.[166] Disagreements become deadly conflicts when you move from rightly pointing out wrong behavior to assuming the ability to completely understand a person's inner purposes, which is something only God can do (Romans 2:16).

Do you exercise proper restraint about reading others' motives? Think of some instances when you misread someone's motives badly.

Prayer: Lord, my need to judge people is unseemly coming from a heart that should itself be judged. You alone are judge and king of hearts. Give me not a naive but a gracious spirit that gives people the benefit of the doubt. Amen.

> Do not say, "I'll do to them as they have done to me; I'll pay them back for what they did." (24:29)

FORGIVENESS: PART 1. What happens when a relationship breaks down? The first thing to do is to forgive. 24:29 shows the psychological structure of resentment. We say inside, *"I'll do to them as they have done to me."* But Proverbs tells us to deliberately refuse that thought—*do not say* it. Why? The desire for vengeance always backfires. Cain's sinful resentment mastered him (cf. Genesis 4:6–7). If someone wrongs you, you start by hoping for that person to be unhappy. But then you may graduate to saying and doing things to hurt them and those around them. What is happening? The evil done to you has come into you and is shaping you. As Hawkeye says about the bitter Magua in *The Last of the Mohicans*, "Magua's heart is twisted. He would make himself into what twisted him."[167]

To forgive is to refuse to hold people liable for what they have done to us. That is God's job, not ours (Romans 12:19). And if Jesus died to forgive you of your infinite debt to him, how can you not forgive the wrongdoer his finite debt to you (Matthew 18:21–35)?

Where have you seen residual resentment toward someone affecting the life of a person you know? Where has it affected your life?

Prayer: Lord, my resentment toward some persons and some kinds of persons shows itself in irritability and abrasive remarks. I admit it for what it is—a failure to forgive as you forgave me. Forgive me for not forgiving! And dissolve my anger with a look at your dying love on the cross. Amen.

August 3

Do not say, "I'll do to them as they have done to me; I'll pay them back for what they did." (24:29)

FORGIVENESS: PART 2. When we are wronged, we want to *pay them back*. Forgiveness, however, is a commitment not to do that but rather to bear the cost yourself.

How? First, by refusing to hurt the person directly. Beware of subtle ways that we can try to extract payment. Don't drag up the past over and over. Don't be more demanding and controlling than you are with others, all because you feel this person still owes you. Don't avoid or be cold to them. Second, by refusing to cut the person down to others. Refuse, by innuendo or hint or gossip or direct slander, to diminish him or her in the eyes of others under the guise of "warning" people or getting personal support. Finally, don't continually replay the memories of the wrong in your imagination in order to keep the sense of loss and hurt fresh and real to you so you can stay actively hostile to the person and feel virtuous yourself.

By bearing the cost of the sin, you are walking in the path of your master (Colossians 3:13).

Think of someone who has wronged you. Have you paid the costs (listed above) to forgive that person?

Prayer: Lord, my forgiveness is skin deep. I refrain from obvious efforts to pay them back, but I simmer. It is far more costly to refuse thoughts of anger and self-pity, to remember I am a forgiven sinner, to pray for them from the heart. But in light of your costly love for me, I resolve to pay the price. Help me, Lord. Amen.

August 4

Whoever would foster love covers over an offense, but whoever repeats the matter separates close friends. (17:9)

FOSTERING LOVE: PART 1. If a relationship breaks down, we should forgive—not repeating the matter to pay them back, as we saw yesterday. But we should not merely refrain from payback. We should also *foster love*. The goal is to still be *friends*, not merely not enemies. How? For the restoration of a relationship, we must let people know they wronged us (Luke 17:3–4). It is never loving to let someone continue to sin against you, nor can the relationship be mended without talking about it. You may learn of something the other person has against you (Matthew 5:24). For more on this, see the reflection of August 5.

What the Bible counsels is almost the very opposite of how we ordinarily operate. When wronged, we burn inside with resentment but say nothing. Instead we are called to forgive on the inside and then speak the truth. Only if you have forgiven deeply will your expression of the truth not be dripping with resentment and thus hard to hear. Only if you forgive will your rebuke be for God's sake and the person's sake rather than for your sake.

Is there someone who used to be a friend but is now just "not an enemy"? What could you do about that?

Prayer: Father, you bring life out of death. I have both family and friendship ties that have essentially died, but I ask you to bring new life to them. Start the resurrection within me, with a new sense of your love on my heart enough to melt the hardness I still have. Amen.

August 5

Whoever would foster love covers over an offense, but whoever repeats the matter separates close friends. (17:9)

FOSTERING LOVE: PART 2. Some signs that you need relationship restoration are when you begin avoiding each other, or are relatively formal with each other, or when you find that you are irritated when *that* person says something more than when someone else says it.

How do we restore things so as to regain our brother or sister (Matthew 18:15)? First, see that it is always your move to go to them (cf. Matthew 5:24 and 18:15). Second, start by admitting anything you did that you think may have contributed to the problem. Then invite them to add anything to the list. Listen respectfully to any criticism. Don't be quick to defend or even to explain yourself. When all that is done, then ask forgiveness and offer any helpful explanations (not excuses) for what happened. Third, if necessary, gently tell the other person where you believe they might have wronged you (Matthew 18:15–19). Invite them to correct you if your understanding is inaccurate. If they agree with you, tell them you are willing to put it behind you. Carefully suggest alternate ways of behaving in the future.

Have you seen anyone try a process like this? Did it work? Why or why not?

Prayer: Lord, there are friends with whom I've had a conflict and now we are cool to each other. Give us the courage and ingenuity to slowly rebuild trust so we can be friends. After all, you were betrayed by your friends, but you loved them to the end. Help me. Amen.

August 6

Through patience a ruler can be persuaded, and a gentle tongue can break a bone. (25:15)

GENTLE PERSISTENCE. A "gentle answer" can quickly de-escalate an angry feud (15:1, July 4). We might infer that gentle speech means being mealy-mouthed, compliant, or pacifying, like saying to a bully, "I give up." Here we see that is not true at all. The metaphor of *breaking a bone* means that *a gentle tongue* is better at breaking down hardened resistance to an idea than aggressive words. You may still argue pointedly, but in a gentle, patient, respectful manner.

This insight fits in well with the New Testament exhortation that no matter how much someone may oppose us or may even have wronged us, we must forgive him or her from our heart, first and unconditionally. This drains out so much of the contempt and disdain (18:3) that can easily creep into our voice when we are contending with someone. Most of us are either temperamentally direct, bold, and persistent *or* gentle, calm, and deferential—but never both. Yet the wise learn to be both. They follow the one who always showed boldness without harshness, humility without uncertainty, who spoke truth but always bathed in love.

Do you tend to be direct and persistent or gentle and deferential? How can you combine them?

Prayer: Lord Jesus, you combined qualities of humility and majesty as no one else has ever done. And through the gospel, which both humbles us into the dust and makes us kings to reign. Make us, in your image, gentle but absolutely insistent on truth. Amen.

August 7

Starting a quarrel is like breaching a dam; so drop the matter before a dispute breaks out. (17:14)

NOT SO FAST. If a *dam* breaks you should be ready for chaos. And if you are entering a dispute, be prepared for what will happen. This is a good example of how Proverbs works. This seems to be a blanket statement, namely that if you have a bone of contention, you should just *drop the matter* rather than get into a dispute. Yet to offer reproof to someone can often be the wise thing to do (15:10, 27:5–6), and to advocate for the oppressed is right (31:8–9).

What do we learn, on the whole, from Proverbs about contentions and disputes? We cannot take this as a blanket prohibition, given the rest of the book of Proverbs. Yet the strength of the warning means entering a dispute should be a last resort, not a natural course of action. We should look at our motives, get good advice, think both about the issues of justice (has a genuine injustice been done?) and about love (would it be good for the person to hear the truth?).

Are you doing everything possible to avoid a dispute—or are you being (or have you been) drawn into one?

Prayer: Father, in conflicts some of us are too ready to contend and others are too reticent. Your Son knew when to call someone a whitewashed tomb and when to refuse to defend himself (Mark 11:33). Teach me the wisdom to know when to do what and the self-control to do it right. Amen.

August 8

In a lawsuit the first to speak seems right, until someone comes forward and cross-examines. (18:17)

BAD REPORTS. We are prone to snap judgments. This text reminds us of a common occurrence. If we hear from a single party, that person's account is almost never a full and unbiased report. We hear from him or her and it is natural to draw our conclusions. But wise people don't do it. They keep an open mind—they know there is always another side, another perspective. It is exceedingly rare for one person in a dispute to be able to represent the opponent's point of view adequately.

So 18:17 directs that, when we hear a complaint or bad report about someone, we remember that we never have all the facts and we never see the whole picture until we investigate further. Instead of drawing a conclusion about the person mentioned in the report and passing the negative information along, we should keep it to ourselves unless it is one of those relatively rare situations in which someone's safety is at stake. In today's world, this principle means we should not get all our world news from one source and slant.

Have you recently made a snap judgment on the basis of a single bad report? How can you avoid that?

Prayer: Lord, your plans and counsels are flawless for you have perfect knowledge of all hearts and things. But drill deep into my consciousness that I don't. Save me from precipitous conclusions, which I am so prone to draw. Make me wiser by reminding me I'm not so wise. Amen.

August 9

What you have seen with your eyes do not bring hastily to court, for what will you do in the end if your neighbor puts you to shame? If you take your neighbor to court, do not betray another's confidence, or the one who hears it may shame you and the charge against you will stand. (25:7–10)

GO WITH DISCRETION. These verses refer not to mutual grievances between two parties who need restoration (August 4 and 5) but to a situation in which you learn of an injustice that someone has done and you decide to accuse him of it before the authorities. This warns about doing so hastily. Kidner summarizes: "One seldom knows the full facts, or interprets them perfectly (8) and one's motives . . . are seldom as pure as one pretends (10). To run to the law or to the neighbors is usually to run away from the duty of personal relationship—see Christ's clinching comment in Matthew 18:15b."[168]

If you hear a bad report, you should suspend judgment until you learn more. If it is something that requires action, you should usually speak to the other party personally first. If that does not help, you should seek to rectify things, always in love, and making sure that in the process other injustices are not done.[169]

Have you seen a situation, either in your own life or someone else's, where complaints were lodged too hastily and injustice was done in the end?

Prayer: Lord, inflammatory images and rhetoric are now shared instantly and passions lead so quickly to legal action. But when I get indignant, slow me down, remind me of my own wrongdoings, and give me the courage to talk to the people personally or drop it. Amen.

August 10

Casting the lot settles disputes and keeps strong opponents apart. A
brother wronged is more unyielding than a fortified city; disputes are
like the barred gates of a citadel. (18:18–19)

TELL IT TO THE CHURCH. A brother wronged can be unyielding. Is there any hope for reconciliation? Verse 18 proposes
that in the bitterest disputes we should cast lots. In the Old Testament, lots were cast to get yes or no answers from God (Joshua
14:1–2). But the last time that method was used in the Bible was
in choosing the replacement for Judas just before Pentecost (Acts
1:26). After that, decisions were made through prayerful coun-
cils (Acts 15:1–29) and elections (Acts 6:1–7) based on the Word
of God.[170]

How do we seek God's will after Pentecost? Consider going to
Christian leaders, presenting your case, and accepting their
decision (Matthew 18:15–18). In our individualistic age, and also
a time in which there are many unhealthy churches, such advice
will not be welcome. But that just puts more responsibility on
Christians to look for churches with leaders they can respect
(Hebrews 13:7,17) and then use these leaders for help in your
relationships. The Spirit is especially grieved by unresolved conflict and bitterness (Ephesians 4:30–32).

Have you seen a situation in which church leaders helped in a
dispute or to restore a relationship? Did it work? Why or why not?

Prayer: Lord, in a time of church decline, biblical calls to respect and submit to church leaders do not sit very well. There is
much malpractice and abuse in the ministry. But how good it is
when godly leaders help people find the wise paths. Raise up
those leaders and put them in every church. Amen.

KNOWING THE TIMES AND SEASONS
Guidance, Planning, and Decision Making

August 11

> The lot is cast into the lap, but its every decision is from the LORD. . . .
> Many are the plans in a person's heart, but it is the LORD's purpose
> that prevails. (16:33, 19:21)

THE GUIDANCE OF GOD. Christians want God's guidance, that is, we want help with what decisions to make. But these verses remind us that he is already guiding us.

God can help us in our decision making if we depend on him. But in another sense we are told God has a plan for our lives and history, and he is working it out. God is all-powerful, infinitely loving, and perfectly wise in how he loves us and in what he brings into our lives. "He works out everything according to the purpose of his will" (Ephesians 1:11), and that is for our good (Romans 8:28). This is the greatest comfort. No matter what others may try to do, God's purposes for you will stand. *It is the Lord's purpose that prevails.* No matter how much Jacob lied and deceived and created havoc in his life, still he could not thwart God's plan for his life, that he be an ancestor of the Messiah. In a sense, for a Christian, there is no "plan B."

How can this truth—that God has a good plan for your life—be a comfort and help as you seek to make wise decisions?

Prayer: Lord, you are completely just and fair and, despite appearances due to our extremely limited vantage point, you have never wronged anyone. Give me the deep contentment and peace that can only come from knowing your designs for me are flawless, though I cannot possibly fathom them. Amen.

August 12

To humans belong the plans of the heart, but from the LORD comes the proper answer of the tongue. In their hearts humans plan their course, but the LORD establishes their steps. . . . A person's steps are directed by the LORD. How then can anyone understand their own way? (16:1,9, 20:24)

CONCURRENCE. Modern people reason that either God is in charge of history, working everything according to his plan, or we have freedom of choice. But the Bible says both are true at once. Theologians have called this "concurrence." Jesus' death on the cross was foreordained, absolutely certain, yet all the people who killed him were responsible for their actions (Acts 2:23).

The plans of the heart belong to us—they are our responsibility. The way God controls history does not force us to act. Yet all we do—every one of our steps—is part of his plan. This seeming paradox, while impossible to completely fathom, is supremely practical. It gives you enormous incentive to take personal initiative—poor choices will create pain and trouble. And yet, if you do fail, remember that you can't truly mess up your life. God will weave even your failings into his plan for you. 20:24 adds that therefore we should not worry about the fact—as others do—that we can't control our future. It is in God's hands.

Have you grasped this unique biblically balanced view of history, or are you more anxious or more passive than you should be?

Prayer: Lord, you are of eternity and I am of time, and that is why I cannot grasp how every detail of history could be under the control of your plan, and yet every human action be free and responsible. Yet they are, and I bow with fear and trembling before the incomprehensible but wonderful wisdom of this. Amen.

August 13

The integrity of the upright guides them, but the unfaithful are destroyed by their duplicity. . . . The plans of the righteous are just, but the advice of the wicked is deceitful. . . . Do not those who plot evil go astray? But those who plan what is good find love and faithfulness. (11:3, 12:5, 14:22)

NOT HOW BUT WHOM. If you survey Proverbs for methods of discerning God's will, you will conclude that the book does not talk about *how* God guides as much as *whom* God guides. What modern people want is almost a form of magic. They want little signs and feelings in order to determine from God the right decision to make. But that is the way you may guide an infant, who cannot understand you and must be carried or led. The way you would guide a youth or adult is to speak to them so they understand and can make decisions without being led by the hand in every instance.

Through a long path and a lot of work (Proverbs 1–4), we develop integrity and righteousness and it is through these character traits that God guides us. The more we know God, ourselves, the human heart, the order of creation, the times and seasons, the more we will have the wisdom to make good decisions. Modern people want a technique for guidance, "five steps to good decisions." God offers wise character, hard won over a lifetime.

Why do you think people prefer to look for signs and feelings rather than relying on wisdom to make decisions?

Prayer: Father, my culture conditions me to desire quick answers that can fit on a slide or a short video. But you are not an answer dispenser or a wisdom cash window. Here I resolve to take the long journey to becoming the kind of person you guide. "I set my heart on pilgrimage" (Psalm 84:5). Amen.

August 14

The way of fools seems right to them, but the wise listen to advice. . . .
There is a way that appears to be right, but in the end it leads to death.
(12:15, 16:25)

REALISM. We tend to think that if we have lived right and followed the Bible and made the right decisions, things will go well. If things are not going well, we may conclude we didn't receive God's guidance. But these two proverbs together give us a sobering fact about our world that you must know in order to be wise.

12:15 says that the path to disaster *seems right* to a fool. That is, fools are terrible at making plans because they reject the way of wisdom (trusting God, listening to good advisers, making careful plans, controlling their emotions and words, knowing their heart, and so on). Absalom comes to mind (2 Samuel 17).

But then 16:25 comes along, which says that sometimes the way to disaster *appears to be right*—period. This highly unwelcome but realistic observation is that in this world you can follow the ways of wisdom and make your plans as well as can be and things can still go terribly wrong. The wise know that sometimes all paths may run ill.[171] Yet God promises that he is working all things for ultimate good and glory (Romans 8:28).

Can you think back on some situation in your life or someone else's in which you now see that there was no choice or option that would have brought a pleasant outcome?

Prayer: Father, I don't want to believe that sometimes every option, even with right action, might lead to a difficult, painful end. But this was the case for your Son—there was no escaping agony and death. But he accepted it and obeyed you faithfully in it, and new life was the result. Help me to do the same. Amen.

August 15

The plans of the diligent lead to profit as surely as haste leads to poverty. . . . Put your outdoor work in order and get your fields ready; after that, build your house. (21:5, 24:27)

PLANNING. A theme of Proverbs is that impulsive *haste* should be avoided and forward-looking, careful planning should be part of making decisions (21:5). We are to be *diligent*, giving attention to detail and patience. Good planning means discerning all possible options and weighing the strengths and weaknesses of each. Even the triune God accomplished our salvation through a brilliant, well-laid-out plan (Galatians 4:1–7).

24:27 warns (using the language of an agrarian culture) that you must evaluate how much income you will make before you know how big a house to build. It is the height of foolishness to fix our hearts on a particular lifestyle and try to live it when we don't have the ability to support ourselves. The verse aligns with C. S. Lewis's observation that in ancient times "the cardinal problem of human life was how to conform the soul to objective reality, and the solution was wisdom, self-discipline, and virtue. For the modern [person], the cardinal problem is how to conform reality to the wishes of man, and the solution is a technique."[172]

When was the last time you saw in your life or someone else's the consequences of poor planning? What went wrong, specifically?

Prayer: Lord, your plans are perfect because you are perfect in knowledge, love, and holiness. And mine are not because I am not. Your Son could not be hurried. He was never early or late, despite appearances (Mark 5:35–36). Save me from my impetuousness. Amen.

August 16

Commit to the LORD whatever you do, and he will establish your plans. (16:3)

TRUST. At first glance, 16:3 seems to say we should pray, "Oh, Lord—bless my plans! Let them succeed!" and he will grant your wishes. But it does not say, "Commit your plans to the Lord." It says, *"Commit to the Lord whatever you do."* The word commit means to roll onto, to put all of your weight onto something. What the proverb is calling us to do is to unconditionally obey and trust him in every area of our lives. It is only if and as you do this that you will find that you are slowly but surely becoming a person who makes wise, realistic plans (February 18).

What turned Joseph into the wise leader who saved Egypt and his own family? He was sold into slavery and sent to prison unjustly, but if he had not trusted God unconditionally through all those dark times, he would never have become the wise man he became. If you trust God, then as time goes on, both your good times and your bad times will turn you into the kind of person whose plans and decisions are more and more wise.

Are you getting more wise in the decisions you are making? Why or why not?

Prayer: Lord, you are completely sovereign—no one can thwart your will. Yet you are infinitely loving and good, so there is nothing to fear from your absolute power. Like Joseph I simply bow in submission and adoration. I submit to your good will. And just doing that will both glorify you and make me wise. Amen.

August 17

For lack of guidance a nation falls, but victory is won through many advisers. . . . Plans are established by seeking advice; so if you wage war, obtain guidance. . . . Surely you need guidance to wage war, and victory is won through many advisers. (11:14, 20:18, 24:6)

CHOOSING WELL. We saw that having *many advisers* across the spectrum of opinion is good policy (July 19). Yet Ahab (1 Kings 22:1–39) and Absalom (2 Samuel 17:1–23), though well furnished with counselors, gave heed to the wrong ones. So advisers are a help, but they are still no substitute for the guidance of wisdom. We must learn to discriminate between bad, good, and best courses of action. How can we choose the right path?

After getting advice from others, choose the best course in light of: any relevant biblical texts, the opinion of authorities (in family, church, and state), your conscience (James 4:17), an examination of your motives, the best use of your gifts and abilities in God's service, and finally an assessment of your decision's impact on others. Look at each factor, and then choose well.

Which of these elements of good decision making (listed above) do you often miss?

Prayer: Lord, you warn against being "double-minded" and indecisive (James 1:8). When I am, it is because I forget that you are powerful and you are loving and so I can't ruin your good plan for me. Give me peace through knowing that, and strength to do your will. Amen.

August 18

A wicked messenger falls into trouble, but a trustworthy envoy brings healing. (13:17)

THE NEWS. In ancient times "messengers possessed an important role scarcely comprehensible to modern people."[173] In our culture of fake news and social media, no one can be sure that the messages they are getting are *trustworthy*. Lewis Smedes wrote: "Truthfulness is one more invisible fiber that holds people together in humane community. When we cannot assume that people communicating with us are truthful, we cannot live with them in trust that they will respect our right to freedom to respond to reality. [*sic*] If we cannot trust each other to respect this basic right, we have lost our chance to be human together in God's manner. . . . Speak the truth, be the truth, for your truth sets others free."[174]

There have been societies in which people couldn't trust what the government told them, couldn't trust what the newspapers told them, couldn't trust what the inspectors and police would do with them. Those societies collapsed. There is no higher priority for a healthy society than to have a truthful communications and news media. Recent technological trends, as well as ideological fragmentation, have made this a challenging goal in our time.

Has the trustworthiness of the news media increased, decreased, or remained about the same in your lifetime?

Prayer: Lord, it is the nature of the human heart to deceive and hide the truth to serve our own interests. By your power and grace restrain that sinful tendency of the human heart in our society. As a body politic, help us distinguish truth from falsehood. And make your people salt and light in a dark world. Amen.

August 19

The bloodthirsty hate a person of integrity and seek to kill the upright.
(29:10)

GOODNESS ATTRACTS HOSTILITY. A young man took a summer job in a company, and on his second day the permanent employees came to him to say, "Don't work so hard—you are making us look bad. Slow down or else." A policeman decided not to take the routine bribes that the pimps spread around the precinct to keep the police from arresting their prostitutes. When the others noticed, they came and said, "If you don't take the bribes, we won't have your back."[175]

Christians are to be the "light of the world" (Matthew 5:14), but light exposes, and people do not want to be exposed. Simply living the way you should live can expose dishonesty in the office, racism in the neighborhood, gossip in your social circle, corruption in your government office. Just living with integrity will irritate many people. This is why simple goodness will attract hostility, just because it is good. People *hate a person of integrity*. The wise person is not surprised at this. We should expect this (2 Timothy 3:12), because our Lord, who was the light who exposed the darkness, got nothing less (John 1:5–11).

Have you experienced hostility for your faith or practice? What did people find offensive or threatening? How well did you respond?

Prayer: Father, I confess that I am shocked when people turn on me for doing right—and then I get scared. Turn my eyes to see your Son taking blows for me, and then make me "rejoice" if "counted worthy of suffering disgrace for the Name" (Acts 5:41). Amen.

August 20

Under three things the earth trembles, under four it cannot bear up: a servant who becomes king, a godless fool who gets plenty to eat, a contemptible woman who gets married, and a servant who displaces her mistress. (30:21–23)

YOU CAN'T BE WHATEVER YOU WANT TO BE. A servant without ability *becomes king.* A *contemptible woman* who will make a bad wife gets married. A maidservant who (it's implied) is unequipped becomes powerful. But these things all bring disaster—the earth cannot bear up under them. What is the point?

Proverbs does not mandate strict social stratification, because 17:2 says that a wise and hardworking servant *should* become prominent. And God loves to raise the needy up (Luke 1:46–55). Rather this saying reminds us that we are not all fitted, by character or capacity, for any role in life we may want. Many roles require talent, gifts, and in some case physical abilities that not everyone has. Modern culture tells children, "You can be whatever you aspire to be," but some of our aspirations are for wrong things and others simply don't fit the reality of what we were designed for. In Christ we will eventually inherit the earth and will rule and reign with him (Matthew 5:5; Revelation 1:6). But until then, we can't be whatever we want to be.

Have you seen, in your life or someone else's, an aspiration that was out of touch with reality and led to a sad result?

Prayer: Lord, "You lift the needy up," but, in this world, not everyone can be a ruler. Give me enough trust in your goodness and wisdom to serve you joyfully in "whatever situation the Lord has assigned . . . just as God has called" (1 Corinthians 7:17). Amen.

August 21

> When you sit to dine with a ruler, note well what is before you, and put a knife to your throat if you are given to gluttony. Do not crave his delicacies, for that food is deceptive. (23:1–3)

MANNERS. You are to conduct yourself properly at the table if you are invited to sit *to dine with a ruler*. Why care about something as seemingly trivial as manners? "Society cannot exist without etiquette. . . . People must agree to restrain their impulses and follow a common language of behavior in order to avoid making communal life abrasive, unpleasant, and explosive. This has its personal drawbacks, of course, but it is considered worth the advantage of living among people who aren't perpetually furious."[176]

Van Leeuwen writes: "Even table manners and food are part of the overall order of things, connecting us to the physical world that sustains us, connecting various people to one another, and giving expression to their varied relationships. . . . In the end, nothing, even table manners, is indifferent to the service of God, even though God gives us servants immense freedom to shape cuisine and culture in various ways."[177] Nothing is trivial. When you comb your hair, you bring order out of chaos, as God did at the beginning (Genesis 1:1–3). Do everything for the glory of God (1 Corinthians 10:31).

Have you overlooked manners and courtesy as a way to be wise and glorify God? If not, how do you do it?

Prayer: Lord, manners and etiquette are considered a discredited marker of class privilege—yet they are more than that. They are love, thoughtfulness, and respect in the smallest and most common things in life. Help me to be kind enough to be courteous. Amen.

August 22

Do not answer a fool according to his folly, or you yourself will be just like him. Answer a fool according to his folly, or he will be wise in his own eyes. (26:4–5)

TEMPERAMENT. While seeming to contradict each other, these two sayings, juxtaposed, are meant to make a point. Sometimes it is best to not engage a fool in an argument, and other times it is. How do you know when to do which?

The markers to help with this discernment are listed. If there is no chance of correction and you will end up giving the foolish person only a greater opportunity to express his folly, then just avoid the engagement. But if there is a chance he may see where he is wrong, then plunge in, using all the insights for speaking and listening we have been discussing. But there is an even larger point to be made. Most of us temperamentally will default to always avoiding engagement, and others will be attracted to debating. Sometimes our instincts will be right, but often they are not. So be wise enough to think things out and sometimes go against your instincts.

To which of these two approaches are you more temperamentally disposed? When was the last time you went against your temperament and it turned out to be a wise thing to do?

Prayer: Lord, I thank you that, because you have led me to accept the authority of your Word, I have had many occasions to act against my temperament, and it has not only made me wise, but saved my life. Amen.

August 23

Mockers stir up a city, but the wise turn away anger. (29:8)

INTERNET CULTURE. We have learned a great deal about *mockers*, those who scoff at all truth claims and virtue. Here we see that their work not only harms personal relationships but can *stir up a city*—that is, undermine an entire social order. Literally, this verse says that mockers "set a city on fire," agitating people, stirring up skepticism, doubt, division, and cynicism. This leads to a breakdown in society, because people who listen to mockers can't really believe or trust in any ideals, noble causes, or moral absolutes.

It could be argued that technology has, in an enhanced way, given mockers a platform to set our society on fire with polarizing, incendiary speech. Internet culture privileges mockers, whose insults and broadsides are click bait. It disadvantages the kind of civil, respectful, patient, and careful back-and-forth that brings a diverse society together. The question is—how do we turn away the anger it causes? That is the challenge for the wise today. Start by not being sucked into its passions yourself.

Have you found yourself upset by what you read on social media? Did you get drawn into it? How can you avoid that?

Prayer: Lord, many try to stir up my anger—to get my support, money, vote, and to buy things. With your help, I resolve resistance. Remind me that you are the judge, and I am the judged, yet absolved in Christ. Let these wondrous truths consume my self-righteous indignation. Amen.

August 24

Gray hair is a crown of splendor; it is attained in the way of righteousness. . . . The glory of young men is their strength, gray hair the splendor of the old. (16:31, 20:29)

BEING OLD. We live in a culture that idolizes the beauty, energy, and creativity of youth. Proverbs, however, takes a remarkably balanced view of the unique *splendor* and *glory* of every age and stage of human life. The young have a *strength* and an unwearied ambition that older people cannot muster. The old have a perspective, wisdom, and dignity that younger people have yet to acquire. These are all distinct goods that should be enjoyed in their time.

This side of a final redemption, however, these glories all can't be combined at once. Only when Jesus glorifies us on the last day (Romans 8:18–21) will they all be united. J. R. R. Tolkien points to this great hope when he describes the death of Aragorn: "Then a great beauty was revealed in him, so that all who after came there looked on him with wonder; for they saw the grace of his youth, and the valor of his manhood, and the wisdom and majesty of his age were all blended together. And long there he lay, an image of the splendor of the Kings of Men in glory undimmed before the breaking of the world."[178]

How can you better enjoy the age stage of life you are in rather than fear it or wish for a different one?

Prayer: Lord, I praise you for the promise of the resurrection, that the long experience and wisdom of our older years will be combined with the creativity, grace, and stamina of our younger ones, together with a glory and beauty we have never known. Until then, help us wait in patient, joyful hope. Amen.

August 25

A heart at peace gives life to the body, but envy rots the bones. . . . A cheerful heart is good medicine, but a crushed spirit dries up the bones. (14:30, 17:22)

REAL MEDICINE. The sages understood the intricate relationship between mental and physical health. Depression (a crushed spirit) literally *rots* or dries up *the bones*, keeping in mind that the term "bone" can signify the whole person, body and soul (17:22).[179] Envy and the resentment it creates do the same thing, particularly affecting the cardiovascular system (14:30).

Wise health care, therefore, must treat human beings as integrated wholes—not merely as physical objects. A young Christian physician was visiting with a prominent doctor and saw that over half his diagnostic notes included comments such as "working too hard," "unhappy in marriage," and other nonphysical conditions. In other words, the physical problems were being aggravated or even caused by problems that were emotional and spiritual. Nevertheless, the older doctor insisted that a physician should ignore the nonphysical issues and just do "real medicine" and not try to counsel people. But the younger doctor argued, rightly, that there was no way to effectively treat sick people without addressing the whole of their lives.[180] Modern medicine, informed by biblical wisdom, should embrace this crucial insight.

Have you seen in your own life or someone else's how a physical illness was complicated by personal spiritual and emotional problems? How did help come?

Prayer: Lord, raise up doctors and medical workers who don't think of us just as flesh but as a complex whole of soul and body. And teach me wise stewardship of my body, your gift. Don't let me abuse it inadvertently by ignoring my emotional and spiritual well-being. Amen.

August 26

> Do not be wise in your own eyes; fear the LORD and shun evil. This will bring health to your body and nourishment to your bones. (3:7–8)

HEALTHY LIVING. We saw yesterday that our souls and bodies—our mental and physical health—are interwoven and must be treated together. How do we do that? The text tells us that if we *fear the Lord* (know God and enjoy fellowship with him) and *shun evil* (change your life to align with his will) it will lead to physical *health*. This cannot be seen as a guarantee that if we have faith, all will go well with us. The entire book of Job opposes "health and wealth" theology, namely, that if you live right, God will keep you healthy and prosperous.

It does, however, mean that "well-being and . . . happiness, when God grants them, are natural by-products of a quest for more ultimate goods."[181] That is, when we seek to know and serve God more than we seek physical and mental health, we are far more likely to receive them than if we seek well-being more than God. And the health and nourishment that come with a right relationship to God are "a state of complete physical and mental well-being, not simply to the absence of illness and disease."[182]

How could spiritual growth and godly, wise priorities contribute to your physical health?

Prayer: Father, first, I ask that I would grow stronger spiritually when I'm weak physically. Let my illness and discomfort be like smelling salts that show me my dependence and need for you more clearly. Second, I respectfully beg you for good health, that I can serve you with all my attention. Amen.

August 27

> Though their speech is charming, do not believe them, for seven abominations fill their hearts. Their malice may be concealed by deception, but their wickedness will be exposed in the assembly. (26:25–26)

WORK ON YOUR INSIDE. People increasingly market themselves. They craft an image through the clothes they wear, goods they consume, and pictures they post. It is the default mode of the human heart to hide what is ugly (Genesis 3:7–8). A person's speech may be *charming*—a word that means eloquent, compassionate, attractive—yet *seven abominations fill their hearts*, such as pride, envy, hate, lust, and greed.

We are shocked when upstanding citizens harbor racial hatred that breaks out in violence, or when respected Christians are found guilty of immorality and corruption. It is because they cultivated their image more than their inner being. One minister caught in adultery said that for years he had preached without praying. "A minister may fill his pews, his communion roll, the mouths of the public, but what that minister is on his knees in secret before God Almighty, *that he is and no more.*"[183] That is true of every person as well. Don't work on your image; work on your heart before God, or your true self will be *exposed in the assembly.*

What bad attitudes or habits that are largely hidden should you be giving to God and working on with his help?

Prayer: Father, give me the insight to see my besetting sins, the inordinate particular attitudes of my heart that lead to wrongdoing. Show me the things I love too little that I should adore, and the things that I adore too much that I should just receive with thanks. Amen.

August 28

My son, do not despise the LORD's discipline, and do not resent his rebuke, because the LORD disciplines those he loves, as a father the son he delights in. . . . The wages of the righteous is life, but the earnings of the wicked are sin and death. (3:11–12, 10:16)

THE TWO GREAT TESTS. 3:11–12 tells us that suffering can be *the Lord's discipline* to us, or it can be despised and nothing learned at all. 10:16 also tells us that prosperity (*earnings*) can lead to *sin and death* (August 29). Why? C. S. Lewis wrote: "If there are rats in a cellar you are most likely to see them if you go in very suddenly. But the suddenness does not create the rats: it only prevents them from hiding. In the same way the suddenness of the provocation does not make me an ill-tempered man: it only shows me what an ill-tempered man I am."[184]

We are blind to our weaknesses. Call them "rats." And there are two basic situations that flush them out, making them visible: prosperity and adversity. Both success and suffering will test you, bring out the worst in you, revealing the rats. They are equal spiritual crises. Will you accept what they show you and change, or deny and repress that knowledge? They will make you better or worse, but you will not stay the same.

How have you seen, in either your life or someone else's, that prosperity and things going well actually bring out the worst in us?

Prayer: Lord, both success and difficulty bring out things in my heart that are appalling. You saw them in there all along, yet you loved me. You saw me to the bottom but loved me into heaven. How great is your love! Amen.

August 29

My son, do not despise the LORD's discipline, and do not resent his rebuke, because the LORD disciplines those he loves, as a father the son he delights in. . . . The wages of the righteous is life, but the earnings of the wicked are sin and death. . . . If you falter in a time of trouble, how small is your strength! (3:11–12, 10:16, 24:10)

PROSPERITY AND ADVERSITY. Both success and suffering test us (August 28). The same financial success that leads to *life* for the wise leads to *death* for the *wicked* (10:16). One of the worst things God can do to people is to let them have what they want, to "give them up" to their desires (Romans 1:24,26). If proud people get success, if greedy people get wealthy, and if lustful people achieve physical beauty, it only confirms them in their illusions about their ability to achieve their own happiness, and that will lead to greater despair in the end when all these supposed paradises become dead ends. Only Jesus' living water will satisfy (John 4:13–14).

On the other hand, how easy it is to *falter in a time of trouble*. How can we pass both tests? By believing the gospel of Jesus. The gospel's message about our utter sinfulness keeps us from letting success go to our heads, but its message of God's unconditional love helps us get through any dark valley.

Looking back on your life, would you say that prosperity or adversity has been the greater spiritual trial and test for you?

Prayer: Lord, as I look at my own heart and the people I know, despite our fears of suffering, "adversity hath slain her thousands, but prosperity her ten thousands."[185] Good times are far more likely to make you unreal to us. Save us, spiritually, from prosperity. Amen.

August 30

Desire without knowledge is not good—how much more will hasty feet miss the way! (19:2)

YOUR MIND MATTERS. *Desire without knowledge is not good.* Zeal without careful analysis and knowledge *misses the way*, chooses the wrong path. Modern culture puts the greatest emphasis on passion and feeling. A great deal of modern Christianity is also anti-intellectual. We want feeling and we want results, but this produces a "simplistic activism that shows zeal without . . . insight into the complexities of life. We want answers and action before we have understood the questions."[186]

This is one reason that Christian churches are constantly being taken by surprise by cultural shifts—we don't understand how complex culture is. It is also a reason Christians often thoughtlessly just imitate the culture. We don't know how to analyze the world around us using biblical theology and doctrine. So anti-intellectualism results in the church being more conformed to the world and the spirit of the age. The wisdom literature of the Bible "insists that God's human servants develop their intellects and use them in every aspect of life so that . . . we may 'destroy arguments and every proud obstacle raised up against the knowledge of God and . . . take every thought captive to obey Christ'" (2 Corinthians 10:4–5 RSV).[187]

In what specific ways do you see anti-intellectualism harming the church? Do you hold the attitude yourself?

Prayer: Lord, my mind is as much part of me as the rest, and my whole self is yours. Give me both zeal and knowledge—not just one or the other. Amen.

August 31

The LORD tears down the house of the proud, but he sets the widow's boundary stones in place. (15:25)

BOUNDARIES. Widows were without social power. So it was possible to move their *boundary stones* and take part of their land. To steal a family's God-allotted land was to trample on their humanity. Today we don't live in an agrarian society, so for us "Proverbs 15:25 must be applied to the boundaries that concern bodies, emotions, jobs, reputations."[188] When we try to have sex with someone without giving them our whole lives in marriage, we violate a bodily boundary and use them rather than serve them. If you are manipulative or verbally abusive, you are not honoring emotional boundaries. When companies get rich selling products that are not good for people—physically, emotionally, and spiritually—they are exploiting people.

Rather, we should look to Jesus, who came not to be served but to serve (Mark 10:45), who not only brings down the rulers and lifts up the needy (Luke 1:52–53) but had all his boundaries—physical, emotional, and spiritual—violated when he took the punishment due for our sins.

In what ways in your own life do you see boundaries violated? What can you do about it?

Prayer: Father, when I see Jesus being so careful, respectful, and kind to all, I am convicted that my words, humor, and actions often fail to honor boundaries. Fill my mind with the truth that "my neighbor" is "the holiest object presented to my senses."[189] Amen.

September 1

There is no wisdom, no insight, no plan that can succeed against the LORD. The horse is made ready for the day of battle, but victory rests with the LORD. (21:30–31)

THE TECHNOLOGICAL SOCIETY. Horses were "high technology" that made foot soldiers almost obsolete. So this proverb "warns against overconfidence in power and technology."[190] Today there are many who believe technology will solve our problems. But while science and technology can tell you what can be done and how to do it in the most efficient way, they cannot tell you whether you should do it or not. They can't tell you if something is good or bad for human life because such things cannot be determined by technology, only by moral wisdom.

Without moral wisdom, cost-benefit analysis becomes ultimate, and economic profit and efficiency become ends in themselves. Sociologist Max Weber argued that technology creates an "iron cage" that traps individuals into depersonalized bureaucratic systems, based purely on efficiency and calculation. Technology, however, will never solve all human problems because we are more than matter. The wise know that our lives are in God's hands. And they remember that an untrained, ragtag group of men and women, believing in Jesus, turned the mightiest human civilization in history "upside down" (Acts 17:6) and that *victory rests with the Lord.*

Where have you seen mere technology and data applied to a human problem that really required moral wisdom?

Prayer: Lord, you are a personal God who created a world of persons in your image, and created a universe that isn't a machine but one animated by your loving hand—even the weather and seasons are ruled by you (Jeremiah 5:24). Yet our society is run increasingly on impersonal, bureaucratic techniques that treat people as numbers, not persons. Save us! Amen.

September 2

Pay attention and turn your ear to the sayings of the wise; apply your heart to what I teach, for it is pleasing when you keep them in your heart and have all of them ready on your lips. So that your trust may be in the LORD, I teach you today, even you. Have I not written thirty sayings for you, sayings of counsel and knowledge, teaching you to be honest and to speak the truth, so that you bring back truthful reports to those you serve? (22:17–21)

ENVOYS. These verses are admonitions to an envoy who will be sent out by those he served and who must be sure to pay attention and remember all he sees and hears so he can bring back truthful reports. What does this have to do with us?

Christians are virtual envoys—ambassadors (2 Corinthians 5:20)—to those whose knowledge of the truth depends on us.[191] We may approach Proverbs asking, "How can this enrich *my* life?" But you should never learn God's truth just for yourself. Others' knowledge of the truth depends on us. Do you understand God's words well enough that they can be quickly accessed (*ready on your lips*—22:18b) either for applying to yourself in a given situation or for passing along to someone else? Does Scripture come to your mind during the day, shedding light on decisions or strengthening you in the moment to trust God or do the right thing (verses 19–21a)? We must be like Jesus, who did not keep God's words to himself but spoke them to us at an infinite cost (John 12:49–50).

How might you be living differently if you took the calling of being Christ's ambassador with greater seriousness?

Prayer: Father, I praise you I'm not saved by my works but by Jesus'. Yet the quality of my life matters immensely, because I represent him. If I do not love, I make Jesus look ugly to the world (John 17:24). Don't let me embarrass my loving Savior. Conform me into his likeness. It is urgent. Amen.

September 3

The righteous detest the dishonest; the wicked detest the upright. (29:27)

INTOLERANCE. Two seemingly contradictory currents mark our society. There is a denunciation of all claims of absolute truth. Yet there is also a "fanaticism in which one position or group is absolutely right, nothing is ambiguous, and divergent views should be destroyed."[192]

The two are interdependent. Relativism actually feeds fanaticism. If there is no objective standard by which we can sift our inward intuitions, then whatever I feel most deeply about is absolutely right. 29:27 says both the righteous and the wicked are capable of intolerance. The righteous, of course, can be disdainful, condescending, and cruel—because of self-righteousness that comes from having the truth. The unrighteous, however, even if they claim to be amoral or freethinkers, can detest those who "think they have the truth." Ironically, *they* think they have the truth, namely, that there is no truth. What's the solution?

The gospel, that we are lost sinners saved by sheer grace, prevents both. It tells us we are sinners, so there is no relativism. But because we are saved by grace and not our efforts, the gospel is inherently humbling. We cannot feel superior to anyone. The gospel erodes both relativism and fanaticism.

Have you seen the marks of self-righteousness in yourself? What brings it out or tempts you to it? How should you deal with it?

Prayer: Lord, in our culture, intolerance is a great sin, but self-righteousness and sanctimony are encouraged. The gospel shows me it's neither. We cannot tolerate sin, but neither can we oppose it with an ounce of superiority. Raise up a whole generation of Christians of whom this is true. Amen.

Marriage[193]

September 4

> Wisdom will save you also from the adulterous woman, from the wayward woman with her seductive words, who has left the partner of her youth and ignored the covenant she made before God. (2:16–17)

COVENANT. Adultery is serious because it breaks *the covenant*. A marriage is a legal bond solemnized by vows. A wedding is not so much a claim of present love as a promise of future love. The vows keep you together despite the ups and downs and changes that would end a normal relationship. Without a covenant that keeps you together, you will be cut off from the peculiar riches of lifelong committed love that survives through thick and thin.[194]

There is a self-interested kind of relationship in which each party says, "I'll be with you as long as the relationship is fulfilling me." What matters then is *me* more than *us*. But a covenant relationship is one in which each party says, "I'll be there for you." Jesus, our true spouse, loved us not because we were lovely and fulfilling to him but in order to make us lovely (Ephesians 5:25–27). The wise person knows that fulfillment does not come from seeking it directly but is, paradoxically, a by-product of keeping promises and sacrificial service.

How does the nature of a vow-created covenant relationship privilege sacrificial service over self-fulfillment?

Prayer: Lord, you were not smitten with our beauty, and yet you made an eternal covenant with us. You came and died and made us your own and now you are patiently making us like yourself. Your covenantal love is my life! Teach me to practice covenantal love in my family and friendships. Amen.

September 5

> May your fountain be blessed, and may you rejoice in the wife of your youth. A loving doe, a graceful deer—may her breasts satisfy you always, may you ever be intoxicated with her love. (5:18–19)

LOVER. A spouse is someone bound to you by covenant, but what is the relationship that the covenant creates? First, a spouse is a lover. In ancient societies the purpose of marriage was to gain security and status for your family. You married the person who helped your family's status the most. That meant that the husband often looked elsewhere for sexual pleasure.

Yet the Bible says your spouse must also be your lover. The husband is to be *intoxicated with* his wife's love. This is not, however, the modern mistaking of sexual chemistry for real intimacy. Only when, because of your covenant bond, you learn to stick with each other through all things, to repent and forgive when wronging each other, does the richest, deepest intimacy grow. Then sex becomes the celebration of your life together. The physical union is a wonderful sign of the union of all the other aspects of your life. True sexual chemistry, then, grows from the whole relationship, rather than the relationship being based on sexual chemistry.

In what ways does the modern belief that you must have sexual chemistry before marrying distort both marriage seeking and marriage itself?

Prayer: Lord, the Scripture says sex is a gift, with wholesome powers unlocked only within the covenant of marriage. Yet intimacy with you is the only one love we truly must have. Let your people live into your Word so that our spouses are lovers and our single people are living in purity. Amen.

September 6

Listen, my son, to your father's instruction and do not forsake your mother's teaching. They are a garland to grace your head and a chain to adorn your neck. . . . For I too was a son to my father, still tender, and cherished by my mother. . . . My son, keep your father's command and do not forsake your mother's teaching. . . . A wise son brings joy to his father, but a foolish son brings grief to his mother. (1:8–9, 4:3, 6:20, 10:1)

INTELLECTUAL PARTNER. Here is another surprise. In ancient times women were generally not given an education. Yet in the very beginning of Proverbs we see both the father *and* the mother teaching their son in wisdom (1:8–9, cf. 10:1). The mother is an authoritative voice right alongside the father. And to be able to instruct someone in the terse and dense poetry of wisdom required education and training. These sayings assume a man's wife was educated and a true partner in learning and instruction.[195]

This does not mean that one spouse may not be much more educated than the other. It does expect, however, that as believers they would be true colleagues and students together in learning God's wisdom from the Word of God. They should be intellectually curious together, fellow travelers in learning biblical truth and brainstorming how to align all areas of their lives with its wisdom. And if the spouses become parents, they should be joint professors in their children's intellectual and moral formation.

If you are married, are you and your spouse real colleagues in learning? If you are not married but would be open to it, have you been as concerned about this as about sexual chemistry?

Prayer: Lord, let your people have marriages—and find marriages—in which spouses both know your Word, love it, and teach it to one another, their family, neighbors, and friends. Let our families be schools of the Bible, and Christian spouses one another's colleagues. Amen.

September 7

The wise woman builds her house, but with her own hands the foolish one tears hers down. . . . She watches over the affairs of her household and does not eat the bread of idleness. (14:1, 31:27)

MANAGING PARTNER. Proverbs assumes, as does the rest of the Bible, that the husband is head of the home (September 18 and Ephesians 5:22–26). This headship will take different forms in different marriages. But however one conceives it, it cannot be taken to mean that the husband alone makes all the "management decisions." *The wise woman builds her house,* and here the word house means not to merely construct a physical dwelling but to lay the foundations for a family's life—socially, economically, materially, emotionally, spiritually. One commentator writes this means that on her wisdom "chiefly depends the family's stability."[196]

What a husband and wife contribute to the affairs of the household will depend on each spouse's gifts and skills. The wife of Proverbs 31 is administrator, broker, philanthropist, and craftswoman (31:10ff.). That is not an absolute template for all wives *or* all husbands. But they both contribute what they have and can to create and manage a household together.

If you are married, are you and your spouse real managing partners in your household? If you are not married but would be open to it, will you make it clear to any prospective partners that this is your expectation?

Prayer: Lord Jesus, though as our true spouse you are our head (Ephesians 5:25), you treat us as friends, not servants, because you include us in your business (John 15:15). We will reign with you (2 Timothy 2:12). May the husbands in our churches be conformed to your image in how they treat their wives. Amen.

September 8

Wisdom will save you also from the adulterous woman, from the way-ward woman with her seductive words, who has left the partner of her youth and ignored the covenant she made before God. (2:16–17)

FRIEND. Though having many wives was common in the ancient Near East, Proverbs prescribes the union of one man and woman, and that union is too fully personal to fit with polygamy. The word for *partner* here (Hebrew *hallup*) means the closest of friends (16:28; 17:9). "This is a far cry from the not uncommon ancient idea of a wife as chattel and child bearer but not companion."[197]

In a culture in which women were seen mainly as possessions, to call men to have wives who were their exclusive lovers (September 5) and best friends disrupted the world's cultural categories. All the marks of friendship—constancy, sensitivity, speaking the truth in love to each other, counseling each other—must be present in marriage. This is the highest view of marriage possible. In an age when people did not marry for romantic joy or for intimate companionship, Proverbs called for both.

If you are married, is your spouse your best friend or nearly so? If you are not married but would be open to it, have you been as concerned about this as about sexual chemistry?

Prayer: Father, out of your divine friendship within the Trinity you created the world. You made us friends of Jesus and you changed us through spiritual friendship in the church. Let Christian marriages be known for this—that the spouses are not just lovers and partners but the greatest of friends. Amen.

September 9

A wife of noble character is her husband's crown, but a disgraceful wife is like decay in his bones. (12:4)

EDIFYING. To crown someone was to lift them up and honor them. It is the opposite of bringing decay in the bones, meaning an inner weakening and fragility as opposed to the inner confidence and resilience that come with a *crown*. A spouse should edify, build up the other. Indeed, your spouse has the power to make or break your dignity, confidence, and sense of self.

Your natural self-image is a compilation of verdicts that have been passed on you by various people over the years. But when you marry, your spouse has the ability to overturn all those verdicts. If the world says you are ugly but your spouse says you are beautiful, you will feel beautiful. Your spouse has the power to massively reprogram your self-image and to heal you of many of the deepest wounds of the past. And when your spouse is also a Christian, not just loving you but pointing you to your identity in Christ (Galatians 3:25–29), your spouse can truly be your *crown*.

If you are married, do you and your spouse build each other up or more often criticize? If you are not married, do you consider when looking at prospective partners the psychological power you will wield in each other's lives?

Prayer: Lord, your word of grace edifies us (Acts 20:32). We are to build each other up formally through the church's ministry and informally through friendships. Send your Spirit of edification so our marriages become preeminently places where people build each other up and not tear each other down. Amen.

September 10

Better to live on a corner of the roof than share a house with a quarrelsome wife. . . . Better to live in a desert than with a quarrelsome and nagging wife. (21:9,19)

NOT QUARRELSOME. Another job of a spouse can be put in the negative: to not be quarrelsome.[198] "*Quarrelsome*" is best conveyed by our word "nagging." To nag is not to do thoughtful criticism (September 11) but to do "drive-bys," making brief caustic or cynical remarks that complain and question motives and character. Two telltale signs of a nagging statement is that it begins, "You *always . . .*" or "You *never . . .*"

The images of living on a corner of the roof and of living in a desert evoke a situation in which we are exposed to the elements. A spouse is to be a crown who builds up (September 9), but nagging tears down. A marriage is supposed to be a haven of rest and shelter from the world, but the attack of nagging makes you feel you have no roof or walls around you, no real home, no shelter from life's storms.

Do you tend to nag people in your family or your friends? Do you know of someone who habitually nags rather than offering respectful criticism? How could you help them?

Prayer: Lord, because of my pride, impatience, and a lack of your lovingkindness in my heart, I often nag rather than lovingly correct. Let your people's marriages and all our churches be free from this sin of the tongue, and put a guard over my lips too. Amen.

September 11

A foolish child is a father's ruin, and a quarrelsome wife is like the constant dripping of a leaky roof. (19:13)

TRUTH TELLING. Water in single drops coming through *a leaky roof* was not only useless but harmful. Nagging is the slow, constant dripping of short, unhappy barbs and arrows, which can wear out the love of a relationship as dripping water can erode even stone.

But the water image also suggests how critique *should* work in a marriage. As friends (September 8), spouses must constructively challenge each other in love (27:5,17). Don't be dripping your criticism in painful little jabs that only evoke similarly brief angry responses in return. Instead, pour. Take time to sit down, to identify the problem behavior instead of attacking character, and to propose practical ways to change, mixing all with often-expressed love and encouragement. Your spouse can see your flaws and sins better than anyone else ever has. You need to hear about them to achieve the self-knowledge available no other way. Together you must learn to do truth telling that builds up, even as Jesus does to us (John 17:17; Ephesians 5:25–27).

If you are married, do you and your spouse mutually give permission to lovingly tell each other the truth about your flaws? If you are not married but would be open to it, have you practiced this truth telling profitably with friends?

Prayer: Lord, we veer between speaking truth unkindly or not at all. Both the harshness and the fearfulness are forms of selfishness. Cure us! Let your people's communities and marriages be places where, in love and wisdom, we exhort one another daily, lest we be hardened by the deceitfulness of sin (Hebrews 3:13). Amen.

September 12

A kindhearted woman gains honor, but ruthless men gain only wealth. (11:16)

GRACE. The Hebrew word that begins this proverb has been translated many ways—*kindhearted*, "charming," or "beautiful." But the word means, literally, gracious. Unlike the ruthless, this woman shows grace to people. Marriage should grow us and change us profoundly, if we speak the truth in love. But some people refuse to critique or confront—out of "love." Others speak "truth" but unlovingly. Truth without love isn't real truth and love without truth isn't real love—and unless they are used together, no real character change is possible.

A third ingredient is necessary. Just as grinding compound goes into a gem tumbler so the stones polish one another beautifully instead of breaking one another, so Christians must inject gospel grace into their marriage. Christians are called to forgive everyone, "just as in Christ God forgave you" (Ephesians 4:32). Marriage requires the ability to forgive freely without a shred of superiority, and to repent freely without begrudging.

If you are married, do you and your spouse show each other grace? Are you good at repenting and forgiving and moving on? If you are not married, are you practiced enough at giving grace within friendships to do it, were marriage a prospect?

Prayer: Lord Jesus, in your marriage with us, you show grace and forgiveness, always with a view to our becoming radiant, stainless, and holy (Ephesians 5:27). By your Spirit enable all believers to love one another in the same way, but especially let the marriages of your people excel in this transformative grace. Amen.

September 13

A wife of noble character who can find? She is worth far more than rubies. (31:10)

VALIANT. Spouses are to build each other up in love, critique each other with truth, and readily repent and forgive each other. Each of these takes great courage. It takes courage to tell the truth and face at least the short-term anger and hurt of your spouse. It also takes courage and fortitude to forgive.

Several times Proverbs speaks of wives *of noble character* (12:4, 31:10, 31:29), a word that means to be courageous or valiant, ordinarily used of warriors. Some say it is surprising for an ancient document to apply it to women. But both spouses must show courage just to do their jobs with each other. And perhaps it is fair to say that in a world in which men tend to put down women, it is important that women realize they have, with God's help, the same calling to be valiant as any man. Life—and family life—requires doing the right thing despite your fears.

If you are married, evaluate in which of the three tasks—edifying, truth telling, and forgiving—you are the weakest. Is the weakness due to a lack of courage? If you are not married, do you lack the courage to consider marriage? What can you do about that?

Prayer: Lord, "it requires more prowess and greatness of spirit to obey God faithfully than to command an army of men, to be a Christian than a captain."[199] And it requires valor both to tell the truth to and forgive your spouse in a marriage. In your people's marriages, give this spirit of courage to both husbands and wives. Amen.

September 14

Her husband has full confidence in her and lacks nothing of value. (31:11)

VULNERABLE. In Hebrew this reads literally, "Her husband entrusts his heart to her." Your spouse has the power to reprogram your self-image (September 9). That is because your spouse knows you so intimately. If someone else says, "You are a kind man," you may be complimented, but then, that person doesn't know you all that well. But if your wife tells you, "You are the kindest man I know," *that* affirms more deeply, because she sees your whole life. But, conversely, that means if your spouse says, "You are stupid," that wounds much more deeply. How do we use this great power to build each other up but survive the inevitable misuses of it?

The way to get the inner security and courage for such an intimate relationship is to remember that a Christian's ultimate confidence and self-worth come from having the Father's strong love because we are in Christ. Christ names us—not our spouse or anyone else (Galatians 3:26–29; Revelation 2:17).

If you are married, have you and your spouse wounded each other but been able to use gospel grace in order to get past it? If you are not married, is your identity rooted in Christ, or are you in danger of taking too much of your self-worth from being a spouse?

Prayer: Lord, you call your people to trust our hearts to one another—confessing sins to one another (James 5:16) and lovingly admonishing one another (Romans 15:4). Let our faith in you enable us to be vulnerable to each other, and let this spirit of mutual trust and openness grow in our marriages. Amen.

September 15

She selects wool and flax and works with eager hands. She is like the merchant ships, bringing her food from afar. She gets up while it is still night; she provides food for her family and portions for her female servants. She considers a field and buys it; out of her earnings she plants a vineyard. (31:13–16)

INDUSTRY. One thing 31:13–16 teaches about marriage is that it is, among many other things, an economic unit. Researchers have noted that married people, in general, do better economically than singles. They stimulate and cooperate in accruing wealth for the family. But this benefit of married life can be realized only by the hard work of both parties. Despite the likely differences in earning capacities, and whether one stays home to keep house, both spouses are ultimately breadwinners.

Some have complained that the woman of Proverbs 31 is idealized and have argued that such a woman doesn't exist. True, but neither does the truly loving person (1 Corinthians 13:4–8a) or godly person (Galatians 5:22–23a) exist. We should read all these texts in light of the gospel. We are not saved by performance, but those saved by grace in Christ love these texts as guides to pleasing and resembling the one who saved us. The gospel produces people who are eager to obey these patterns and not be crushed by them.

How do you see the biblical standards for life? Do they seem unreasonable? Crushing? Beautiful? Other?

Prayer: Father, I confess in my heart I do not rest entirely on the righteousness of Jesus. Because I still look to my performances to give me a sense of being presentable, I find the law burdensome. Give me rest in Christ so I can obey your law with eagerness and gratitude. Amen.

September 16

She brings him good, not harm, all the days of her life. . . . She sets about her work vigorously; her arms are strong for her tasks. She sees that her trading is profitable, and her lamp does not go out at night. (31:12,17–18)

STAMINA. This wife is indefatigable—*her lamp does not go out at night* (31:18). This describes physical stamina, but more than that is in view. Her loving service lasts *all the days of her life* (31:12).

When contemporary people write their own wedding vows, they may say things like, "I love you," "You are wonderful," and "I want to be with you." But traditional vows don't mention feelings at all. In marriage vows we do not merely express present love— we promise future love. We promise not to always feel loving but rather to *be* loving, faithful, tender, and compassionate no matter how we feel at the time. Marriage is a covenant; it requires lifelong endurance, strengthened by our vows. How else can we trust the other person enough to give ourselves wholly to them? But to get your strength, look not only to your spouse's vow but to your true spouse, who loved you to the very end, no matter what he faced (John 13:1).

If you are married, have you and your spouse *both* completely owned your wedding vows, to be faithful to the end? If you are not married, don't even think about marrying someone unless you are willing to make a promise like this.

Prayer: Lord Jesus, "you loved us to the end" (John 13:1). You kept your vow to the end of your life and now are committed to us until the end of time. Let us too be known as people who keep their word, who finish what they start. Especially reproduce this long-term love in our marriages. Amen.

September 17

She opens her arms to the poor and extends her hands to the needy.
(31:20)

MINISTRY PARTNERS. This wife is actively concerned with
the needs of *the poor*. Proverbs teaches that the wise and righteous are generous to and advocates for the poor (11:24, 28:27,
29:7,14), and so the husband should be no less committed to justice than his wife. But this text does not mean simply that a wife
and husband should be marked by social concern as individuals.
The implication is that the family has a ministry to the poor.

Jesus challenges us to open our homes to those in need (Luke
14:12–13). That could mean the elderly, the chronically sick, single parents, or new immigrants. John Newton wrote about these
verses, "I do not think it is unlawful to entertain our friends; but
if these words do not teach us that it is in some respects our duty
to give a *preference* to the poor, I am at a loss to understand
them."[200] A husband and wife should have a strategy for together
extending practical love, especially to their needy neighbors
(Luke 10:25–37).

If you are married, does your family have a ministry to those
in need? If you are not married, how are you obeying Jesus' call
to love your neighbor in need?

Prayer: Father, make our families and our churches ministry
centers of our streets, neighborhoods, and cities. Let us be like
your son, known as people who live not just to please ourselves
but our neighbors, and especially the weak (Romans 15:1–3).
Amen.

September 18

Her husband is respected at the city gate, where he takes his seat among the elders of the land. (31:23)

HONORING YOUR HUSBAND. *The city gate* was the public meeting area where cases were decided and so functioned as what we today would call "city hall." To *take his seat among the elders*, not just of the city but *of the land*, means he commands so much esteem that he has become one of the leaders of the country. This most "noble woman" has many accomplishments. Yet here we see that her achievements have led to her husband's ascension into a place of power and influence, and there is no indication of her resentment. The background here is what the rest of the Bible says about a wife's willingness to follow her husband's leadership (Ephesians 5:22–24).[201] In this she also assumes the Jesus role to which St. Paul points (Philippians 2:6). Though he was in every way equal with the Father, Jesus took the role of service, just as the Holy Spirit glorifies Jesus rather than himself (John 16:13–14).

To serve someone else's promotion and success does not compromise your dignity and greatness. Rather, it establishes it. Have you settled that last principle in your mind? Without it, a marriage can't thrive.

Prayer: Lord Jesus, in our culture people so often enter marriage expecting to fulfill and further themselves rather than to sacrifice in order to advance their spouse's honor and standing. But when you committed to us, you lost glory that we could gain it. Fill our churches with spouses who do the same for each other. Amen.

September 19

Her children arise and call her blessed; her husband also, and he praises her: "Many women do noble things, but you surpass them all." (31:28–29)

HONORING YOUR WIFE. The husband and children of this ideal, noble woman *call her blessed*, and this means far more than just a claim that she's a good person. The Hebrew term translated as "blessed" refers to the multidimensional flourishing or shalom that results when we live wisely (3:2,17)—physically, psychologically, socially, spiritually. This woman's children and husband are saying that they are all reaping the benefits of her godly life. The husband goes beyond this and praises her—the Hebrew word *hallah* used for praising the Lord ("hallelujah").

It is sometimes said that men are not as emotionally affirming and do not express affection and praise as well as women. That may be true in a given culture, or for men of a certain temperament, but it is never right. All Christians are called to praise and honor one another (Romans 12:8; 27:2 on May 22). How much more should husbands regularly praise their wives? Think of how our great husband, Jesus Christ, blesses us.

If you are married, do you and your spouse intentionally and thoughtfully bless each other? If you are not married, do you practice blessing others in the family of God's church?

Prayer: Lord, you call Christians to outdo one another in praising one another and deferring to one another. At a time when many fear marriage is stifling or oppressive—how much more should Christian husbands honor their wives? Lord Jesus, show husbands how to love their spouses as you love us. Amen.

September 20

She speaks with wisdom, and faithful instruction is on her tongue. (31:26)

SHEPHERDS. This wife and mother speaks with wisdom and gives *faithful instruction*—the Hebrew *torat chesedh*, teaching filled with lovingkindness. This fits the biblical idea of a pastor. We think of a "pastor" as an ordained minister in the church. But the word means to shepherd—to lovingly but directively care for people. The Bible calls all Christians to mutually shepherd one another. We are to bear the burdens (Galatians 6:2), admonish and counsel (Romans 15:14), exhort and correct (Hebrews 3:13), encourage and strengthen (1 Thessalonians 5:11), teach the Bible (Colossians 3:16), confess sins (James 5:16), forgive and reconcile with one another (Ephesians 4:32).

This one-another ministry is given to all believers, so how much more should a husband and wife shepherd not only each other but especially their children! In a sense every Christian family is a small church. This does not mean that the family can ever replace the church, but it does mean that worship and prayer, teaching and instruction, evangelism and mission should all occur at the family level.

Have you understood and embraced the responsibility to engage in one-another ministry? If you are married, have you and your spouse embraced it within the family?

Prayer: Lord, make our Christian families not merely loving places but also disciple-forming communities. Make parents priests and shepherds who lead each other and their children into "the stature of the fullness of Christ" (Ephesians 4:13). Amen.

September 21

When it snows, she has no fear for her household; for all of them are clothed in scarlet. She makes coverings for her bed; she is clothed in fine linen and purple. . . . She makes linen garments and sells them, and supplies the merchants with sashes. She is clothed with strength and dignity; she can laugh at the days to come. (31:21–22,24–25)

DOMESTICITY. Many criticize the "cult of domesticity," the emphasis on the creation of the perfect house and home. It is seen as a responsibility traditionally given exclusively to women in order to so absorb them that they have no energy for public life. Some women have deliberately lived in absolute domestic squalor as a protest against such social confinement.[202]

Proverbs 31 shatters these either-or categories. It depicts a wife who is deeply involved in public commerce, yet in a way that takes nothing from home life. Rather it enhances it. Kidner writes that this chapter "shows the <u>fullest</u> flowering of domesticity, which is revealed as no petty and restricted sphere, and its mistress as no cipher."[203] For a home to be a true haven, it must be as well ordered, visually appealing, and restorative a place as possible. It does not necessarily require affluence to create such a place, but it does take creativity, ingenuity, and constant work. Such women are the creators and maintainers of civilization.

Do you pay enough attention to your living space so that it is a restorative place to live or even visit?

Prayer: Lord Jesus, life here wears us down and exhausts us until you give us the final rest and rich suites of your Father's house (John 14:2). Teach us how to create homes that are places of order and refreshment that are foretastes of that, in which our families and friends can find haven. Amen.

September 22

He who finds a wife finds what is good and receives favor from the LORD. (18:22)

MARRIAGE SEEKING. In a time when many marriages were arranged by parents, Proverbs counseled us to go *find* a spouse. How should a Christian go about seeking a mate? First, look for a fellow believer (1 Corinthians 7:39; 2 Corinthians 6:14). If the fear of the Lord is the very foundation of a wise understanding of reality, how could you look for anything but another Christian? Second, look for a person of such spiritual character that it evokes your admiration and praise. The fruit of the Spirit in their lives (Galatians 5:22–23) should be a thing of beauty.

Third, get advice, not only about the prospective spouse but also about your own readiness for marriage. If you are listening only to your heart and not to advice, you have left the path of wisdom. Finally, remember Paul's teaching in 1 Corinthians 7, namely, that we do not need to be married to be a fully completed person. Only union with Christ can do that. So never marry out of desperation. You have the only spouse who can truly fulfill you (Ephesians 5:25–33).

Are you more in danger of overdesiring, or overfearing, or undervaluing marriage? If you are married, what is the main advice you'd give to marriage seekers?

Prayer: Lord, marriage is a great good, but not the ultimate good. Because our enjoyment of your love is so weak, we become too desperate and, therefore, also too fearful of marriage. Lord, there are many not finding marriage who should, and many you have called to singleness who are discouraged by it. Help them all. Amen.

September 23

Charm is deceptive, and beauty is fleeting; but a woman who fears the LORD is to be praised. (31:30)

ATTRACTION. Proverbs does not attach much value to physical *beauty*. Here, in fact, it is seen as *deceptive*, because it promises far more than it can deliver. Studies show that we tend to trust attractive people more than unattractive ones, assuming their insides match their outsides, which is not true in the slightest. And when thinking about marriage, we tend to simply screen out the less attractive without giving them serious consideration at all. This is profoundly unwise. Physical beauty is fleeting, and for the great majority of us, it won't be around for most of our marriages.

Instead we should seek a comprehensive attraction to someone we marry. Certainly there should be a physical attraction, but that should not be primary. Attraction to the beauty of someone's love, courage, servant heart, humility, joy, and peace should have pride of place. And we should also be drawn to what a person is becoming, what God is making them through his Spirit (Ephesians 5:25–27; Philippians 1:6). If this comprehensive attraction is more important than the physical, the attraction will deepen and increase as the years go by and your physical youth and beauty wane.

Have you embraced this countercultural approach to attraction? If not, you will have trouble as you and your marriage partner age, or, if you are not married, you may choose a partner poorly.

Prayer: Lord, we talk about not judging a book by its cover and yet when choosing a spouse we moderns are overwhelmed by looks and appearance. The results are many mistaken assessments, and so many overlooked people. Give us eyes to see people truly, and not just for marriage seeking! Amen.

Sex

September 24

> Drink water from your own cistern, running water from your own well. Should your springs overflow in the streets, your streams of water in the public squares? Let them be yours alone, never to be shared with strangers. May your fountain be blessed, and may you rejoice in the wife of your youth. A loving doe, a graceful deer—may her breasts satisfy you always, may you ever be intoxicated with her love. (5:15–19)

SEX AS BLESSING. This passage forbids adultery but also celebrates sex within marriage. There is barefaced rejoicing in sexual pleasure here, using vivid images. Female sexuality is likened to a *well* into which there is descent; male sexuality is called a *fountain*. The husband is to be attracted to his wife's *breasts*. To *drink water* is to quench sexual thirst through lovemaking. Verse 18 actually asks for divine blessing on sex. While the passage shows a reverence for sex, there is not a hint of prudishness. The New Testament agrees sex within marriage is crucial and not optional (1 Corinthians 7:2,5).

In that day it was expected that the husband would find supplemental sexual pleasure elsewhere, but the Bible allows no double standard. *Should your springs overflow in the streets?* Rather, the wife's sexuality belongs to her husband (*your own well*) even as the husband's to the wife (1 Corinthians 7:4–5)—an expression of equal sexual authority within marriage that, especially for its time, was striking. Within that bond, sex can truly flow and sing.

Are the people in the churches you know too prudish about sex? On the other hand, do they lack a reverence for sex, not seeing it as for marriage alone?

Prayer: Lord, your Word's teaching on both the sexuality's meaning and practice was a bombshell in the ancient world and is again today. It infuriates and confounds both the prudish and the licentious. Give your people the wisdom to see and love your wisdom about your creation, the gift of sex. Amen.

September 25

"There are three things that are too amazing for me, four that I do not understand: the way of an eagle in the sky, the way of a snake on a rock, the way of a ship on the high seas, and the way of a man with a young woman. This is the way of an adulterous woman: She eats and wipes her mouth and says, 'I've done nothing wrong.'" (30:18–20)

SEX AS CONSUMPTION. The first three pictures in this passage are of one penetrating into the realm of another. When *the way of a man with a young woman* is added, it is clear that these are poetic images likening sex to wondrous things like soaring (*eagle*) or sailing (*ship*). Then verse 20 is jarring. Sex is likened not to flying but to sloppy eating. This is sex as no big deal, nothing special, nothing to get all breathless about. It's just a minor high we enjoy a bit, just something people do.

Sex outside of marriage inevitably diminishes it to that level. A consumer transacts with a vendor as long as the produce is good enough in quality and price. Sex apart from marriage becomes a product we consume if we find someone attractive enough in quality and low enough in price. But if the quality goes down or the cost goes up, we can walk away, because there was no covenant. If sex comes only with the radical self-giving and whole-life commitment of marriage, that takes sex off the market, as it were, and makes it priceless. Sex on the market no longer soars. It only *wipes its mouth*.

Have you seen, in your life or others', this diminishment of sex?

Prayer: Lord, when your church was born, sex was nothing special, something done routinely with prostitutes, at parties, with domestics, and it was no big deal. Please protect your people from this same devaluation today. Don't let us be robbed of the joy and pricelessness of sex. Amen.

September 26

"There are three things that are too amazing for me, four that I do not understand: the way of an eagle in the sky, the way of a snake on a rock, the way of a ship on the high seas, and the way of a man with a young woman. This is the way of an adulterous woman: She eats and wipes her mouth and says, 'I've done nothing wrong.'" (30:18–20)

SEX AS APPETITE. 30:20 has a contemporary sound. Many see sex as nothing but appetite. Why feel more guilt about it than you would if you've had a good meal? "I've done nothing wrong." But it takes time to become so insouciant about sex. Our natural impulse is to find sex a very big deal and to become emotionally involved. Our hearts go along with our bodies. Only after you train yourself to take physical pleasure without the full personal commitment of marriage do the soul and body become detached. Then you can have sex without being too emotionally involved, and you just *wipe your mouth*.

Sex should instead be a way to both display and deepen full trust. It is a radical, unconditional, deeply personal means of self-donation. It is God's created way to say to someone else, "I belong wholly and exclusively to you." If you use it to say that and mean that, as time goes on it will enable spouses to indeed become more indissolubly one and each other's. If you don't use it like that, you've turned it into groceries. It will be routine, then boring. There will be no wonder left.

This view of sex and marriage is radically countercultural. Does it make sense to you? Why or why not?

Prayer: Lord, the stories our society bombards us with make sex either too transcendent or too common. Preserve your people, Lord, from these distortions of mind and heart so that both married and single Christians may understand sex in its true nature as covenantal love. Amen.

September 27

Like a gold ring in a pig's snout is a beautiful woman who shows no discretion. (11:22)

OVERVALUING SEX: PART 1. Our culture has found a way to both undervalue and overvalue sex at the same time. By treating sex as just an appetite or commodity that can be had without lifelong commitment, it undervalues sex. But it also overvalues it. This satirical proverb begins with the picture of a beautiful *gold ring*. It's so lovely you want to take hold of it. But if you don't notice that it is connected to a pig covered in mud and slop, suddenly you will have a mess in your lap. You reached for something beautiful and got a pile of filth.

You ask, "What fool would do that?" But the sage is saying if you enter into a relationship with someone who is physically and superficially attractive and polished but who is selfish, immature, and cruel, it is you who are the fool. Only an idiot would let the gold ring obscure the fact that this is a pig. Only a fool counts outer beauty as more important than inward character.[204] Many people missed the true beauty of Jesus because outwardly he was nothing to look at (Isaiah 53:2).

What bad effects have you seen, in your life or others', of an overvaluing of sexual attractiveness?

Prayer: Lord, you were infinitely lovely in your character but not in your body. Teach us how to discern true beauty and not be distracted by the superficial. Let this spiritual insight infuse not only our Christian marriages, but also the way we conduct all relationships. Amen.

September 28

Like a gold ring in a pig's snout is a beautiful woman who shows no discretion. (11:22)

OVERVALUING SEX: PART 2. Men especially tend to evaluate women on their looks, hence this verse's metaphor. Today we consider how this harms everyone. It damages relationships between the genders. Women see clearly how men react to beauty and it rightly lowers their respect for men. Also, it distorts women's self-images and lives. It is difficult for them not to overvalue thinness and shapeliness, high cheekbones and great skin. It's a huge temptation for women to say, "Why should I care about my character when everyone else—men and women—is evaluating me on my looks?"

Addiction to beauty fuels the pornography industry, which confirms men in their delusion that only young and beautiful women are sexually alluring. Pornography also gives men a way to get quick sexual pleasure without the messy, frightening work of building a real relationship with someone. Finally, many men fail to see wonderful prospective spouses—women who would be absolutely terrific partners—right under their noses. They are "screened out" for not being as good-looking as the pictures in porn. The idolatry of beauty is ruining us individually and as a society.

Can you think of any other ways that our culture's overvaluing of physical attractiveness is harmful?

Prayer: Lord, we are to pray against the evils of the age, that you protect not only your people but also all that you have made. I pray that the people who promote the pornography industry would be convicted of its malevolence. I pray that its effects would be curbed and people saved from its dehumanizing power. Amen.

September 29

> Listen to your father, who gave you life, and do not despise your mother when she is old. Buy the truth and do not sell it—wisdom, instruction and insight as well. The father of a righteous child has great joy; a man who fathers a wise son rejoices in him. (23:22–24)

TEACH YOUR CHILDREN WELL. Traditionally parents used strict discipline. The modern view is that parents should mainly be supportive and allow children to do self-discovery.[205] Proverbs teaches that the ultimate goal of parenting is neither mere control nor affirmation but to teach their children to become wise and righteous.

It is folly to expect a child to work out for him- or herself the moral wisdom of the ages. What makes a person capable of coming up with a standard of right and wrong is not that their parents taught them exactly right but that their parents *did* teach them. If their parents held a coherent account of good and evil and tried to impart it, even if later it is rejected in whole or part, at the very least the child will have developed a critical moral faculty. If instead the parents just let their child grow up as a detached, autonomous self, that's parental malpractice. We should do for our children what our heavenly Father did for us when he sent Jesus to us with his fatherly teaching (John 14:24).

How does this view of parenting undercut both traditional and modern views of parenting? What families have you seen do this well? What can you learn from them most?

Prayer: Lord, our societies are filled with many powerful influences so antithetical to the teachings of your Word. More than ever, parents need to be teachers of their children, but how can they compete with social media? We need your wisdom and the Spirit's work in our children's hearts. Amen.

September 30

My son, do not despise the LORD's discipline, and do not resent his rebuke, because the LORD disciplines those he loves, as a father the son he delights in. . . . May your father and mother rejoice; may she who gave you birth be joyful! My son, give me your heart and let your eyes delight in my ways. (3:11–12, 23:25–26)

MUTUAL DELIGHT. The main job of parents is to teach their children about right and wrong, good and evil. But this must be done in an environment of mutual *delight*. A teacher can have a good grasp of the material but still create a harsh atmosphere in which the students will not really want to learn, even if out of fear they try.

Proverbs directs parents to do discipline and punishment, but behind it all must be a love and delight in the children that is obvious to them. A family needs the constant, every-hour expression of love, joy, and wonder. You must "catch your child being good" and jump on every opportunity for praise. Avoid falling into a habitual, ongoing tone of mutual exasperation and complaint (Ephesians 6:4; Colossians 3:21). If you have a father and mother who are firm, have a coherent understanding of right and wrong, and delight in you, then even if you grow up and do not follow all their values, you've still been trained to be a competent adult. If parents don't show delight to the children they are training, they fail in their job.

What families have you seen do this well? What can you learn from them most?

Prayer: Lord, you said your prophets would turn the hearts of parents toward the children and the hearts of children to their parents (Malachi 4:6). Now, by your grace, put that spirit in our Christian families, and in all believers, that we might take delight in one another across the generations. Amen.

October 1

Discipline your children, for in that there is hope; do not be a willing party to their death. (19:18)

DISCIPLINE YOUR CHILDREN. The word *discipline* means to punish. While the primary goal of parents is to teach what is right (September 29) in an environment of love and delight (September 30), one of the main ways to do that is to establish both boundaries and consistent consequences for trespassing those boundaries for your children. Why?

There is a design in the world, and to go against it brings natural consequences. If parents do not bring carefully controlled, unpleasant consequences into the children's lives, they will go out into the world and bring far more painful and harmful results onto themselves later. Inflicting minor sadness now avoids great despair later. If you do that when they are young there is hope that the child will internalize your training and learn self-control. If you don't, you are a willing party to their death. Strong words, but fair. God's parenting is perfect, and he disciplines us for our good. He knows we hate the consequences he brings into our lives now, but later they will bear enormous fruit (Hebrews 12:9–11).

What families have you seen do this well? What can you learn from them most?

Prayer: Lord, the world that you made punishes foolishness and sin with the most deadly natural consequences. Help your people, then, to exercise discipline in our homes and discipline in our churches—in order to encourage self-discipline in our lives and hearts, that we may live at peace in this world. Amen.

October 2

A rod and a reprimand impart wisdom, but a child left undisciplined disgraces its mother. (29:15)

THE ROD. Proverbs' call to use the *rod* concerns today's readers. Child abuse is indeed a great evil, and the modern debate over corporal punishment is a good one but too complicated to present here. What we can learn from Proverbs includes these things. First, because the rod was literally used to punish criminals in ancient society, it came to be a symbol of authority and of discipline in general. So when Proverbs tells parents to use the rod, it does include the possibility of corporal punishment, but it means much more.[206] Second, Proverbs never sees the rod as a magic bullet. No one should look to discipline as the essence of child rearing, or to overrely on corporal punishment as the essence of discipline. 29:15 says that along with consequences must come the verbal, reasoned reprimand.

The entirety of the book of Proverbs implicitly condemns the harsh disciplinarian by its entire tone, that is, "by its own reasonable approach, its affectionate earnestness," and by the warmth and love that come out in the parents' addresses.[207] Bruce Waltke writes that "parents who brutalize their children cannot hide behind the rod-doctrine of *Proverbs.*"[208]

What do you think of the wisdom of corporal punishment for children? How can it be overrelied on?

Prayer: Lord, you save us by your grace, yet you love us too much to let us acquiesce in sin, and so you discipline us (Hebrews 12:4–11). You are never, ever, too lax or too harsh, combining affectionate care with firm discipline. Let our churches and families do the same. Amen.

October 3

Whoever spares the rod hates their children, but the one who loves their children is careful to discipline them. (13:24)

DON'T BE BLACKMAILED. While parenting requires far more than *discipline*, it never requires less. Boundaries must be absolutely clear and consequences absolutely consistent, imposed with gravity but not with exasperation and withering remarks. That way the child can grow to see that the real conflict is not a battle of wills with the parents but a fight for self-control, without which the world and life itself will punish them forever. Yet discipline is hard *not* just on the children but also on the parents. When punished, your children will instinctively cry out in self-pity and anguish, "You don't love me!" But Proverbs warns that *not* to discipline is to *hate* them and *to* discipline is to *love* them. So don't let children emotionally blackmail you. If you crumple and refrain from discipline, you are loving only yourself, not them.

Child discipline also demands parental discipline. It is easy to punish in anger rather than in love. Rather than sitting on the couch, shouting unfulfilled threats with increasing irritability, parents must respond instantly to any disobedience while they are still calm, and see that consequences are imposed.

What families have you seen do this well? What can you learn from them most?

Prayer: Lord, it's costly to love imperfect people. You could not call us to repentance and save us without suffering. And we cannot discipline our children (or admonish our friends) without paying a cost as well. But as we look first to you, and then to those we love, make us able to pay the price. Amen.

October 4

Folly is bound up in the heart of a child, but the rod of discipline will drive it far away. (22:15)

REALISM. Many assume that children are naturally innocent and pure, and that only society teaches us to hate. But this verse says *folly* is natural to us. Foolishness is to be destructively out of touch with the reality of God's created order. Children are naturally self-centered, they don't understand how other people feel, and they don't know how their behavior will affect others—all of these basic things must be taught.

We must learn this lesson again and again. Arthur M. Schlesinger, who grew up in the early twentieth century, wrote, "We had been brought up to believe in human innocence and . . . the perfectibility of man. But nothing in our system prepared us for Hitler and Stalin, for the death camps and gulags."[209] It is just as disastrous if parents do not know the potential for folly and evil that every child's heart contains. We have said that the rod of discipline is not necessarily corporal punishment, but it *is* punishment—real consequences with teeth in them. If sin and folly are deep in every child's heart, it will take more than words to root them out.

This view of human nature and child rearing is radically countercultural. Does it make sense to you? Why or why not?

Prayer: Lord, our children are infinitely precious image bearers and hereditary sinners. In our churches help us to raise our children with both truths about them solidly in view, with love and firmness, with truth and tears. Amen.

October 5

> For I too was a son to my father, still tender, and cherished by my mother. Then he taught me, and he said to me, "Take hold of my words with all your heart; keep my commands, and you will live. . . . The righteous lead blameless lives; blessed are their children after them. (4:3–4, 20:7)

DO AS I DO. How can we pass our wisdom on to our children so they make it their own? There are three factors here. The first is *words* (4:3). We must open our mouths and instruct. The second is a parent's *blameless life* (20:7)—a word that means not perfect but consistent. Children are highly sensitive to perceived hypocrisy, which will undermine all efforts to pass on your wisdom. Are your actions consistent with your professed beliefs? Do you repent and apologize to others, including your child, when you have wronged them?

The third and most important, you must *cherish* your children (4:3). The verse literally says, "I was the only one in the sight of my mother." A child should feel they are the object of powerful, unconditional love from the parent. One researcher interviewed youth who had continued in their parents' Christian faith as adults. The key factor was not church attendance or family devotions or strictness of discipline. The main thing they said was that they felt they could talk to their parents about anything and they would still love them.[210]

What families have you seen pass on their faith and values well to their children? What can you learn from them?

Prayer: Lord Jesus, you awakened love for your name in us through the wisdom of your words, the beauty of your life, and the unconditional nature of your love. Oh, teach us how to do the same! Let us as parents, aunts and uncles, friends and neighbors, draw our children to you, we pray. Amen.

October 6

Start children off on the way they should go, and even when they are old they will not turn from it. (22:6)

OUTCOMES. Some think that to set children *on the way they should go* means we must respect their individuality and help each find their own way. Other interpreters think "the way they should go" simply means the right path for all people. But it may be that the ambiguity is deliberate, because one of the great mysteries is why some children when they are old embrace their parental training and others do not. Whose fault is it if a child's life goes "off the rails"? Sometimes a foolish adult is the result of parental failure (29:15). But some children simply don't respond to the rightful reproof parents give them (13:1, 17:21). Their choice—to listen or not—determines the course of their life (1:10–18).

So according to Proverbs, there are three factors that determine the way a child grows up—the hearts they are born with ("nature"), the quality of the parenting they receive ("nurture"), and their own choices. The three interact in complex ways that no one can control, except God himself (cf. 21:1). A parent's final but most powerful resource, then, is prayer to the God who opens hearts.

What families have you seen *not* pass on their faith and values to their children, though apparently they did things right? What can you learn from them?

Prayer: Lord, we can feel either too responsible for our children's choices—or too little. We know you put us as parents and adults in their lives to point them to you, but their hearts are in your hands, not ours. Give us more consistent, godly lives for their sake, and help us to entrust our children to you. Amen.

October 7

A wise son brings joy to his father, but a foolish man despises his mother. . . . "There are those who curse their fathers and do not bless their mothers. . . . The eye that mocks a father, that scorns an aged mother will be pecked out by the ravens of the valley, will be eaten by the vultures." (15:20, 30:11,17)

HONOR YOUR FATHER AND MOTHER. How should children relate to their parents? "Honor your father and your mother" (Exodus 20:12). It does not say "love" or "admire" your parents, because some of us have foolish or even evil parents. And it doesn't say "obey" your parents, because at a certain point you should grow up and no longer be under their tutelage (Matthew 19:5; cf. Galatians 3:23–25).

There is only one thing you should do for all kinds of parents, no matter what they are like and how old you are—honor and respect them. Don't *despise*, *curse*, or *mock* them, but *bless* them. This is what your conscience and heart need and what society needs. Find ways to show them respect at holidays, at gatherings, with phone calls, and even with social media. Give credit where it is due: "I learned that from you." Let them change if they are trying—don't stereotype them. And forgive them for things they may have done wrong. This honors the sacrifices they may have made for you that you know nothing of, and it models for the younger generations how they should treat you when you are older.

Looking back at the last paragraph, have you honored your parents in these ways? Is there any way you could improve?

Prayer: Father, many have mixed feelings about their parents. But help us look over their shoulders to you, our true Father, who gives us the love we need, and has given us our parents to serve us in so many ways. In the light of these truths, show us how to honor them. Amen.

October 8

A wise son brings joy to his father, but a foolish son brings grief to his mother. (10:1)

THE SOCIAL DIMENSIONS OF SIN. Your sins always have a social effect. A man may consume pornography privately. But not only does it influence the way he relates to women in society, it also creates a market for it, making it available to others. A woman may insist that she has a right to commit suicide because she belongs to no one but herself. Yet even at the human level, that is wrong. What right does she have to darken or even ruin the lives of those who love her and who will be devastated by her suicide?

The fact is that we are unavoidably interdependent. We became what we are not simply through our choices but through how we were loved and treated by others, for better and worse. We owe others much, and they us. And so your sins and follies are doubly guilty because they always *bring grief* to others. So here is the reality that 10:1 gives us. "Without the ties by which people are members of one another, life would be less painful but immeasurably poorer."[211] If we pull away, there is less *grief* but less *joy*.

Have you seen the social effects of your sins? What are they?

Prayer: Lord, no one is an island, and what I do in private affects how I live with others around me. My sins are first and foremost against you (Psalm 51:4), but second, and seriously, they are against my fellow human beings. Impress this on me, as one of the many ways you keep me from sin. Amen.

October 9

A prudent servant will rule over a disgraceful son and will share the inheritance as one of the family. (17:2)

THE LIMITS OF FAMILY. Traditional societies are far more family oriented than modern ones, but they can make an idol of it. Often in those settings unqualified but blood-related people are chosen for leadership. Proverbs, for all its high regard for the importance of family, still puts individual worth ahead of pedigree.

"It's not what you know but who you know," goes the cynical modern saying, but that is not the guidance of the book of Proverbs. In this text, the wise head of an estate will recognize that one of his employees is much better at running his enterprise than his son, and so will elevate the servant and even make him an heir (*will share the inheritance*). So character and ability outweigh blood and family ties. This principle works itself out in the New Testament, where we see it is never race and social standing but faith in Jesus Christ alone that brings you an inheritance in God's family (Matthew 8:11–12; 1 Corinthians 1:27–31; Galatians 3:26–29). Privilege and insider status mean much to the world but nothing to God.

Where have you seen things go wrong when pedigree was put before worth and merit?

Prayer: Lord, centuries before the famous words that the "content of our character" is more crucial than racial and family ties, your Word said the same.[212] Do not let us be blinded by family loyalty and love to the flaws and shortcomings of our kin. Amen.

October 10

Children's children are a crown to the aged, and parents are the pride of their children. (17:6)

GRANDCHILDREN. A *crown* speaks to the unique joy of grandchildren. In the harried, day-to-day maelstrom of raising one's own children, it is hard to stand back and take in the wonder of a new life growing up out of your parental and spousal love. But the faces of your grandchildren evoke memories of your children, spouse, parents, and own childhood in a way that nothing else does. Grandchildren open a room in your heart that could not be unlocked by anyone else.

Nevertheless, Bruce Waltke reminds us that while in the Old Testament childlessness was a curse, it is never spoken of that way after Christ. "By contrast . . . Jesus Christ, who had no biological children, blessed the Church to reproduce spiritually, not physically (see Matthew 28:18f; Luke 24:50f; John 20:22)."[213] In *The Great Divorce* the childless Sarah Smith of Golders Green is surrounded in heaven by countless men and women who she spiritually mothered.[214] One's spiritual family includes all who trust in Christ (Mark 3:31–34). And you can have far more spiritual children and grandchildren (1 Corinthians 4:14–15) than you ever could physical ones.

Do you know Sarah Smith–type believers, with far more spiritual children than physical?

Prayer: Lord, those of us who have lived to see children and grandchildren praise you for the peculiar joy of seeing new generations. But remind and teach us that yours is the true family, and helping people grow in faith creates children who will live with us in fellowship with you forever. Amen.

October 11

A friend loves at all times, and a brother is born for a time of adversity. (17:17)

WHEN FAMILY COMES THROUGH. The Bible keeps us from making an idol out of the family, even as it lifts up its importance. There are friends who are better than siblings (18:24) and colleagues who are as well (17:2). Our truest brothers and sisters, sons and daughters, are other believers in Christ (John 1:12–13; 1 Timothy 5:1–2). So family relationships should not always take precedence.

And yet family ties can be uniquely deep and they often shine brightest in times of trouble. Unlike a friend who is around at all times, there are members of your family who may not want to hang out with you socially—and you may not find them to be people you would choose as friends. But when the chips are down, in a time of *adversity*, family members will often stand with you even to the point of great sacrifice. Like Jesus himself, they will walk through fiery furnaces with you (Daniel 3:25).

When have you seen, in your life or someone else's, an example of the truth of this proverb?

Prayer: Father, we thank you for our families and friends who walked with us through the dark valleys. But most of all we thank you for Jesus, the one who truly "sticketh closer than a brother" (18:24) for he alone can walk with us through death's door into the light he has won for us. Amen.

October 12

To have a fool for a child brings grief; there is no joy for the parent of a godless fool. (17:21)

YOUR UNHAPPIEST CHILD. This text homes in on just one of the more diabolical effects of sin. In judo the key is to use your opponent's strength and momentum against him. In the family, evil uses one of the features of love against you. *There is no joy for the parent of a godless fool.* When you love someone, you essentially put your happiness into the happiness of the one you love. That is, you make the other person's joy and peace a part of your own. You cannot be fully happy unless the loved one is happy as well.

Once a child is born to you, your heart will be naturally bound to him or her. This means, first, that you cannot rest contently if any of your children is in difficulty. It also means that, for the rest of your life, you can be only as happy as your unhappiest child. Children should be aware of the power they have to bless or curse their parents, just by the way they live. Parents should let the pain they may feel for their child become a spur to extraordinary prayer, not worry (Philippians 4:6).

Where, in your own life or the lives of others, have you seen children's power to bless or curse parents? How are you using that power?

Prayer: Lord, our family ties are—by their very intimate nature—often painful. But teach us how to use these bonds for spiritual growth and ministry. Let anxious parents be motivated to powerful prayer for children; let thoughtless children realize their power to bless parents with encouragement and love. Amen.

October 13

If someone curses their father or mother, their lamp will be snuffed out in pitch darkness. . . . Like a bird that flees its nest is anyone who flees from home. (20:20, 27:8)

RECONCILIATION. 20:20 speaks of those who are angry at and bitter toward their parents. The consequences of an unreconciled relationship with one's family are serious. *Their lamp will be snuffed* out means, at least, that their happiness will be extinguished. 27:8 does not mean that there may not be a good reason for leaving one's home, only that there is no real replacement for home and family. To be alienated from family is a deep sadness.

But what if your parents *have* truly wronged you—how can you get the freedom to not resent them? It comes only by grasping the ultimate parental love of the Father through Jesus (John 1:12–13). If parental care and approval are the main source of self-worth and security, then you will be overdependent on your parents if they are relatively good parents, and unbearably angry with them if they are not. If, however, through Jesus Christ, your true brother, you have come into the ultimate family and received the ultimate fatherly approval, you will have the freedom to not need your parents so much, and to forgive them. In Jesus you are always home.

Have you tended to be either too resentful of or too dependent on your parents? What effects of that have you seen in your life?

Prayer: Father, many are bound and shaped by bitterness toward family members. Perhaps no resentment can distort our lives and relationships more. Show us your grace—which both chastens us and lifts us up—so we have enough humility and joy to forgive even the most grievous sins by our family. Amen.

October 14

A man who loves wisdom brings joy to his father, but a companion of prostitutes squanders his wealth. (29:3)

THE PRODIGAL SON. Proverbs gives us small hope that young people, having gone down the path to foolishness, can come back. Yet this verse is almost a miniature version of Jesus' parable of the Prodigal Son (Luke 15:11–33). The younger son in Jesus' story was a fool. Rejecting wisdom and bringing sorrow to his father, he "squandered [his] property" on "prostitutes" (Luke 15:30). But in Jesus' parable the two antithetical clauses become one—the *companion of prostitutes* becomes the son who brings joy to this father (Luke 15:22–24).

How is such a turnaround possible? The answer is in Jesus himself. Jesus, like the prodigal son, was a companion of sinners and declared that prostitutes could enter the kingdom of heaven (Matthew 21:32). He became weak and despised, he stood in our place and took the punishment and the rod that fools deserve (26:3), so that he could forgive and draw the worst sinners and fools to himself. No wonder the cross is true wisdom but looks like foolishness to the world (1 Corinthians 1:18–25).

Have you seen this turnaround? What brought it about?

Prayer: Lord, we know of prodigal sons or daughters, either our own or a friend's, whose foolish paths are breaking hearts. Give us a resolve to pray extraordinarily for them. Then use our prayers in our lives and theirs. Get glory for yourself and joy for us by bringing them home—not just into our families but into yours. Amen.

October 15

I love those who love me, and those who seek me find me. With me are riches and honor, enduring wealth and prosperity. My fruit is better than fine gold; what I yield surpasses choice silver. . . . The blessing of the LORD brings wealth, without painful toil for it. (8:17–19, 10:22)

WEALTH IS A GOOD. Proverbs is full of references to economic life. Although, as we will see, the dangers of wealth are great, nonetheless wealth is a great good. Wisdom's self-control and self-knowledge, its ability to plan and to take advice, all tend to bring about greater prosperity. *With me are riches.*

But 10:22 introduces the crucial factor of priorities. *Painful toil* connotes the life-crushing sorrow of overwork, of the craving for power and wealth that comes from selfish wickedness (10:3). God condemns self-wounding labor (20:21). The wise person does not do painful overwork but simply works hard and lets the blessing of the Lord determine how wealthy the work makes them. The fear of the Lord, the intimate relationship the wise have with God, is *better than fine gold.* Wealth is a great good as long as it does not become your *summum bonum*—your greatest good.

Where in your life or someone else's life have you seen what happens when we rely more on painful toil than on the blessing of the Lord for our money?

Prayer: Lord, may I be neither envious nor disdainful, neither too overawed nor intimidated, by wealth. You blessed Abraham, Job, and David with great wealth but only as they put it second to faithfulness to you. Make me like them. Amen.

October 16

The wealth of the rich is their fortified city, but poverty is the ruin of the poor. (10:15)

PRIZE BUT DON'T TRUST. Half of the times the Hebrew word for *wealth* is used in Proverbs, we are told to prize it. Strikingly, the other half of the times the word is used, we are told not to trust it (12:27, 13:7, 19:14, 29:3, cf. 19:4).[215] That remarkable, nuanced balance expresses the essence of wisdom's approach to money. The great problem is that money can lead the wealthy to see it as their security, *their fortified city*, rather than looking to the Lord.

But there is no reason to romanticize poverty, for it is a kind of slavery (22:7). Abraham was fabulously wealthy by the blessing of God (Genesis 20:14–16), as were Joseph, Job, and David. Accumulated wealth or large incomes are not evil in themselves. Yet of those to whom much has been given, much will be required. The rich are stewards of their wealth, not owners of it. And Jesus vividly supplements this proverb in his interview with the Rich Young Ruler (Mark 10:17–31). There he shows us how easily great wealth can be our ruin as well.

Where have you seen the lack of money having ruinous effects on someone? Where have you seen the abundance of money having ruinous effects?

Prayer: Father, it is easy to be a Rich Young Ruler who trusts his money too much to lose it in sacrificial giving. But your Son was the true Rich Young Ruler, for his wealth was infinite, his sacrifice unimaginable, and all for us. Make us like him in our stance toward our money. Amen.

October 17

Diligent hands will rule, but laziness ends in forced labor. . . . All hard work brings a profit, but mere talk leads only to poverty. . . . The appetite of laborers works for them; their hunger drives them on. (12:24, 14:23, 16:26)

HARD WORK. What are the factors that, in general, bring greater prosperity? The first is simple *diligence* and *hard work*. At one level, hard work is inspired by simple *hunger*, the need for the basics of physical survival (16:26). It is a perfectly legitimate reason we should get and hold a job—to eat—whether it is fulfilling or not (2 Thessalonians 3:10). If you don't take the initiative to find work you choose to do, you will in the end find yourself doing work you are forced to do (12:24).

But the deeper background behind work in Proverbs is the book of Genesis, where we see God with his hands in the dust (Genesis 2:7,19), creating a paradise for human beings in which work itself is one of the good things (Genesis 2:15). God is happy in his work, and we are made in his image. No wonder there is nothing more humanizing than good work, and no wonder God rewards it.

Where in your life or someone else's have you seen that unless we seek out work we want to do, we will be forced to do work we do not want to do?

Prayer: Lord, I love, dread, and can't live without work. It is an irreplaceable part of my humanity and yet something that now wears us down (Genesis 3:17–19). Lord, it is not work for pay, but only work for you—for your eye and your honor—that will enable me to work well. Amen.

October 18

Those who work their land will have abundant food, but those who chase fantasies have no sense. . . . Those who work their land will have abundant food, but those who chase fantasies will have their fill of poverty. (12:11, 28:19)

INTEGRITY IN WORK. A second factor that can bring prosperity is work that is not just diligent but done with integrity. These texts warn about *chasing fantasies* but don't say what they are. However, many examples are clustered in Proverbs around 28:19. Some ways to make money involve bribery (28:21). Others seek to make a profit mainly through sheer "stinginess," an unwillingness to pay well or spend and invest at appropriate times (28:22). Other people use deceptive business practices (28:23) or exploit vulnerable populations (28:24) or evoke hostile opposition by being too ruthless (28:25). All these approaches are being pursued with real labor, yet they will lead to poverty.

In modern books on business ethics, these practices are condemned as being "bad business." They are, as Proverbs attests. But anyone who complies with ethical guidelines only out of self-interest will almost certainly fail morally. If the only motivation for honesty is fear, it is inevitable that you will be dishonest in those situations where there is no fear or possibility of detection. Christians know that, despite no fear of final condemnation (Romans 8:1), all things lie open to the eyes of "Him to whom we have to give an account" (Hebrews 4:13).

Where have you seen these kinds of "fantasy" business practices? Have you used any of them?

Prayer: Father, root out the motives of fear, pride, and self-pity that can make me dishonest. And make me as unlikely to believe lies as to tell them. Make me like your Son my Savior, who told and held to the truth to his own hurt. Amen.

October 19

Like an archer who wounds at random is one who hires a fool or any passer-by. . . . Be sure you know the condition of your flocks, give careful attention to your herds; for riches do not endure forever, and a crown is not secure for all generations. (26:10, 27:23–24)

HARD-NOSED REALISM. Wealth can come about through hard work, integrity, and hard-nosed realism. Forms of unrealistic work are described in 27:23–24, where we see owners who are out of touch with the condition of their sources of income (*the condition of your flocks*), perhaps because they delegated too much, or because they did not do sufficient research before making investments in new herds.

Verse 24 goes on to warn against smugness, the belief that without staying in touch with changing realities, their wealth will simply endure. 26:10 is an interesting study in hiring practices. We all know that to hire a fool will be disastrous. It is like an archer who wounds at random because the devastation will be impossible to predict. But it is just as destructive to hire any passer-by, that is, to employ someone without performing due diligence. Don't just call a person's references; call her references' references' references to get an accurate picture of whom you are hiring. How striking is wisdom's combination of assurance that only God is the ultimate source of abundance, along with the strong call for steely-eyed realism.

Where have you seen this kind of steely-eyed realism practiced and rewarded?

Prayer: Lord, you call me to careful, painstaking due diligence in all things, and then you assure me it is all under your sovereignty and according to your plan. Strengthen awareness in my mind and my heart for both the solemn charge and the wonderful assurance. I cannot work well without both! Amen.

October 20

Do you see someone skilled in their work? They will serve before kings; they will not serve before officials of low rank. . . . Do not wear yourself out to get rich; do not trust your own cleverness. Cast but a glance at riches, and they are gone, for they will surely sprout wings and fly off to the sky like an eagle. (22:29, 23:4–5)

SKILLFULNESS. Another factor that promotes economic prosperity is being *skilled in [your] work.* The word *skilled* here means experienced. This is not necessarily calling for everyone to be what today we would call a "professional" or "white-collar worker." Rather, it is a call for excellence of workmanship. House-keepers, for example, through years of experience can come to do excellent work and be in such demand that kings and queens will indeed fight to employ them (22:29). The Son of God himself lived in the world as what we would call a "blue-collar worker" (Matthew 13:55; Mark 6:3).

Only a few verses after this paean to the craftsman is a warning to not trust your own *cleverness*—your own insights and skillfulness (23:4). What is the lesson? God wants you to value workmanship over success. He wants you to take enormous pride in work well done and give far less thought to how much money the work makes. This follows St. Paul's admonition to do work excellently, looking to please God and not for the applause or reward of human beings. We are to "serve wholeheartedly, as if you were serving the Lord, not people" (Ephesians 6:7).

Where in your life are you doing some task or work that is unrewarded or unrewarding? How can you use the wisdom of these verses to help you?

Prayer: Lord, give me the wisdom to seek skillfulness, but not be taken with my own cleverness. Give me the discernment to perceive excellence, but not be enamored of pedigree and credentials. And with this wisdom, make me a better worker, to your glory and to the good of my neighbor. Amen.

October 21

Dishonest money dwindles away, but whoever gathers money little by little makes it grow. . . . The wise store up choice food and olive oil, but fools gulp theirs down. (13:11, 21:20)

THE DANGERS OF WINDFALLS. The word *dishonest* translates a Hebrew phrase that means literally "money out of the air," meaning wealth that comes suddenly rather than gradually. The warning is this: If you don't grow wealth over years through diligence, vigilance, and skillfulness, you may not have grown the character and habits necessary to manage the money well.

Children who inherit money without earning it often *gulp it down*, running right through it because they have not learned habits of self-control, wise management, and the virtue of delayed gratification (21:20). Young celebrity athletes or entertainers—and unusually gifted (and lucky) young people who have made fortunes in finance or technology—run the same risk. This proverb suggests that wealth be gathered slowly so that the character that greater assets require grows along with your wealth. If riches come quickly, assume that the money will make you lose your sense of proportion without help from many advisers (15:22) and from Jesus himself, who warned that wealth so distorts spiritual perspective that it requires God's divine intervention to free us (Mark 10:24–26). Yet there's much hope. "All things are possible with God" (Mark 10:27).

Have you seen the danger of windfalls play out in your life or someone else's?

Prayer: Lord, save me—and those I know and love—from prosperity, and especially sudden success or fame. What our society covets, your Word warns against. Let those among your people, who come by your Providence into more riches and power than the rest, receive a due sense of their heightened responsibility as servants before you. Amen.

October 22

The LORD detests dishonest scales, but accurate weights find favor with him. . . . Differing weights and differing measures—the LORD detests them both. . . . Food gained by fraud tastes sweet, but one ends up with a mouth full of gravel. (11:1, 20:10,17)

WEALTH CAN MAKE YOU DISHONEST. Proverbs names several significant spiritual dangers that wealth brings. The first is this: Money has the power to corrupt your integrity. You might be a person of honesty and character, but in the presence of a lot of money, it is remarkable how many people will make compromises.

In ancient times the seller might label a one-pound weight as two pounds, place it on the scale, and lead the buyer to pay more for the grain than he should. *Dishonest scales* refers to dishonest business practices. Jesus denounced religious leaders—men who should have been moral examples—for succumbing to the power of money by twisting the law to increase their profits (Mark 7:11–12). Today there has been an explosive multiplication of ways to hide from either customers or investors the information they ought to have, without which you can take advantage of them and exploit them. Money has never had so many ways to tempt you. Don't be naive about its power. Wealth gained by fraud will never satisfy. You will end up with a mouth full of gravel (20:17).

In your life or someone else's, where have you seen the power of money to make us dishonest?

Prayer: Lord, I can feel the power of wealth to corrupt me even when I do my taxes, or when I just don't want to know how my bank uses my savings. Protect me from the small compromises and slow hardening of the soul that money can bring. Amen.

October 23

> People curse the one who hoards grain, but they pray God's blessing
> on the one who is willing to sell. (11:26)

BOTTOM LINES. 11:26 describes a man who, in a time of food
scarcity, holds on to his grain to raise the price higher. This is
not illegal. Yet this man is rightly being *cursed*. Why? Because he
is acting as if the *only* bottom line is financial profit.

If all we own belongs to God and is given to us only as stewards (1 Chronicles 29:14), there is always another "bottom line"
in our financial dealings: the good of others, the good of the
community. You can't live without breathing, but no one wants
to live just to breathe. And you can't have a business without
profit, but no one should be in business simply to make money. If
business leaders choosing between two companies ask only
which is more profitable—and not "Which company gives us a
product that helps the town, society, and people more?"—they
have been corrupted by the power of money, according to the
book of Proverbs.

Have you ever seen an instance in which the "bottom line" of
the common good was chosen over profit—and not simply
because it was thought to be good public relations?

Prayer: Lord, give men and women in business—whether by
conscience (Romans 2:14) or the regenerating power of the
Spirit—the understanding and moral conviction that commerce
is not, ultimately, about profit. Amen.

October 24

"It's no good, it's no good!" says the buyer—then goes off and boasts about the purchase. . . . Whoever increases wealth by taking interest or profit from the poor amasses it for another, who will be kind to the poor. (20:14, 28:8)

MONEY CAN MAKE YOU RUTHLESS. Money can make you dishonest, but more often it makes you ruthless. 20:14 depicts a practice that many would call simply "sharp dealing." A buyer bidding on an item publicly insists it is of little worth but privately reveals his knowledge of its true value. 28:8 assumes the teaching of God's law to Israel, namely, that loaning at interest is proper if it is a business transaction (Deuteronomy 23:20), because both parties stand to profit, but you should not charge interest to a poor fellow believer who needed help just to survive (Leviticus 25:35–36). Jesus condemned those who legally but heartlessly "devour widows' houses" (Luke 20:47). You must not make money by taking advantage of vulnerable populations.

What we have in these cases is a heartless individualism, in which personal profit is put ahead of the good of others. Today the huge economic inequalities are the result of "not a market trend but . . . a new permissiveness, financial rather than sexual."[216] Money has the power to make you think that ruthlessness is just normal.

Where have you seen the power of money to make us ruthless?

Prayer: Lord, give us a conscience and concern for the vulnerable so that we don't make a profit from the young by selling corrupting entertainment, or from the elderly people by selling useless products, or from poor people by selling them mortgages they can't afford. I pray that you would move us to do justice as a nation. Amen.

October 25

Wealth is worthless in the day of wrath, but righteousness delivers from death. (11:4)

WEALTH CAN MAKE YOU DISTRACTED. Wealth has the power to absorb your time, energy, and imagination so you have too little left to pay attention to more important things. No one on their deathbed cries out, "I wish I'd spent more time at the office, making more money." *The day of wrath* is Judgment Day. Judgment Day questions are "What is my life amounting to? Whom am I really living for—God and my neighbor, or myself? What contribution am I making?"

Wealth blinds you to Judgment Day questions. It sucks you into a frantic cycle. It goes like this. "I've earned more, so I'm going to spend more. But now that I'm spending more, I need to earn more." And all the time you feel strapped and not that well-off, which leads you to work even more. Wealth has the power to make you far too busy with things that are less important. Jesus' version of this proverb is given in Luke 12:16–21. You are a fool if you are absorbed in "storing up things for [yourself]" that you cannot keep but are not "rich toward God" in things you cannot lose.

In your life or someone else's, where have you seen the power of money to distract us from the big questions and issues?

Prayer: Father, I don't want to be like the fool who broke his back to build up his business, all with a view to future years of ease that never came. Make me "rich toward God" now. Meet me in prayer. Conform me into the image of your Son. Grow me in the fear of the Lord. Amen.

October 26

"The rich are wise in their own eyes; one who is poor and discerning sees how deluded they are. . . . I may have too much and disown you and say, 'Who is the LORD?'" (28:11, 30:9)

WEALTH CAN MAKE YOU PROUD. We naturally take credit for wealth. Instead of acknowledging the enormous number of factors outside your control that brought the money to you, even with all your work, you attribute it all to your cleverness and discipline. Thus you become *wise in your own eyes*, the essence of foolishness (28:11). This pride will lead you to put too much faith in your instincts. You won't listen to others. Making money does not make you a great judge of character or wise about everything—but many wealthy people feel it does. Bernard of Clairvaux is reputed to have once said, "To see a man humble under prosperity is the greatest rarity in the world."

The ultimate danger of wealth is it leads us to say, "*Who is the Lord?*"—"Why do I need God?" Jesus insisted that we do not feed and clothe ourselves any more than the birds or the flowers do (Matthew 6:25–34). It is only when, in the Spirit's power, we realize we are saved only by grace that we can see God's grace in everything, and escape this deadly power of money.

Where have you seen the power of money to make us proud?

Prayer: Lord, how quickly we take credit in our hearts for a little financial success. So Lord, I thank you for any successes, any goals attained, and any blessings I wasn't capable of attaining, yet you sent to me. Amen.

A person's riches may ransom their life, but the poor cannot respond to threatening rebukes. (13:8)

THE BURDEN OF WEALTH. The situation in 13:8 could be a kidnapping or perhaps blackmail. A wealthy family pays the demanded sum. This seems to be an argument for having a lot of money. Commentators point out that the poor cannot respond to such threats, but on the other hand they don't need to as no one would try to get a ransom out of them.[217] The wealthy are subject to dangers "to which a poor man offers too small a target."[218]

The wealthy have stresses and burdens others do not have. They are barraged with requests for gifts and investments in new projects. They may become lonely because it is difficult to know who their friends truly are. Also, wealth needs constant attention and care just to maintain and manage (27:23–24). So riches bring cares, burdens, and responsibilities that others do not face. Living life with money actually requires greater faith and dependence on God, not less. Look to David for the proper attitude toward your wealth (1 Chronicles 29:10–19) and to the greater David's attitude toward his (2 Corinthians 8:9).

Whom have you seen shoulder the burden of affluence well? Whom have you seen do it not so well? What were the differences?

Prayer: Lord, there is a kind of justice in that those with the greater blessings also receive greater responsibility and burdens. I ask by your grace that if you deign to bless me with greater success, I might grow in the greater wisdom, humility, and love necessary to bear it. Amen.

October 28

My son, if you have put up security for your neighbor, if you have shaken hands in pledge for a stranger, you have been trapped by what you said, ensnared by the words of your mouth. So do this, my son, to free yourself, since you have fallen into your neighbor's hands. Go—to the point of exhaustion—and give your neighbor no rest! (6:1–3)

GAMBLING OR INVESTING? A young man has agreed to put up money for a business deal with someone he hardly knows—*a stranger*. He is admonished for entering into an unwise, overly risky financial transaction (11:15, 17:18, 20:16, 22:26–27). When it comes to financial dealings, "Scripture establishes prudence as one of the virtues. . . . [This] does not banish generosity; it is nearer to banishing gambling."[219] Many supposedly financial deals are so risky and imprudent that they are as much gambling as playing a slot machine.

The moral problems with gambling, in any form, are many. It is an effort to do an "end run" around the hard work, due diligence, and time investment that ordinarily is required to make wealth grow. Magic is condemned in the Bible because it is an effort to get power without discipleship, so we don't have to rely on God. Gambling is the same. Any money that we really can afford to essentially throw away on a risk we should instead be willing to give away to help others, which is always a sure thing. Jesus "threw away" his wealth and power, but to enrich us—not himself (Romans 15:1–3a).

What are the varied forms of gambling available to us in our society? Have you ever been drawn into any of them?

Prayer: Lord, make me prudent with regard to money, not prone to impulsive or risky endeavors. At the same time, give me foresight and a lack of fear and worry about money, knowing that you supply me with what I need even as you do the birds and flowers (Matthew 6:25–34). Amen.

October 29

How much better to get wisdom than gold, to get insight rather than silver! . . . Better a dry crust with peace and quiet than a house full of feasting, with strife. . . . Better the poor whose walk is blameless than the rich whose ways are perverse. (16:16, 17:1, 28:6)

WEALTH IN PERSPECTIVE. Money is not as important as *wisdom* and *insight* (16:16 and 8:19). Why not? The advantages of wealth seem to include safety and comfort for your family and the ability to do good in the world. Yet wealth without wisdom means the dangers and difficulties that wealth inevitably attracts will make us *less* secure and useful. Without wisdom, wealth cannot truly give us anything good.

Money is not as important as relationships (17:1). It is only love and right relationships—with God and with others—that can give us a meaningful life, yet wealth, as we have seen, can put a strain on relationships, disrupt them, and leave us lonely. Money is not as important as integrity of character (28:6). A good conscience before God and human beings (Acts 24:16) is crucial, yet, as we have seen, money puts great pressure on our integrity. The bottom line: Wealth is an extremely useful thing, but it can give you nothing of lasting value or happiness.

Has wealth gotten out of perspective in your life?

Prayer: Lord, wealth seems to offer such good things—security, consequence, and power to do deeds of mercy. Yet without wisdom it can deliver none of them. Therefore, Lord, I ask that you not grant me any financial success unless you bless me with character, a good conscience, and strong relationships. Amen.

October 30

> The wealth of the rich is their fortified city, but poverty is the ruin of the poor. (10:15)

THE IDOL OF WEALTH: PART 1. We return to this important proverb. Why does wealth have all the power over us that we have been describing? In ancient times, because walled and *fortified cities* were so safe, the wealthiest wanted to live in them and the poor could not afford to. The city dwelling meant high status. But 10:15 does not say merely that the rich live *in* the city. It says their wealth *is* their city. That is, wealth can become your identity.

When wealth becomes your identity, you come to feel that people are not just below you economically; they are *below* you. This is spiritually lethal. In the parable of the Rich Man and Lazarus (Luke 16:19–31) the "rich man" in hell has no name because that was all he was—just a rich man. If you make wealth your very identity, and something takes the money away, there is no "you" left. You are prosperous and successful or you are nothing. But for the wise, the fear of the Lord *is* their treasure (Isaiah 33:6). To those who believe in Jesus, he is surpassingly precious (1 Peter 2:7).

Have you had enough success in life to be tempted to make your career or wealth your identity? Have you seen others give into this temptation? How can it be defeated?

Prayer: Lord, it takes little to make my social class into my identity. Pride in my credentials, or in the neighborhood I live in, become more important to my "name" than my true name in Christ. Let me instead rest my hope and find my worth in you. Amen.

October 31

The wealth of the rich is their fortified city; they imagine it a wall too high to scale. (18:11)

THE IDOL OF WEALTH: PART 2. 18:11 says wealth exerts its power over us through our imagination. We *imagine* all the ways it will save us—it will be *a wall too high*—from the things we fear or dread. Thus our daydreams and fantasies about money not only show us that wealth can be an idol but they can also reveal our other idols to us. What your heart most loves and adores, what it most rests in, is where you most effortlessly, joyfully, almost addictively spend your money.

Some people put their money most effortlessly into savings, in order to feel safe. Others put it most readily into clothing or things that make them appear attractive and sophisticated, in order to get people's approval and admiration. Others put it into homes and membership in clubs, in order to get status and power. "Where your treasure is, there your heart will be also" (Matthew 6:21). What will help break the hold that money has on our hearts? Radical generosity to God and the poor is a critical starting place. For idolatrous hearts it will be painful, but "one who cannot cast away a treasure at need is in fetters."[220]

How have you seen the truth of Jesus' saying "Where your treasure is, there your heart will be also" worked out in your life or others' lives?

Prayer: Lord Jesus, what a revealer money is! If I look at what I spend money on most effortlessly, almost without thinking, I see the real functional joys and trusts of my heart. Let me behold your glory (2 Corinthians 3:18) until these other things lose their grip on my heart and desires. Amen.

November 1

A wicked person earns deceptive wages, but the one who sows righteousness reaps a sure reward. (11:18)

UNREAL WEALTH. Without a relationship with God, your income is *deceptive*, literally, "unreal" (Hebrew *seqer*). Why? As we have seen, money's spiritual power lies in its ability to make us think it can give us far more than it can. We slip into believing that we could have a better life if we were just a little bit richer. We think that with the money will somehow come life and peace, but that is not true at all.

The only true solution to the power of money over you is to see yourself rich in Christ. In him we are "rich toward God" (Luke 12:21; cf. 2 Corinthians 8:9). Riches on earth bring some short-lived status, but we are children of the King of the universe. Riches on earth bring some security, but "in all things God works for the good of those who love him, who have been called" (Romans 8:28). Riches on earth bring power, but we will rule with Christ (2 Timothy 2:12). Christ has paid the only debt that could destroy us (Luke 7:42–43), which makes all other debts inconsequential. In Christ you are truly rich.

In your life or the life of someone else, have you seen the false promises of wealth being exposed for what they are? How?

Prayer: Lord, real wealth is to be wealthy toward you (Luke 12:12) and real fame is to be praised by you (Romans 2:29). I thank you that, in your grace, you added to the lasting treasures of my salvation some of the world's fading goods. Let me never lose track of which kind of wealth is which! Amen.

November 2

One person gives freely, yet gains even more; another withholds unduly, but comes to poverty. (11:24)

SCATTERING AND GATHERING. The more you scatter your wealth, the more you gather it, and the more you try to keep it for yourself, the more it dissipates. How could that be? Think of farmers. The more they scatter seed, the more they will reap. And keep in mind that seed comes back in a better form, as harvest you can eat and sell. In the same way, spiritually wise people realize their money is seed, and the only way for them to turn it into real riches is by giving it away in remarkable proportions (cf. 2 Corinthians 9:6).

This is *not* a promise that the more you give away, the more money you will make. Rather the more you give away wisely to ministries and programs that help people spiritually and physically, the more your money becomes the real wealth of changed lives in others and of spiritual health in yourself. And you will be walking in the footsteps of the one who was literally broken and scattered so he could gather us to himself.

Where have you seen this principle of scattering and gathering illustrated? How?

Prayer: Lord Jesus, your infinite loss on the cross has led to resurrection and infinite gains for us. Give me the faith to follow your path, to disburse and scatter my goods and time for others, and thereby see your grace and life grow in the lives of people around me. Amen.

November 3

The generous will themselves be blessed, for they share their food with the poor. (22:9)

THE BLESSING OF GENEROSITY. *The generous will themselves be blessed* when *they share their food with the poor.* Of what does this blessing consist? Generosity that breaks the power of money over you may make you wiser in your financial dealings.

But the *blessing* here is surely the increase in the true wealth of love. Even at the level of common sense, we feel the most rich when we most love and are loved. Radical generosity is an act of love toward God and toward others that exponentially increases love. It moves us from seeing money as a currency of status and power to instead seeing it as a currency for loving God and others. We love God with our money when we treat it as his, not ours, and send it out to the things he loves. We love people with our money when we heal and repair lives with it. And in the Bible we are blessed the more like God we become. God originally gave us our own lives. Then he gave us his Son's life. The more we give away, the more like our God we become. And that is blessed.

How have you seen the blessing of generosity illustrated?

Prayer: Father, there is only one true "currency" of value—love. In love you made the world and sent your Son. Let me never put financial security before love. Let me use my money to love people who are poor, to love people who don't know you, and to love people with needs in my family and Christian community. Amen.

November 4

Those who give to the poor will lack nothing, but those who close their eyes to them receive many curses. (28:27)

I SHALL NOT WANT. If we are generous with wealth, we will *lack nothing*. While this cannot mean that all generous, righteous people become more prosperous (15:15–17, 16:8,19, 19:22), the second clause gives us a hint at why financial generosity can enhance material security. Selfish people get *curses* from the community around them. Thus the generous get the blessings of the community.

In Mark 10:29–31 Jesus says that if, through generosity, you lose "homes" or "fields" for his sake, you will receive new ones "in this present age." The reason that Christians are free to radically give away money when needs are evident is because they are now members of a community that will do the same for them, should they be in want. This gives us every incentive to maintain Christian communities of mutual, practical love, like the early church, where "no one claimed that any of their possessions was their own, but they shared everything" (Acts 4:32–34). This is how believers can be radically generous without excessive worry. Because they are embedded in a community of believers they will lack nothing they really need.

In your life or the life of someone else, have you seen how the strength of the bonds of a Christian community encourages and supports generosity?

Prayer: Lord, to live as a rugged individualist is not your will for me, and it leaves me vulnerable. Change my heart and strengthen the church so we, your people, can truly be members of one another. Amen.

November 5

Honor the LORD with your wealth, with the firstfruits of all your crops; then your barns will be filled to overflowing, and your vats will brim over with new wine. (3:9–10)

HOW MUCH IS ENOUGH? How much of our money should we be giving away to follow the biblical direction to be generous? When Proverbs tells us you must *honor the Lord with your wealth*, it speaks against the backdrop of the biblical "tithe." God required Israelites to give 10 percent of their annual income to the Levites and the priests to support both the temple and the poor. God saw this proportion of their wealth as his, and therefore the failure to give it was seen not as stinginess but as robbery (Malachi 3:6–12).

The New Testament nowhere explicitly requires tithing. But in Matthew 23:23 Jesus castigates listeners for not being willing to go beyond the tithe when there are needs. This is only reasonable. We have greater privileges, joy, knowledge, and power than our ancestors in the faith, so how could we be expected to be *less* generous with our possessions? So the tithe is best seen as a minimum rule of thumb for Christians who want to give in gospel proportions to the church, the poor, and others.

Do you think that it is reasonable to see the tithe as a minimum standard for Christian generosity? Why or why not?

Prayer: Lord, my culture presses me to spend and spend in order to be happy and secure. But remind me that I have joy and peace in you, and then help me be open to constantly giving a greater and greater percentage of my income away as the years go by. Amen.

November 6

"Keep falsehood and lies far from me; give me neither poverty nor riches, but give me only my daily bread. Otherwise, I may have too much and disown you and say, 'Who is the LORD?' Or I may become poor and steal, and so dishonor the name of my God. (30:8–9)

GLAD SIMPLICITY. Money can corrupt us not only by its presence but by its absence. The poor are tempted to crime as a means for income (*I may become poor and steal*). They are often excluded unfairly from the economy, and in their hearts there can arise self-justification for illegal and even violent action. We have already seen the dangers and burdens of wealth.

But we must not read this as a "middle-class" ideal. "My daily bread" (cf. 1 Timothy 6:8) refers to a modest lifestyle, lower than what we would call middle class. Does this mean Christians should divest themselves of all money beyond a "simple life-style"? Not necessarily, because we need Christians in all places and social circles. What it does mean is at least this: Our homes, clothing, and lifestyle should be modest within our circle and neighborhood so we can be as generous as possible. The Christian community should model to the world a society in which wealth and possessions are seen as tools for serving others and not as means of personal advancement and fulfillment.

Do you live as modestly as possible within your vocation and neighborhood, in order to be as generous as possible?

Prayer: Lord, don't let my heart regard my money and possessions as my treasures and you as just a means to various ends. Rather, direct my heart to make you my most precious treasure (1 Peter 2:7) and so see and use my worldly things as mere tools for serving others. Amen.

November 7

The lazy do not roast any game, but the diligent feed on the riches of the hunt. . . . An unplowed field produces food for the poor, but injustice sweeps it away. (12:27, 13:23)

GOD'S ECONOMY. 12:27 tells us that the lazy do not eat because they do not pursue the quarry. Many see that as the explanation for poverty—a lack of personal initiative. But 13:23 tells us that a family might have extremely fertile land yet injustice may take their profits away. The Bible's view of wealth and economics does not fit neatly into either socialism or capitalism. Poverty cannot be reduced to either a simple lack of initiative or to unjust social structures. Hard work and private property are highly valued, yet property rights are not absolute, because we are only stewards of what God has entrusted to us.

Deuteronomy 23:24 says you may walk through a neighbor's vineyard, and if you are poor you may eat "all the grapes you want," but you may put none in a basket. In a fully communitarian society, the grapes would belong to the state. In a fully individualistic society, any taking of grapes would be robbery. The Bible's vision for interdependent community, in which private property is important but not an absolute, does not give a full support to any conventional political-economic agenda. It sits in critical judgment on them all.

If Christians believed that the Bible does not support fully either a pure liberal-socialist or a conservative-capitalist approach to economics, how would that make the church different from what it is today?

Prayer: Lord, the wisdom of your Word can be reflected but never fully captured by any human political project or economic system. May your people love their neighbors, and give themselves to be salt and light in society (Matthew 5:13–14), yet never put our hopes too much in any social program. Amen.

November 8

By me kings reign and rulers issue decrees that are just; by me princes govern, and nobles—all who rule on earth. (8:15–16)

LEADERSHIP. Proverbs does not ignore the reality of power and speaks constantly to those who wield it. Leadership has never been more difficult than it is today, yet no society can function without it. Here speaks God's wisdom, through whom the Lord made the world (8:25–31), and says, *By me kings reign.* What does it mean? On one level it means that all leaders are effective only to the degree that they acknowledge at some point the givens of God's wisdom—that they are not too wise in their own eyes, that they are relatively free from the power of money, that they know themselves and the times and seasons and how relationships work.

On another level, however, *reigning by me* means all leaders, whether they know it or not, exercise authority by the permission and power of God himself. Jesus told Pilate he had no power but that which was given to him by God (John 19:11), and he told him this even as Pilate was about to commit a great injustice. Even leaders without much wisdom or virtue, though they don't know it, are ruling by God's appointment and ultimately furthering God's plan (Genesis 50:20; Acts 2:23; Romans 8:28).

How should Christians regard good leaders who are not believers and bad leaders who are?

Prayer: Lord, instead of grumbling about our civic leaders, move your people to both thank you and pray for those in authority, that they would be given enough wisdom that we may live peaceful and quiet lives in all godliness and holiness (1 Timothy 2:1–2). Amen.

November 9

Eloquent lips are unsuited to a godless fool—how much worse lying lips to a ruler! . . . By justice a king gives a country stability, but those who are greedy for bribes tear it down. (17:7, 29:4)

CHARACTER. Although Proverbs usually uses kings and rulers as case studies in power, the basic principles apply across all forms of leadership—from parenting to leading a small group to supervising employees.

The first mark of a wise leader is evident strength of character. 17:7 speaks of *lying lips* on a *ruler* as profoundly incongruous (though, sadly, not at all rare). 29:4 urges rulers to not be greedy or corrupt and open to bribes. Leadership certainly can and should make use of formal legal obligations. You are required to grant authority to many who have the power to penalize you legally or financially if you do not follow their direction. But the most powerful leaders are those whom people trust so much that they *want* to follow them. The New Testament tells church leaders to not "[lord] it over those entrusted to you, but [be] examples" (1 Peter 5:3). You can have trustworthy character and not have the gifts or skills to be a strong leader, as we will see. But the reverse is not true. You cannot be a real leader without character that all can see, respect, and therefore trust.

Thinking of the best leaders you have known, how has character been important to their effectiveness?

Prayer: Lord, I pray for the leaders of our states and nations, of business and commerce, of the arts and cultural institutions, of scholarship and the academy, and of social and welfare institutions for their honesty, wisdom, skill, and virtue in their duties, that their work would be a public blessing. Amen.

November 10

When a king sits on his throne to judge, he winnows out all evil with his eyes. (20:8)

READING CHARACTER. A second mark of a good leader is the ability to assess the character of others. A leader who cannot read people's hearts, who cannot *winnow out all evil*, will not govern well. She cannot recruit the right people to serve with or under her. She cannot discern good partners for her institution or organization. Either naïveté or cynicism about people—habitually overtrusting or undertrusting motivations—will greatly hinder leadership effectiveness.

In 1 Kings 3 the new young king Solomon refrains from praying for wealth or power and instead asks for "a discerning heart to govern your people and to distinguish between right and wrong. For who is able to govern this great people of yours?" (1 Kings 3:9). God is pleased. Immediately after this prayer, Solomon is faced with two women, both with newborn sons, one of whom has tragically, accidentally killed her infant. Each claims that the living child is hers, and Solomon is able to cut through the contradictory testimony and expose the hearts of the women, distinguishing good and evil where it was unclear and rendering a just judgment. Just as Jesus could read hearts (John 2:24–25), so can good leaders.

Thinking of the best leaders you have known, how has the ability to judge character been important to their effectiveness?

Prayer: Father, as your Son could read people's hearts but did not despise them, but rather died for them, so enable me to discern the good and the bad in people. Let such insight, a gift from you, move me only to love them more deeply and more wisely. Amen.

November 11

A wise king winnows out the wicked; he drives the threshing wheel over them. (20:26)

DECISIVENESS. A third mark of good leadership is decisiveness. The *threshing wheel* was fitted with sharp iron blades that separated the wheat from the chaff. The wicked are likened to chaff, but the image does not mean they are to be literally tortured. It means that leaders are not to be afraid to "clean house" and make judgments, especially with regard to matters of right and wrong.

We must not think that any human leader has the insight to completely remove wickedness from a church or organization. Jesus warns that only he will be able to do that, and not until Judgment Day (Matthew 3:12, 13:24–30). Yet good leaders are able to see past appearances and make judgments. They are not afraid to take bold action. Indecisiveness is often due to fearfulness. In Jesus' parable of the talents, the steward who is afraid to invest the master's money is called "wicked" and "lazy" (Matthew 25:26). Indecisiveness may also result from an excessive need for approval. We don't want to appear bossy or hurt the feelings of others. But when people in an organization are not quite sure what was decided or exactly what they are expected to do, that's a failure of leadership.

Thinking of the best leaders you have known, how has decisiveness been important to their effectiveness?

Prayer: Lord, help me overcome both the fearfulness that leads to indecision and the pride that leads to stubbornness. Give me sound judgment, oh Judge of all the earth, who can only do right (Genesis 18:25). Amen.

November 12

Love and faithfulness keep a king safe; through love his throne is made secure. (20:28)

POWER IS NOT ENOUGH. Covenant *love and faithfulness* is a phrase often used in the Bible to describe God's relationship to his people. God loved us so much that he came into the world and sacrificed himself for our good. That's how relentlessly faithful and loving he is to us. This saying, then, means that even a king's leadership must be characterized by a love for his people that is evident to them. That is, they must see that in the end he would sacrifice himself for them, rather than sacrifice them to save himself.

A leader is like a true husband who leads his wife only to serve her, even to his own detriment (Ephesians 5:25), not like the false husband who sacrifices his wife to save his own skin (Judges 19:22–28). The most powerful kind of leader is one who uses his or her authority ultimately to serve the ones being led. A leader must be decisive, and that includes making the tough decisions (November 11). But in the end, exercises of power are not enough. The greatest leaders are the greatest servants (Mark 10:45; Luke 22:27).

Thinking of the best leaders you have known, how have evident love and a servant heart been important to their effectiveness?

Prayer: Father, we pray that our leaders in the nation would seek loving service instead of power and glory, and that our leaders in the church would fully conform to the pattern of your Son, who came not to be served but to serve. Amen.

November 13

Where there is no revelation, people cast off restraint; but blessed is the one who heeds wisdom's instruction. (29:18)

VISION. We turn now to what leaders *do*. Here we are told that *people cast off restraint*—they scatter in all directions and wander from the path—if they lack something, but what? The Hebrew word describing it is literally "vision"—to see ahead—but it can also refer to the *revelation* that prophets receive from God. Translators are therefore divided, but it may be best to take the senses together. "Those who don't have a goal and/or a plan for the future have nothing to guide them onward, so they go every which way."[221]

Christian leaders, guided by the wisdom of God's Word, must set before people goals that honor God and serve others. And indeed the best leaders are those who can paint a compelling picture of the future, who can say, "This is the world I want to see. Who's with me?" Organizations can become calcified when they become selfish—no longer serving a vision, a cause outside themselves, but only maintaining their own power and turf. Good leaders not only are servants but make their organizations into servants as well.

Have you seen a leader cast a vision or paint a picture of the future in a compelling way? How was it done?

Prayer: Lord, may our nation's leaders not be motivated mainly by a desire for personal advancement. Let them be animated instead by a vision for peace (the end of violence and conflict), for prosperity (the lifting up of the poor, sick, and hungry), and for freedom (the breaking of systems of injustice). Amen.

November 14

A king delights in a wise servant, but a shameful servant arouses his fury. . . . The plans of the diligent lead to profit as surely as haste leads to poverty. . . . Like an archer who wounds at random is one who hires a fool or any passer-by. (14:35, 21:5, 26:10)

ORGANIZING. A leader may have a servant heart and a compelling vision. Yet 14:35 and 26:10 tell us nothing will be accomplished if the king has selected his servants poorly. Some leaders are good at "catalyzing" but not good at organizing. Organizing includes finding coworkers who can actually do the job. Organizing also means the ability to devise wise, strategic plans (21:5).

Finally, organizing is a matter of . . . being organized. Disorganization is selfishness, a lack of sacrificial love in little things. Good leaders will find and give time to the most important things. Jesus started the day this way: "Early in the morning, while it was still dark, . . . [he] left the house and went off to a solitary place, where he prayed" (Mark 1:35). When the time had come to go up to Jerusalem, he set his face (Luke 9:51). All this shows a mastery of his time in complete service to the calling upon him. So we were saved. Ask him to help you bring your time into the service of his calling upon you.

It is one thing to say, "Here's where we need to go"; it is another thing to know how to actually get there. Are you better at setting goals than at reaching them? How can you change?

Prayer: Father, I have had many captivating ideas for new projects, but too often I lack the wisdom to know how to make the dreams a reality. By your grace, help me be organized enough to finish what I start so I become like your Son, Jesus Christ. Amen.

November 15

The lips of a king speak as an oracle, and his mouth does not betray justice. Honest scales and balances belong to the LORD; all the weights in the bag are of his making. Kings detest wrongdoing, for a throne is established through righteousness. Kings take pleasure in honest lips; they value the one who speaks what is right. A king's wrath is a messenger of death, but the wise will appease it. When a king's face brightens, it means life; his favor is like a rain cloud in spring. (16:10–15)

BEFORE GOD. In these verses "'The LORD' could be inserted wherever 'king' is found."[222] Even though all human authority is limited (Matthew 22:21), and we must obey God over human beings (Acts 5:29), leaders in authority do stand in God's place (Romans 13:1).

What this means is that if you have been given authority—whether as a parent, a teacher, a government official, or a small group leader—it is something God gave to you (Daniel 4:17), and God holds you fully responsible for what you do with it (Deuteronomy 17:18–20). You now must, as much as possible, represent him in your leadership. Here indeed is a reason for fear and trembling before the Lord. But remember that Jesus put the failed Peter into leadership (John 15:15–25), showing that it is not ability but humility and dependence on him that matter most. As Aslan said to Prince Caspian: "If you had felt yourself sufficient, it would have been proof that you were not."[223]

Have you seen that your failures and weaknesses have made you more, not less, qualified to lead?

Prayer: Lord, leadership made me anxious that I wouldn't look good, but now it brings, I hope, a godly anxiety that I won't represent you as I should. Give me all the integrity, unpretentiousness, love, and decisiveness I need to be a good leader. Amen.

November 16

By justice a king gives a country stability, but those who are greedy for bribes tear it down. . . . If a ruler listens to lies, all his officials become wicked. (29:4,12)

A CULTURE OF TRUTH. *Bribes* may vary from small "tips" enabling you to skip to the head of a queue to large sums in order to secure government contracts. Bribes can be legal or illegal depending on the situation and the country, but the Bible universally condemns the practice (Deuteronomy 10:17–18; 2 Chronicles 19:7; Proverbs 17:23, 29:4). It does so not just for the sake of honesty but for the sake of justice. The poor cannot afford to bribe, and so bribery is a way of privileging the rich unfairly. It makes advancement out of poverty impossible.

If corruption comes from the bottom of a society, those in power might with difficulty root it out. But if it comes from the top (29:12), it becomes endemic and impossible to change. "One form of this top-down corruption . . . is the ruler who is soothed by lies, who surrounds himself or herself with underlings who will say only what he wants to hear."[224] Be thankful that at the pinnacle of the true kingdom is the incorruptible one. Jesus endured three powerful bribes from Satan (Matthew 4:1–11) and resisted them for his Father's sake and ours. Now we should resist bribes for his sake.

In what forms have you seen bribes extended and taken? Have you been offered a bribe? What did you do?

Prayer: Father, there are so many forms that a bribe can take! Don't let me defer to those with wealth and power, even in subtle ways. Let me remember your Son, who left the wealthiest neighborhood in the universe, to live with us, the powerless and poor. Amen.

November 17

Many seek an audience with a ruler, but it is from the LORD that one gets justice. (29:26)

LEADERS ARE HUMAN. The Bible calls for respect of authority (Romans 13:1–9). Fools and mockers bristle at any exertion of authority over them. Nevertheless, this text warns of the opposite error. We may pin all our expectations for *justice* on an audience with a ruler, when it is only from the Lord that we can be sure it will come. Put another way, we must never forget that leaders are still limited human beings, often subject to appetites and pressures (Acts 24:25–27), irrationality (1 Corinthians 2:6, 8), and instability (Psalm 146:3–4).[225] They are always imperfect, and we must refrain from looking to them more than God.

That means, practically, that we should not be overly shocked and disillusioned when our leaders are revealed as having clay feet. Nor should we be blasé and shrug. If we are to trust God as our only true hope for social order and peace, we must avoid either adulatory naïveté or bitter cynicism about human leaders. Not only are both attitudes deadly for political and civic life, but they also dishonor the God behind all human authority.

Have you been disillusioned by leaders? How? And how have you responded?

Prayer: Lord, I confess to being shaken when some of my most admired leaders were revealed to have feet of clay. The result was I became too cynical and unwilling to trust and follow anyone. But save me from each form of sin, remembering that both are failures to trust you, my Rock and my Refuge. Amen.

November 18

Fear the Lord and the king, my son, and do not join with rebellious officials, for those two will send sudden destruction on them, and who knows what calamities they can bring? (24:21–22)

CITIZENSHIP. These verses could look like mere pragmatism, a warning against being part of a rebellion that could get quashed. But 1 Peter 2:17 ("fear God, honor the emperor") and Romans 13:1 ("Let everyone be subject to the governing authorities") show that good citizenship is not merely pragmatic but part of a wise and godly life.

The Bible's view of government is uniquely balanced. In Romans 13 and 1 Peter 2, Christians were called to respect the authority of emperors whose government was idolatrous. Jeremiah 27:1–7 called believers to participate supportively in the affairs of a pagan culture. Yet we see the civil disobedience of the Hebrew midwives (Exodus 1:17), who remind us of those who hid Jews from the Nazis in World War II. So Christians respect and love their country, but never uncritically. Christians are slaves of God alone (1 Corinthians 7:22) and therefore of no human being (1 Corinthians 7:23), and this undermines the impulses of our heart toward racism and nationalism. It is because we were purchased with Christ's precious blood (Acts 20:28; 1 Corinthians 6:19–20) and so we are not our own.

Do you see Christians today showing respect and love for country and avoiding political extremes?

Prayer: Lord, let me rejoice in my country, in its geographical places, and in its people. But let me remember that the glories I see and joys I feel are but foretastes of my true home and people (Philippians 3:20). Then I can take proper pride and true comfort in my country, neither idolizing nor disdaining it. Amen.

November 19

It is the glory of God to conceal a matter; to search out a matter is the glory of kings. As the heavens are high and the earth is deep, so the hearts of kings are unsearchable. (25:2–3)

INTELLIGENCE. 25:2 tells us *it is the glory of kings*—it is both a means and a mark of leadership greatness—*to search out a matter.* Leaders' intelligence should be both formal and informal. They should make moves based on extensive research, and informally they should always have their ear to the ground. Good leaders should be like David, who had "wisdom like that of an angel" because he knew "everything that happens in the land" (2 Samuel 14:20).

At the same time, a wise king should not be too easy to read himself; he should not run at the mouth. Until the right time he should play his cards close to his chest (25:3). Kenneth T. Aiken notes that this vision of leadership teaches that the government that wins public respect is one that shows that its decisions are based on careful consideration of the evidence, "with the interests of truth and the people uppermost," rather than on "partisan interests, narrow political ideology or short-term political expediency."[226]

Do we have a government today that puts the interests of truth over partisan ideology and short-term expediency?

Prayer: Lord, we long for leaders who put the people's good ahead of personal political gain, and who put truth ahead of ideology. We ask that you would raise up such leaders, and meanwhile prevent us from thinking we would do a far better job, and thereby to despise the leaders we have. Amen.

November 20

Like a roaring lion or a charging bear is a wicked ruler over a helpless people. A tyrannical ruler practices extortion, but one who hates ill-gotten gain will enjoy a long reign. (28:15–16)

GOD HATES TYRANNY. Here again we see Proverbs castigating leaders who are not, at heart, servants to their people. This foreshadows the more extensive teaching of the New Testament on leaders as "stewards." Stewards were household managers—with complete authority over all members of the household—but they were not the owners. They managed the assets for the benefit of the owner. A steward, then, was both a ruler "in charge" *and* a servant (Luke 12:44–45). Paul considered authoritative leadership in the church to be a "stewardship" (1 Corinthians 9:17; Titus 1:7).

Steward-leaders can fall into two opposite errors. They can be too weak and unassertive (Matthew 25:14ff.). But they can also become oppressive, *tyrannical*, using their power over *a helpless people* and forgetting their servant status under the Lord, the owner of all things. In Luke 12:45 Jesus speaks of a steward who beats the other servants. He says that when the true owner returns, the unjust steward will be "cut . . . to pieces" (Luke 12:46). Jesus' denunciation of an oppressive leader is every bit as devastating as his denunciation of a weak one. Jesus is no ideologue. He does not fear strong leadership on principle nor countenance tyrants or oppression.

As a leader, which of the two steward-leader errors are you most likely to fall into?

Prayer: Lord, I say I only want to witness to the truth but it is often just a way to exert power. I express grief and outrage but it too is sometimes a way to exert power. Let all I do be fueled by a desire for love and service rather than power and control. Amen.

November 21

Do not spend your strength on women, your vigor on those who ruin kings. It is not for kings, Lemuel—it is not for kings to drink wine, not for rulers to crave beer, lest they drink and forget what has been decreed, and deprive all the oppressed of their rights. Let beer be for those who are perishing, wine for those who are in anguish! Let them drink and forget their poverty and remember their misery no more. (31:3–7)

LEADERS ARE ALONE. This is the advice of a royal mother to her son, the young King Lemuel (31:1–2). Proverbs is filled with warnings against sexual immorality and abuse of alcohol, but leaders have even more need for self-control, because of their power to do good or ill. When Lemuel's mother proposes that those without power drink till they are drunk, she is actually making a rhetorical point. Others might have a drinking binge or a wild affair, but leaders must not do this, for it could destabilize a whole nation.

Leadership, then, is lonely. Leaders cannot allow themselves many of the indulgences others have. Because of the peculiar stresses and sacrifices leaders make, they can be prone to self-pity, to engage in a secret affair or addiction, because they say to themselves, "After all I've done, I deserve this." But they must not do this. After all, the *rights of all the oppressed* are on their shoulders. John the Baptist was unjustly executed by a sovereign whose pride and fears were out of control (Mark 6:21–29). Don't be a leader, or in ministry, unless you accept the high standards for self-control and dependence on God.

Have you been in positions in which you sensed the loneliness of leadership? Can that help you imagine what it is like higher up?

Prayer: Lord, I have come to see that doing right, telling the truth, going against the evil tide—can be so lonely. When I'm tempted to give in, help me to remember your loneliness. In order to save me, you bore rejection not only of enemies and of friends, but of your Father—and all for me. Amen.

> A king's rage is like the roar of a lion, but his favor is like dew on the grass. . . . A king's wrath strikes terror like the roar of a lion; those who anger him forfeit their lives. (19:12, 20:2)

TACT, NOT PANDERING. These two proverbs give advice to those who engage powerful people. When formidable people get angry, their *wrath* understandably strikes terror. These texts do not tell us if the anger is justified or unjustified. Rather, they warn us to show due respect, realizing the enormous good powerful people can do if persuaded. Their favor is like dew on the grass, and the morning dew in those arid lands was life-giving.

Yet in the end, Proverbs' insistence on integrity and truth telling means we are called not to pander to those in power. We must never sell our souls to get favor with them. Jesus, though he was meek before them (Isaiah 53:7), did not tell the powerful people what they wanted to hear, and they slew him. When believers speak truth to power, they must do so with respect but without compromise (Daniel 3:16–18). Many people are either too disdainful or too servile to engage powerful people well. But the wise can do it.

Have you seen examples of people who were too tactless or too pandering to power? Which of these errors are you most prone to?

Prayer: Lord, when Daniel spoke to the king, he was genuinely distressed for him (Daniel 4:19), yet called him to repent and stop oppressing the poor (Daniel 4:27). How rare to see genuine love for an oppressor—and bold truth telling, all at once. Be pleased, Lord, to reproduce this in me. Amen.

November 23

In the LORD's hand the king's heart is a stream of water that he channels toward all who please him. (21:1)

KING OF KINGS. Farmers could dig irrigation canals and *channel streams of water* where they could do the most good. This proverb tells us that no matter how powerful and proud persons become, they cannot escape the supervision of God. In some cases this means that God may take a person with great power and wealth and actually convert her or him. That is one way the king's heart can be changed.

But the text indicates that the Lord has *every* ruler's heart in his hand. Each powerful person will be only an instrument for the accomplishment of God's plans (Isaiah 10:6–7, 41:2–4). The civil rulers thought they were conspiring against the Christian movement, but ultimately they did only what God's "power and will had decided beforehand should happen" (Acts 4:28). What, then, is practical wisdom regarding intimidating power brokers? On the one hand, don't be intimidated yourself. Christians can call those in power to honor justice and truth as Daniel did (Daniel 4:27). On the other hand, never be in despair. There is a King of kings.

Do you get discouraged about the state of leadership in our country? How does this reflection help you?

Prayer: Lord, you warn us against showing too little respect, even for tyrants (Romans 13:4), or too much (Acts 5:29). Even so, help me to show both a godly courtesy and a godly frankness in all my dealings with powerful people. Amen.

November 24

> When the righteous prosper, the city rejoices; when the wicked perish, there are shouts of joy. (11:10)

THE PUBLIC GOOD: PART 1. These two proverbs talk about the *righteous*. The Hebrew word is *tsaddiqim*, literally, those who are "just." We have seen that this term means those who believe in God and who therefore disadvantage themselves to advantage those around them. Here we are told that this group of people, the righteous, *prosper*. That is, they grow in numbers, they thrive economically, they rise to the top of their respective fields. They are successful in every way. Yet in response the rest of the city does not resent it or shrug, they *rejoice*, a word describing a shout of triumph when a battle is won.

What is going on here? The verse means that if a group of people in a city are truly living "righteously," as Proverbs defines it, they will be such a benefit to the public good of the whole city that the entire populace will exult, feeling that their prosperity is a victory for everyone.

Are you the kind of person, and is your church the kind of church, about which others in your community might say, "I don't share their beliefs, but I shudder to think about what this city would be like without them"?

Prayer: Lord, if I live a godly life I will be persecuted (2 Timothy 3:12) and yet I will also lead people to glorify God (Matthew 5:16; 1 Peter 2:12). I confess that neither of these things is happening to me! And so, Lord, make me more godly until I am both more offensive and attractive to the world. Amen.

Through the blessing of the upright a city is exalted, but by the mouth of the wicked it is destroyed. (11:11)

THE PUBLIC GOOD: PART 2. 11:10 gives us a startling standard. If believers were simply living life as they should, it would create such public good that those around them would rejoice in their prosperity and success. 11:11 tells us that believers should be *blessing* the city.[227] How?

We can infer how they would be doing that from the rest of Proverbs. Their relationships would be marked by justice and fair dealing. In business they would be known to be smart but not ruthless, and people of high integrity. In civic life they would be the most generous and philanthropic with their assets, the most concerned that the poor and immigrants be lifted up out of poverty. The neighborhoods in which they lived would thrive, be great places to live, and not only for those who had the same faith. In politics they would never be vicious. If their community were attacked, they would never retaliate but would respond with forgiveness. They would also be known as peacemakers, doing everything they could to broker relationships and maintain peace among various communities and groups within the city. Finally, the strength of their family lives would be evident to all.

Is this how your city sees your Christian community?

Prayer: Father, your Son said that the church's love relationships should be so powerful that they lead the church to see the truth of the gospel (John 17:20–23). Yet it is the rare church that is seen by its community in this way. Do whatever it takes to raise up churches that glorify you through their good deeds. Amen.

November 26

The violence of the wicked will drag them away, for they refuse to do what is right. . . . The rich rule over the poor, and the borrower is slave to the lender. Whoever sows injustice reaps calamity, and the rod they wield in fury will be broken. (21:7, 22:7–8)

DOING JUSTICE. In 22:8 the word for justice is *tzadeqah*. *Tzadeqah* means "primary justice": giving people fair, equal treatment regardless of their racial, social, or economic status. In 21:7 the word for justice (what is right) is *mishpat*. *Mishpat* means "rectifying justice": putting things right for those being exploited.

If everyone was living a life of primary justice and generosity, there would be no need for rectifying or reparative justice—but there is. So God constantly calls us to "do justice" (*mishpat*) to widows, orphans, immigrants, and the poor (cf. Zechariah 7:9–10; Psalm 82:2–4). That entails defending them before the law (Deuteronomy 10:18–19) and sharing our goods with them so they have enough (Isaiah 58:6–7). Any mistreatment or even neglect of the needs of the members of these groups is called not just a lack of charity but sowing injustice. All believers, as citizens, should be deeply concerned for the poor and doing both primary and rectifying justice in their societies, because God is (14:31; Psalm 146:7–9). It should also be noted that if we exploit others, the violence unleashed in society will rebound on us in some way. *The violence of the wicked will drag them away.*

Have you seen examples recently of people showing primary justice? Rectifying justice?

Prayer: Lord, the word "charity" strengthens my desire to see care for the poor as merely optional, something I can do if I am having a very good year. However, it is unjust not to share what I have with those who have less. Help me to truly live a righteous life toward those in need. Amen.

November 27

Speak up for those who cannot speak for themselves, for the rights of all who are destitute. Speak up and judge fairly; defend the rights of the poor and needy. (31:8–9)

HUMAN RIGHTS. Does the Bible give us a basis for believing in human *rights*? Yes, it does. Here King Lemuel is being urged to defend the rights of *the poor and needy. Rights* translates a word that simply means a claim. Genesis 1:26–27 tells us God made all human beings "in his image." Because of this, every human life is sacred and inviolable (Genesis 9:6), and every person has a dignity and worth that must be respected. James 3:9 says that even to curse someone made in the image of God is a great sin, as is showing favoritism to the rich over the poor (James 2:1–9).

According to the Bible, then, your neighbor comes into your presence with certain claims on you. Negatively, she has the right to not be assaulted, defrauded, or killed. Positively, she has the right to be treated with fairness and respect. These verses again show us it is the poor and needy who cannot assert those rights without help. Perhaps they *cannot speak for themselves* because they aren't instructed enough in the complicated ways of the law, or they can't speak the language well enough, or they are too poor to get good help and counsel. We must champion the causes of those who do not get a fair hearing in courts of law or of public opinion.

Think of a way you could speak for those who cannot speak for themselves, then do it, knowing that Jesus speaks for you before the Father.

Prayer: Lord Jesus, you are my advocate (1 John 2:1). You speak for me before the throne of God to which, otherwise, I would have no access. Now, Lord, show me how I can be an advocate for the poor and marginalized. Give me the wisdom to know how to help them get justice. Amen.

November 28

If you falter in a time of trouble, how small is your strength! Rescue those being led away to death; hold back those staggering toward slaughter. If you say, "But we knew nothing about this," does not he who weighs the heart perceive it? Does not he who guards your life know it? Will he not repay everyone according to what they have done? (24:10–12)

THE DAY OF ADVERSITY. It always costs time and money to do justice (November 27). And yet there are times when doing justice *really* costs. These verses talk about *a time of trouble—* literally, "the day of adversity." In times of crisis, from recessions to government coups, the most vulnerable are most endangered, and to defend them puts you in the way of harm as well. During World War II many German, French, and Dutch families saw their Jewish neighbors *being led away to death* and slaughter. Many afterward claimed, *"But we knew nothing about this."* Yet they were guilty because they did not want to know, for fear of what it might cost them. Similarly, when Kitty Genovese was attacked and left to die on a New York City street, neighbors hearing her cries ignored them out of fear. Viktor Frankl, who survived the Nazi death camps, described how many moral, upstanding citizens turned into collaborators with the enemy in order to survive. These situations can reveal the deep selfishness in our hearts that we otherwise keep hidden. "The true test of a person's strength or mettle is adversity; almost everyone can survive the good times."[228]

How are you building your character and your relationship to God now, so that you will be able to do the sacrificial thing when the time comes?

Prayer: Lord, yesterday I asked you to give me the wisdom to be an advocate for the marginalized, but today, I ask for the courage. Give me such grateful joy for what it cost you to be my High Priest, that I will sacrifice for those who have less of the world's goods and power. Amen.

An unplowed field produces food for the poor, but injustice sweeps it away.... The poor plead for mercy, but the rich answer harshly. (13:23, 18:23)

POVERTY AND OPPRESSION. What causes poverty? As we have seen, the Bible's view of economics does not fit neatly into the current liberal or conservative models (November 7). Some reduce the causes to unjust economic and political systems while others to a failure to build healthy families and live responsibly. In contrast to both, the Bible sees a matrix of interacting causes.

In these two proverbs we see that poverty can indeed be caused by unjust social conditions. 13:23 speaks of a field so fertile it grows food without cultivation. That represents any wealth-producing asset. Yet *injustice* takes these assets *away* and makes the person poor. These conditions cause the poor to plead for help, and 18:23 rightly observes that, in general, those with power and wealth tend to blame the poor for their condition. We take far more credit for our prosperity than we should. When we flatter ourselves that our assets are the result of our work, it leads us to believe any lack of such assets must be the result of laziness. But though David had come to his wealth through enormous risk and effort, he recognized it as fully a gift of God's grace (2 Chronicles 29:14). When we refuse to see or hear the pleas of the oppressed, we are unlike God, who always does (Psalm 28:2,6, 34:6).

Where is there a crying need in your town or social circle that you could be meeting?

Prayer: Father, my heart wants to take full credit for my financial standing and security. Open my eyes to see that my bank account—if there is anything in it at all—is there only through your manifold gifts. Let my generosity to the poor be as unstinting and manifold as your generosity to me. Amen.

November 30

All the days of the oppressed are wretched, but the cheerful heart has a continual feast. Better a little with the fear of the Lord than great wealth with turmoil. Better a small serving of vegetables with love than a fattened calf with hatred. . . . Better a little with righteousness than much gain with injustice. . . . Better to be lowly in spirit along with the oppressed than to share plunder with the proud. . . . Better the poor whose walk is blameless than a fool whose lips are perverse. . . . What a person desires is unfailing love; better to be poor than a liar. (15:15–17, 16:8,19, 19:1,22)

POVERTY AND CHARACTER. Unjust social systems are often the cause of poverty. Examples include unjustly low wages (Jeremiah 22:13), loans with excessive interest (Exodus 22:25–27), a legal system in which the wealthy get far better outcomes than the poor (Leviticus 19:15), and social prejudice against immigrants or minorities (Exodus 22:21, 23:9). There are few societies in which these conditions have not existed.

And while there is poverty caused by foolishness, Proverbs insists that poverty is not always shameful. In every poor population there are many of strong, even *blameless* (19:1) moral character who have been swept up in the complex forces that create poverty. These "better than" proverbs show that it is quite possible to be poor and still a man or woman of *love* rather than *hatred* (15:17), of humility rather than pride (16:19), of righteousness rather than injustice (16:8), and of honesty rather than lying (19:22). But the well-off should not indulge self-justifying fantasies of the "happy" poor. There is always a misery and wretchedness (15:15) around poverty that all who love God will want to remove (Psalm 41:1).

Compared with those who are truly poor, most of us are wealthy in the eyes of the world. How are we being judged as believers for our use of the resources God has given us?

Prayer: Lord, it is easy for us who are not poor to indulge in self-justifying fantasies about those who are. Prevent me from either feeling superior to the poor or forgetting their pain. Any of these attitudes will make me a bad neighbor to those in need. Amen.

December 1

Whoever mocks the poor shows contempt for their Maker; whoever gloats over disaster will not go unpunished. (17:5)

POVERTY AND MISFORTUNE. A third cause of poverty is *disaster*. Notice that to *mock the poor* and *gloat over disaster* is the same thing, because so often poverty is caused by some kind of calamity or catastrophic event. The most common, especially in ancient agrarian societies, was famine (cf. Genesis 47). Most people were subsistence farmers, and if weather conditions wiped out just one year's crop, poverty could be immediate and the family's very life was at risk.

But there is an almost infinite number of other circumstances that can create poverty. There are floods and fires, disabling injuries and crushing medical bills, the death of a family's main breadwinner. There can also be slower-moving disasters, such as a town's economy going under when the local mines or oil fields are tapped out. Some countries are richer and others much poorer because of differences in natural resources. Believers must never look at those with worse circumstances and quietly gloat over our better ones. Christians must weep with those who weep (Romans 12:15).

How does compassion for the poor express itself in your life?

Prayer: Lord Jesus, in this world there is spiritual, moral, and physical devastation everywhere. Your mission of salvation was the ultimate disaster response, and you are the ultimate rescue worker. Help me and my church to never become hardened to the constant reports of catastrophes that need our generosity and help. Amen.

December 2

Lazy hands make for poverty, but diligent hands bring wealth. . . . Whoever loves pleasure will become poor; whoever loves wine and olive oil will never be rich. . . . Do not join those who drink too much wine or gorge themselves on meat, for drunkards and gluttons become poor, and drowsiness clothes them in rags. (10:4, 21:17, 23:20–21)

POVERTY AND RESPONSIBILITY. As we have seen, Proverbs promotes hard work and frugality and rightly observes that, in general, these qualities usually lead to some degree of prosperity (10:4). It is true that poverty can be caused by a lack of self-discipline or the inability to endure delayed gratification (21:17). Tragically, addictions can also be part of the iron cage of poverty (23:20–21).

But in many cases all the factors we have discussed—oppression, calamity, responsibility—are tightly merged and intertwined. A person born into a poor community is likely to experience poor health and social pressure to dabble in crime and drugs. He or she may not have literate parents and so enter pre-K at a marked disadvantage for future learning. The schools in these neighborhoods are often of low quality. Some will rightly point to the unjust social systems at play, and others will rightly point to the breakdown of the family. But in any case, we can never fault the children themselves. And so we should show the poor compassion (14:20), never contempt (17:5).

Do you need to confess any ways in which you have believed that the poor have brought their poverty on themselves by their agency alone? What have you deserved at the hands of God for your sins? What have you received?

Prayer: Lord, if you had come to earth in order to save only those who did not bring their spiritual poverty upon themselves, you could have saved yourself a trip! Though we did not ask for your help, or deserve it, you extended it, at great cost. Help me extend my help to people in need in the same way. Amen.

December 3

> Do not withhold good from those to whom it is due, when it is in your power to act. (3:27)

WHAT YOU OWE YOUR NEIGHBOR. The word *good* here refers to tangible material goods. Do you have an elderly acquaintance who can't afford to clean her own house, or neighbors who can't afford college for their kids? If you have more worldly goods, it is your responsibility to share. Why? The phrase *to whom it is due* translates a single Hebrew word that means, simply, the "owners." The needy, then, have some claim on your assets.

The world is God's, and if he has given you more of it to steward than someone else, that does not mean it belongs wholly to you. Like any steward, you must use the true owner's wealth as he wishes it to be used. God loves everything he has made (Psalm 145:9) and especially those who "fall and . . . are bowed down" (Psalm 145:14). To quote Basil the Great (AD 329–79), "The bread which you keep belongs to the hungry; the coats in your closet, to the naked; those shoes . . . to the shoeless; the gold you have hidden . . . to the needy. Therefore, as often as you were able to help others, and refused, so often did you do them wrong."[229]

What possessions of yours belong to others? How will you get them to those people?

Prayer: Father, my culture tells me that my money is all mine. But this day's reflection shows me that is wrong. Drill this truth down into my heart so I can walk in the way of your Son, who scattered his wealth to others with both hands. Amen.

December 4

Do not move an ancient boundary stone or encroach on the fields of the fatherless, for their Defender is strong; he will take up their case against you. (23:10–11)

FATHER TO THE FATHERLESS. It remarkable how often God is introduced as "a father to the fatherless, a defender of widows" (Psalm 68:5). When you are introducing yourself to someone, you ordinarily mention your vocation: "I'm John Doe, and I'm a physician in town." This tells people what you spend most of your time doing in public life. So when God is introduced as *Defender* of the poor, it shows that it is one of the main things he is concerned about in the world.

It is not easy for modern people to realize how revolutionary this was. In ancient societies, the gods were especially identified with the upper classes. People assumed that the elites were the most virtuous and so were divinely blessed with power and wealth. Job's friends believed this too, that God was on the side of the prosperous. How astounding to have a God who instead identified with the powerless and worked for their interests! When Job said that he "rescued . . . the fatherless who had none to assist them" and "made the widow's heart sing," he was simply seeking to imitate God (Job 29:12–13).

Do you know and care for any widows and fatherless? If not, why not?

Prayer: Father, the more I read through your Word, the more struck I am by how often and how strongly you talk about the poor and call us to do justice for them. Lord, help me to love more the things that you love! And show me how I too can be a defender. Amen.

December 5

One who has no sense shakes hands in pledge and puts up security for a neighbor. (17:18)

HELPING THAT DOESN'T HURT. In a society not based on capitalism, the majority of loans were not business investments but given to friends and neighbors to relieve need. In such a situation, while the motivation may be admirable, to give a loan when the neighbor will never be in a position to pay it back shows *no sense*. Many churches have offered loans to poor people from church funds, and when they could not repay, the results were destructive. People in the church felt deceived, and the poor family was shamed and alienated. Better to have made it an outright gift. It is easy, when trying to help those in need, to show no sense, and make things worse.

On a larger scale, there have been well-meaning schemes for helping poor neighborhoods that have led to unsustainable dependency or uncontrolled gentrification and angry people. We must help but not make things worse. Merely throwing money at a problem can soothe your conscience, even if it does more harm than good.

How can you grow in practical wisdom so that your helping does not hurt?

Prayer: Lord, I tell myself I care about the poor, but it hasn't affected my lifestyle or my relationships. I know it takes much wisdom to help in a way that is fruitful—but give me that wisdom and show me those ways. Amen.

December 6

The righteous care about justice for the poor, but the wicked have no such concern. (29:7)

SOCIAL CONCERN. The word *care* translates a Hebrew term that means to search out a matter, to do exhaustive research. The term for *justice* literally is "the claims." To be *righteous,* according to Proverbs is to know the specific kinds of problems and needs that the poor face in your region, as well as their rights, needs, and opportunities. This is far more (though not less) than collecting food or toys for families at holidays.

And here we see that it is not only wrong to directly exploit and trample on the poor. To even simply have *no . . . concern* for the poor, to just fail to pay attention to their needs, is wicked! If you (perhaps) make an occasional contribution to charity but you don't give your mind and heart to furthering justice for the poor in your region and society, you are not one of the righteous. You are too concerned with your own affairs, happiness, and advancement.

Are you, by this definition, righteous? Are you researching for ways to lift up the poor in your community?

Prayer: Lord, "the poor" exist in my mind as a faceless entity, and so I can't begin to know how to help. Send me instead some friends who, with me, can see the faces of actual poor people with concrete needs, so I can see a way forward for answering your call to care about justice. Amen.

December 7

> The poor are shunned even by their neighbors, but the rich have many friends. It is a sin to despise one's neighbor, but blessed is the one who is kind to the needy. . . . Wealth attracts many friends, but even the closest friend of the poor person deserts them. (14:20–21, 19:4)

NEIGHBORING. We seek relationships on a cost-benefit basis. With the rich we want to be as close friends as possible; the poor we don't even want living in our neighborhood (14:20). It hurts real estate values! And relationships with poor people don't benefit us. So they *are shunned*.

Our social systems quarantine the poor. We protect ourselves from the impositions that their needs would bring upon us. We force them to live all together, so that the poor have no neighbors with the resources and connections to be kind to them. This, of course, only deepens poverty. Whole neighborhoods and communities of the poor lack what is called "social capital," the informal networks of friends and colleagues who trust one another and share goodwill and assets by making referrals, offering free advice, opening doors, and entering into partnerships with one another. Again we see that to turn our backs on the poor of our municipalities, avoiding them and maintaining their isolation, is not just being uncharitable. It is a sin (14:20).

With the help of your church, can you partner with a church in a poor neighborhood, listening and learning before leaping into action and becoming their neighbors?

Prayer: Lord, since I was a child I have been inspired by the parable of the Good Samaritan, who loved his needy neighbor. Yet I have no idea how to truly be a neighbor to the poor, rather than just a donor. Show me and my church how to do that wisely yet sacrificially. Amen.

December 8

Do not exploit the poor because they are poor and do not crush the needy in court, for the LORD will take up their case and will exact life for life. (22:22–23)

OPPRESSING THE POOR. If we want to help the poor, we must become aware of the ordinary ways that society *exploits* them. One way is mentioned here: *crush[ing] the needy in court.* The poor who are accused of a crime are far more likely to be convicted and receive greater penalties than others accused of the same things but who have the money to pay for a good legal defense. Governments often are pressured by more well-off neighborhoods to put low-income housing or shelters in already-poor areas, which simply isolates the poor even further (December 7). Banks "redline" poorer communities, making it difficult for individuals or families to get mortgages or business loans. (When one of our pastors moved to a "bad" zip code, his wife found her credit card canceled.) Landlords in the poorest communities can charge a great deal without providing good services because the people of the neighborhood have nowhere else to go.

There are no easy solutions to these problems because they are systemic. These social systems consist of many people who benefit from the exploitation of the poor, but who simply don't ask questions about the social effects, and who would not be able to easily change things if they did. We would be too discouraged to even try to make changes, if we did not know that the Lord *will take up their case* with us.

Do you really believe that God holds you accountable for the systems that oppress the poor? Does your stock portfolio reflect that? Your use of free time and disposable income?

Prayer: Lord, I am a participant in society's systems that push the poor out and keep them down. The things I can do about it will not be dramatic but small. Don't let me "despise the day of small things" (Zechariah 4:10); don't let me think they aren't worth doing. Give me the wisdom to see what they might be. Amen.

December 9

Whoever oppresses the poor shows contempt for their Maker, but whoever is kind to the needy honors God. . . . Whoever is kind to the poor lends to the LORD, and he will reward them for what they have done. . . . Rich and poor have this in common: The LORD is the Maker of them all. (14:31, 19:17, 22:2)

RESPECTING THE POOR. These three proverbs demand deep respect for the poor. If you insult and disdain the poor, you *show contempt* for their creator. If, on the other hand, you are *kind to the poor*, you are being kind to the Lord. Family members know what it is like to be so closely identified with one another that an attack on a spouse, sibling, or child feels exactly like an attack on them. Here God says he's so closely identified with the poor of the earth that whatever we do to them we are doing to him.

Practically, this means we cannot be paternalistic with the poor, seeing them simply as "cases." It is common for well-off people to show charity to the poor in a completely self-serving way. If we give small gifts, we do it to feel good about ourselves; if we give big gifts, we want to have some control over the program. Instead we should respect the poor as persons, expect to learn from them rather than thinking we can simply fix them like a mechanical object.

Do you know any poor people well enough to see and respect how they face their problems?

Prayer: Father, you call us not just to pity the poor but to love and respect them. I confess my patronizing attitudes. I admit how often I have condescended to the needy I've known over the years. But to insult them is to insult you! How you love them! Let this mind be also in me. Amen.

December 10

Whoever shuts their ears to the cry of the poor will also cry out and not be answered. (21:13)

THERE WAS NO ONE TO OBJECT. The sin described is not overt ruthless exploitation of the poor. Rather, the evil is to simply *shut [your] ears to the cry of the poor*. It is to simply be insensitive, to not give the needs of the poor your time or attention. The result will be that some day you *will also cry out and not be answered*. This is not so much a threat as a statement of how the world works. On one level it is obvious—haters are hated, ruthless people are treated ruthlessly, gossips are gossiped about.

But on another level, if we don't create a society that defends the weak, there may be no one left to defend us. So 21:13 predicted what Martin Niemöller said happened in Germany when the Nazis came first for the socialists, then for the Jews and other unwanted citizens, and hardly anyone spoke up. And so "[W]hen they came for me . . . there was no one left to speak for me."[230]

A society is as strong as its care for its weakest members. What can you do to make it possible for you and our whole society to hear the cry of the poor?

Prayer: Lord, all sin is also stupidity, and a society that doesn't care for the poor will ruin itself. Our every-man-for-himself culture is indeed coming apart. Save us, Lord. Ignite a spirit of loyalty to others in our individualistic hearts. Amen.

December 11

A ruler who oppresses the poor is like a driving rain that leaves no crops. . . . If a king judges the poor with fairness, his throne will be established forever. (28:3, 29:14)

PUBLIC POLICY AND THE POOR. The proper function of rain is to make the ground capable of growing things. *A driving rain*, however, can actually do the opposite of what precipitation should do. It can destroy a crop instead of watering it. The implication is that the very purpose and function of government is to do justice, and in particular to protect the poor from being exploited by powerful interests. This also tells us that poverty cannot be addressed fully by private charity but requires, as we have seen, changing social structures and laws. Social reform moves beyond relief of immediate needs and seeks to change social conditions that aggravate or create that need.

Job not only clothed the naked but "broke the fangs of the wicked and snatched the victims from their teeth" (Job 29:17). The prophets denounced unfair wages (Jeremiah 22:13), corrupt business practices (Amos 8:2,6), legal systems weighted in favor of the rich and influential (Deuteronomy 24:17; Leviticus 19:15), and a system of lending capital that gouged the person of modest means (Leviticus 19:35–37, 25:37; Exodus 22:25–27). Daniel calls a pagan government to account for its lack of mercy to the poor (Daniel 4:27).

Citizens often feel helpless to change something as complex as public policy. If you knew God was going to help you succeed, where would you start?

Prayer: Lord, you want all of society's main institutions to take their part in lifting up the poor. It seems like such a huge undertaking! But show me practical ways for moving my family, my church, and my government toward active compassion for those in need. Amen.

December 12

Whoever increases wealth by taking interest or profit from the poor amasses it for another, who will be kind to the poor. (28:8)

BUSINESS PRACTICES AND THE POOR. These texts tell us that poverty cannot be addressed only by private giving and public policy. There are many business practices that must be changed. Many are perfectly legal and yet are not *kind to the poor.* Many people believe that there is nothing wrong with paying employees as little as one can possibly pay them and still retain them—while charging customers as much as one can possibly charge them and retain them—thereby maximizing profits to the greatest degree, as long as you are charitable with your income. But 28:8 says it is wrong to abuse people in that way.

Part of the Mosaic law was the law of gleaning. Farmers were not allowed to gather all their grain but had to leave some of it for the poor to gather (Leviticus 19:9–10, 23:22). This was not "charity"—this was a way to voluntarily limit profit taking and do it in such a way that the poor did not get a handout but were able to work for their food. Gleaning is not directly commanded in the New Testament, because it was simply one way (in an agrarian society) for business practices to address the needs of the poor.

Can you think of a modern adaptation of the law of gleaning?

Prayer: Lord, it is hard for me to think about justice without being pulled into today's partisan fighting over the very definition of it. Help me immerse myself in your Word so I can imperfectly but better see the world through your eyes. Amen.

December 13

Righteousness exalts a nation, but sin condemns any people. (14:34)

JUDGING A NATION. Some say that we can't judge the moral character of a whole nation, especially today, when so many nations are pluralistic and do not share a single religion or set of moral standards. But that is not what Proverbs says. It says that *righteousness exalts a nation*. If we remember that the definition of *righteousness* is to disadvantage oneself to advantage the whole community, then we begin to see how it would be possible to evaluate the heart of a society.

Daniel calls on a pagan king to act justly toward the poor and oppressed (Daniel 4:27; cf. Jonah 3:1–10), and the prophet Amos held pagan rulers accountable—not to a full Christian standard of faith but to a golden-rule standard of justice and fairness (Amos 1–2). In other words, if a nation treats its weakest members with deference and respect, with fairness and compassion, it is exhibiting righteousness.

How are we doing as a nation?

Prayer: Lord, bring my country, by your grace, to be more conformed to your Word in how it practices justice on the earth. Amen.

December 14

The righteous care for the needs of their animals, but the kindest acts of the wicked are cruel. (12:10)

KIND TO ALL THINGS. This proverb says that loving and caring for *animals* is a mark of being righteous. Deuteronomy 25:4, for example, requires that farmers "not muzzle an ox while it is treading out the grain." When farmers used oxen to drag sledges over the sheaves of grain, to sever the grain from the stalks, they often put a muzzle on the animals so they didn't eat any of the grain and thereby diminish the farmer's profits. But God commands that the farmers share the grain with their animals, that they show kindness to them. Even animals are not to be exploited to maximize profits.

Indeed, Deuteronomy 20:19 goes so far as to warn soldiers that besieging a city, "Do not destroy its trees by putting an axe to them. . . . Are the trees people, that you should besiege them?" Believers have been recipients of mercy and grace and new life, so our instinct should be to be merciful to everything. And we want to be like our Lord, who "has compassion on all he has made" and "satisfies the desires of every living thing" (Psalm 145:9,16).

Care for our natural world and everything in it should be a hallmark of believers. In what way do you demonstrate your care for God's creation?

Prayer: Lord, "man with dog closes a gap in the universe,"[231] meaning that you created us to be keepers and lovers of the non-human world. We are not to worship nature but to worship you by caring for it. Show me ways and give me opportunities to do that. Amen.

KNOWING JESUS,
THE TRUE WISDOM OF GOD

December 15

> When the Sabbath came, he began to teach in the synagogue, and many who heard him were amazed. "Where did this man get these things?" they asked. "What's this wisdom that has been given him? What are these remarkable miracles he is performing?" (Mark 6:2)

THE ULTIMATE TEACHER. Job's friends didn't see how God could be perfectly just and yet bless imperfect sinners. Their lack of wisdom came from not understanding the gospel. To the Pharisees—the "Job's friends" of his day—Jesus answered. God can be just and a justifier of believers (Romans 3:26) because he was our substitute (Mark 10:45). "The essence of sin is we human beings substituting ourselves for God, while the essence of salvation is God substituting himself for us. We . . . put ourselves where only God deserves to be"—in charge of our lives—while "God . . . puts himself where we deserve to be"—that is, being punished on the cross.[232]

So Jesus was the ultimate teacher of wisdom. Like Proverbs 2:1-5 he too presents "two paths" (2:1–5 and Matthew 7:13–14), but he shows that the path to life is the gospel. This explains how we can at once be both sinners deserving punishment and God's children under his care. Martin Luther summarized the gospel as *simul justus et peccator*—in Christ we are simultaneously spiritually lost sinners yet fully justified in God's sight and loved.

How does the gospel produce the "fear of the Lord"?

Prayer: Lord Jesus, the more I contemplate the gospel—how I am sinful yet fully loved—the more I love you with fear and trembling. The gospel answers so many of the deepest riddles. I praise you for its infinite wisdom. Amen.

December 16

> The Queen of the South will rise at the judgment with the people of this generation and condemn them, for she came from the ends of the earth to listen to Solomon's wisdom; and now something greater than Solomon is here. (Luke 11:31)

THE BETTER SOLOMON. Proverbs was assembled by Solomon. Solomon said to wait for God to punish the wrongdoer (24:12), but Jesus took their punishment himself. Solomon said that God is a defender of the oppressed (23:10–11), but Jesus came to become a victim of injustice and stand in the very place of the oppressed. Solomon calls us to write his teaching on our hearts (3:3), but Jesus sends his Spirit to write God's word on our hearts (2 Corinthians 3:3).

Solomon calls us to exercise our wills to obey (1:20–21), but Jesus sends his Spirit to enable us to both want and do obedience (Romans 8:1–8). Solomon paints a picture of the ideal king (16:10–15), but Jesus is the true King (Matthew 27:37). Solomon failed to obey his own wisdom (1 Kings 11:9–10) and put a heavy yoke on people (1 Kings 12:4), but Jesus is the perfect example of God's wisdom (Luke 2:52, Hebrews 4:15) and died to free us from all enslaving yokes (Matthew 11:28–30).[233] Jesus is the better Solomon.

Can you think of any other ways Jesus fills out and completes the wisdom of Proverbs?

Prayer: Father, when I see your Son standing behind the Proverbs, taking my punishment for failing to obey them, and promising to heal my heart with his gospel and Spirit so I can more and more follow them, I find myself eager to read and apply them. How wise your salvation is! Amen.

December 17

"For John came neither eating nor drinking, and they say, 'He has a demon.' The Son of Man came eating and drinking, and they say, 'Here is a glutton and a drunkard, a friend of tax collectors and sinners.' But wisdom is proved right by her deeds." (Matthew 11:18–19)

WISDOM IN PERSON. In Proverbs 8 wisdom is depicted as an actual person with whom God created the world. Also in Proverbs 1–9 God's wisdom is personified as a woman whom we must know personally if we are to live a wise life. And here Jesus makes a remarkable reference to his wisdom and then speaks of wisdom as "her," thereby identifying himself with God's wisdom in Proverbs.

Colossians 1:15–17 and John 1:1–6 tell us that it was Jesus himself who was present with the Father at creation. And as Woman Wisdom offers her disciples food and drink (9:1–3), so Jesus offers himself as the Christian's food and drink (John 6:53). In short, as Proverbs calls all people to become wise by entering into a relationship with the wisdom that created the world, so the gospel calls all people to get the consummate wisdom, the gospel and the indwelling Spirit of God, through a relationship with Jesus Christ.

See how *personal* Christianity is, for its deepest secret of wisdom comes not through massive learning and education but through an intimate relationship with a humble man who was as willing to identify with a wise woman as with Solomon and the kings of old.

Prayer: Lord Jesus, if you had stayed in heaven, you would have been a glorious abstraction. But in the pages of the gospel I see perfect holiness in human form. I long for closer personal intimacy with you. Speak to me through your Word. Be real to me in prayer. Amen.

December 18

"Come to me, all you who are weary and burdened, and I will give you rest. Take my yoke upon you and learn from me, for I am gentle and humble in heart, and you will find rest for your souls. For my yoke is easy and my burden is light." (Matthew 11:28–30)

WISDOM AND REST. In Jewish writings God's wisdom is depicted as calling people to take on wisdom's yoke and to get the rest of soul that comes to the wise.[234] Fools are wise in their own eyes—and so they are always chafing because they feel they are not getting respect, or not getting their due. They also want instant gratification. In all these ways a lack of wisdom means a lack of restfulness and contentment.

When Jesus calls us to take on his yoke and come to *him* for rest, he is saying, "*I* am the true wisdom." Do you want the ultimate rest? Only when you see Jesus dying on the cross for your sins can you lay down the ultimate burden, of trying to prove and justify yourself, of trying to earn your self-worth and salvation. The gospel of the cross is the only true wisdom that will give you this rest. "Lay your deadly doing down—down at Jesus' feet. Stand in him, in him alone, gloriously complete."[235]

Jesus' yoke is easy and his burden is light, or so he tells us. Anything else in the world will enslave you. Have you willingly enslaved yourself to something other than Jesus?

Prayer: Lord, I am weary, and I blame how hard I'm working, but it is more of an inward, spiritual condition. I am working to prove myself, to win approval, to make a name for myself. I am ready to lay down that burden and receive the deep rest that comes from the gospel. Help me to do that. Amen.

December 19

The Son is the image of the invisible God, the firstborn over all creation. For in him all things were created: things in heaven and on
earth, visible and invisible, whether thrones or powers or rulers or
authorities; all things have been created through him and for him. He
is before all things, and in him all things hold together. (Colossians
1:15–17)

THE TRUE KING. A department will be in disarray and un-
productive until a good executive is appointed. Then, under her
management, everything "holds together" and people thrive and
are productive. The same happens to a sports franchise under a
good coach or to a government under a great elected leader. We
all know that leadership heals what is broken by uniting what
was fragmented.

In Jesus, the true wisdom through whom the world was created, things *hold together*. When the world was created and fully
under the divine lordship, all was paradise. Because of the rebellion of sin, the order of creation is disrupted and we now have
disorder and death. Jesus defeated sin and death on the cross and
someday will return to heal the world completely. Outside of
Jesus is chaos and disorder. To choose that instead of choosing
to be under the lordship of the one who created you and all
things is folly. To the degree you are under Jesus' lordship, you
will grow in wisdom and see your life being healed.

Inside each of our sinful hearts is a desire for no rules, no master. Thank Jesus that we have not found what we were looking for.

Prayer: Lord Jesus, there is a part of my heart that desires a
king to guide and protect me, and another part that fears and
resents such authority over me. But you are the true King my
soul desires, one altogether trustworthy and lovely because of
your sacrifice for me. I kneel to you. Command my heart. Amen.

December 20

My goal is that they may be encouraged in heart and united in love, so that they may have the full riches of complete understanding, in order that they may know the mystery of God, namely, Christ, in whom are hidden all the treasures of wisdom and knowledge. (Colossians 2:2–3)

TREASURE CHEST. Jesus is not like other teachers, whose principles we simply memorize and try to live by. Rather, infinite treasures of wisdom and knowledge are *in* him. The wisdom of Christ comes as much through communing with him in our hearts as through studying him with our minds.

In 2 Corinthians 3:18 we are told that to "contemplate [his] glory" actually makes us like him. Proverbs tells the wise to have courage and forgive others. But courage is best developed as we, in love and wonder, reflect on Jesus' courage in going to the cross for us, and a forgiving spirit is best produced in us truly as we joyfully think of Jesus forgiving us on the cross. So true wisdom is not a set of principles but a supernatural person. And we receive this wisdom not simply through acts of the will but through the transformation of our heart and desires by worshipping him.

Proverbs constantly insists that wisdom takes time to develop, and this makes sense if wisdom is a person and we have to learn how he thinks, what his attitudes are, and what actions would please him. Will you make the time to know Jesus in his Word and become wise?

Prayer: Lord Jesus, I have so little idea of what it really means to "contemplate [your] glory" (2 Corinthians 3:18), but I now ask you to teach me. I will try to do it, but I feel like a child learning to speak his first words. I pray Moses's prayer: "Show me your glory." Amen.

December 21

For the message of the cross is foolishness to those who are perishing, but to us who are being saved it is the power of God. . . . Jews demand signs and Greeks look for wisdom, but we preach Christ crucified: a stumbling block to Jews and foolishness to Gentiles, but to those whom God has called, both Jews and Greeks, Christ the power of God and the wisdom of God. For the foolishness of God is wiser than human wisdom, and the weakness of God is stronger than human strength. (1 Corinthians 1:18,22–25)

CHRIST'S FOOLISHNESS: PART 1. This passage is an extended reflection on an important truth, namely, that Christ's wisdom is not the world's common sense. To the world the gospel seems unrealistic, the very opposite of wisdom. Salvation by the cross is the gospel, but the default mode of the human heart is to want to earn our own salvation. Proverbs, taken out of the context of the whole Bible, could be read as a way to do that.

But the cross shows the upside-down nature of divine wisdom. The way up is down. The way to lead is to serve. The way to get happiness is to seek happiness not for yourself but for others. The way to be truly rich is to give wealth away. To the world all these practices seem foolish, but the cross shows them to be ultimate reality. When applied to daily life, they are consummate wisdom. And of course, divine wisdom begins with giving yourself completely to Jesus as he has given himself to you. To the world that looks like a kind of suicide, but it is the way to life.

Where have you seen "the foolishness of Christ" turn out to be great wisdom?

Prayer: Lord, how wise you were in your creation of the world. But, if possible, the wisdom of your redemption is even more stunning, as the cross made it possible for you to be perfectly holy yet love us—to be both just and justifier of those who believe (Romans 3:26). Who can praise your wisdom enough? Amen.

December 22

Brothers and sisters, think of what you were when you were called. Not many of you were wise by human standards; not many were influential; not many were of noble birth. But God chose the foolish things of the world to shame the wise; God chose the weak things of the world to shame the strong. God chose the lowly things of this world and the despised things—and the things that are not—to nullify the things that are, so that no one may boast before him. (1 Corinthians 1:26–29)

CHRIST'S FOOLISHNESS: PART 2. Great people are wise and influential, wealthy and accomplished by human standards. But God deliberately chooses people the world dismisses to show how his salvation works. The "Gideon principle" (Judges 6:15) is that God chooses the weakest and least likely to succeed, so that all glory is clearly his and does not come through the agency of men and women.

This is also a biblical "Peter principle." Of the eleven surviving disciples, Peter failed most egregiously during Jesus' arrest and execution. Yet in John 21 Jesus forgives him and makes him the leader. It is as if Jesus said, "Because you have been the biggest failure, you have the potential to be the greatest leader. Plunge your failures into my grace and it will make you both astonishingly bold and profoundly humble at the same time—and so profoundly wise." The Christian's identity is rooted in God's grace and regard rather than in any worldly factors. And that brings an enormous freedom.

Are you weak enough for God to use? Will you let him use your weakness to make you wise?

Prayer: Father, the sight of your Son dying because of me, for me, is both convicting and wonderful, and that changes me at the core of my being. "With pleasing grief, and mournful joy, my spirit now is fill'd; That I should such a life destroy, yet live by Him I kill'd!"[236] Amen.

December 23

It is because of him that you are in Christ Jesus, who has become for us wisdom from God—that is, our righteousness, holiness and redemption. Therefore, as it is written: "Let the one who boasts boast in the Lord." (1 Corinthians 1:30–31)

CHRIST'S FOOLISHNESS: PART 3. Here Paul ties true wisdom tightly to a strong grasp of how Jesus is our advocate and substitute. We are in Christ Jesus. And we do not get there by accumulating our own righteousness, holiness, and redemption. Rather, Jesus becomes for us these things. When the Father sees us, he loves us as if we had done everything Jesus had done. He loves us "even as" he loves his Son (John 17:23).

Do you know that Jesus lived a perfect, righteous, and wise life *for* you, so God embraces and accepts you fully and loves you infinitely for Jesus' sake? That gives you what you need to become wise yourself. You don't have to constantly prove yourself to others as the fools and mockers do. You can't be wise in your own eyes because you know you are a sinner saved by grace. And you won't try to find your heart's rest in riches, or in your work, or in sexual, romantic love—because in Christ you have the ultimate riches and love. The requirements for wisdom are found through faith in the gospel.

Do you feel rich? (In Christ, you are.)

Prayer: Lord, I am spiritually rich but I live poor in fears and resentments. Your gospel "is like a deep, deep mine; and jewels rich and rare are hidden in its mighty depths for every searcher there."[237] Help me to use its riches in my everyday life. Amen.

December 24

A wise son brings joy to his father, but a foolish son brings grief to his mother. (Proverbs 10:1) He came to that which was his own, but his own did not receive him. Yet to all who did receive him, to those who believed in his name, he gave the right to become children of God—children born not of natural descent, nor of human decision or a husband's will, but born of God. (John 1:11–12)

CHRIST'S FAMILY. Proverbs constantly tells the wise to honor parents, but family relations are often difficult. We may be overly dependent on our parents' approval, or we may be too angry at and bitter toward our parents for failing us. Or we may have destructively foolish parents who are difficult to love.

For each case, we have seen (October 13) we need the assurance of God's perfect parental love. That frees us from being either overly dependent on or overly angry at our parents. How do we get this? Because Jesus experienced the loss of the love of his Father—on the cross—we can be adopted into God's family (John 1:12–13). When his mother and brothers came to see him (and take him home, because he was embarrassing them), Jesus said that his mother and brothers and sisters were those who did the will of the Father (Mark 3:31–35). That was not a metaphor. Hebrews says he is not ashamed to call us his brothers (Hebrews 2:11), for we are all children of God (Galatians 3:26). Your family of origin may be great, or not so great, but the family you have been adopted into, with God as your Father and Jesus as your older brother, is the greatest.

How has knowing God is your Father been of practical benefit for you?

Prayer: Father, I praise you that the one who made the whole universe and upholds it by a Word of your power—would be my Father. Your infinite majesty and might are all now in service of your gentle, fatherly love. Give me the endless rest and joy that should come from knowing this. Amen.

December 25

"I am the LORD your God, who brought you out of Egypt, out of the land of slavery. You shall have no other gods before me." (Exodus 20: 2–3) Folly is an unruly woman. . . . But little do they know that the dead are there, that her guests are deep in the realm of the dead. (9:13,18)

KEEP YOURSELF FROM IDOLS. Tremper Longman makes the case that if Woman Wisdom in Proverbs 1–9 ultimately points to Jesus, then Woman Folly represent idols and idolatry.[238] The first of the Ten Commandments is "I am the Lord your God. . . . You shall have no other gods before me." Either you worship God or you will be worshipping something else—there is not the alternative of not worshipping. Either you will be looking to God for your significance and security or you will be looking to something else (even if it is your own abilities).

From a New Testament perspective, everyone looks to something to justify him- or herself. Either we let Jesus be our wisdom, righteousness, holiness, and redemption—and are saved by faith in him—or we look to something else to be that, and we are saved by works. So true wisdom is to accept salvation by grace, and the heart of folly is to try to save yourself. The gospel is the consummate wisdom.

Oh, the riches of wisdom available to us! Praise the one who came as a baby and who will come again in strength and power.

Prayer: Father, "The dearest idol I have known, whate'er that idol be—help me to tear it from thy throne, and worship only thee. Then shall my walk be close with thee, and calm shall be my frame; So purer light shall mark the road that leads me to the Lamb."[239] Amen.

December 26

Whoever is kind to the poor lends to the LORD, and he will reward them for what they have done. (Proverbs 19:17) For you know the grace of our Lord Jesus Christ, that though he was rich, yet for your sake he became poor, so that you through his poverty might become rich. (2 Corinthians 8:9)

CHRIST'S POVERTY. Proverbs constantly shows us that God identifies with the poor (December 9). To disdain the poor is to disdain the Lord (14:31), and to lend to the poor is to lend to the Lord (19:17). But it is only in the New Testament that we see how much God identified with the poor. In Jesus Christ he literally became a poor man. He was born in an animals' feed trough, he grew up without money, he had his last supper in a borrowed room, and he was buried in a borrowed grave. His only possession was his garment. He was also the victim of injustice.

Why did he do it? Jesus became poor, taking our punishment, so that we could get the eternal spiritual riches. Jesus took the condemnation we deserved so we could get vindication. Proverbs tells us we must care for the poor—and that is wise. But we will never embrace the poor with love and respect for them until we see that we were spiritually poor and we live only by God's grace.

How will you remember and care for the poor in the name of the one who was born in a manger for you?

Prayer: Lord, I live in a society that loudly proclaims its concern for the poor and oppressed, but few of us become personally involved with their plight or give much more than a token of time and money. Give me the grace to be different, in light of your love for those who do not have the world's goods. Amen.

December 27

Blessed are the poor in spirit, for theirs is the kingdom of heaven. (Matthew 5:3)

GENEROSITY. Jesus' Sermon on the Mount (Matthew 5–7) is a reissuing of the book of Proverbs. Like Proverbs, Jesus is taking the principles of the Ten Commandments and applying them to the practical matters of daily life (Matthew 5:17). Proverbs was assembled by and for Solomon, who could only urge us to follow his rules. But in Jesus, the true Solomon, we have one who has fulfilled the rules of wisdom for us, and now, knowing that, and through faith in him, we can live into the wisdom of God.

This is seen in the opening verses of the sermon—the Beatitudes. Each of them calls us to something, yet we can answer the call only because Jesus has already fulfilled each of them for us. Begin with the first. We are called to be poor in spirit—both spiritually humble ourselves, and committed to the poor of the world. If we do that, we will be truly rich—*for theirs is the kingdom of heaven.* But Christians know that we will be rich as kings only because Jesus became poor, spiritually and utterly poor, for us. Knowing that humbles us into being truly poor in spirit and generous to all in need.

No one is a believer unless you're poor in spirit. How has God brought this condition into your life?

Prayer: Lord, "But drops of grief can ne'er repay the debt of love I owe; Here Lord, I give myself away: 'Tis all that I can do."[240] Amen.

December 28

Blessed are those who mourn, for they will be comforted. (Matthew 5:4)

ADVERSITY. The wisdom literature calls the wise to be patient in suffering. And the second Beatitude tells us that if we mourn, God will comfort us. But this is not just a promise for some generic spiritual strength to be communicated to us from heaven. It is through God's salvation we are promised "peace . . . like a river" and that "as a mother comforts her child, so will I comfort you; and you shall be comforted" (Isaiah 66:12–13).

But why can you and I be so assured of such infallible comfort? In ourselves we don't deserve it. It is only because Jesus mourned, because he was a "man of suffering, and familiar with pain" (Isaiah 53:3), because he wept inconsolably and died in the dark for us, that we can be comforted. The tears of Jesus are the deepest consolation possible. See him weeping at the tomb of his friend Lazarus (John 11:35), even though he knows he is about to raise him from the dead. And so, even though he will eventually raise us up, he is still moved by our suffering in this life. Proverbs calls us to be strong in adversity, but the gospel gives us what we need to do so.

Recall a time in which God comforted you when you were mourning.

Prayer: Lord, I don't want suffering in my life, and I know you don't want me to have its pain either. Yet the various comforts you give me in my trials change me in ways I would never want to lose. I don't thank you for the evils that have hurt me, but I praise you with the ways you make me more happy and holy through them. Amen.

December 29

Blessed are the meek, for they will inherit the earth. (Matthew 5:5)

INHERIT THE EARTH. Proverbs says that right living will bring blessedness—*shalom* and flourishing. It says that the righteous will never be uprooted (10:30 cf. Psalm 37:29). But we know that we can't be as righteous as we ought to be. Even here we are told that the meek—the humble and lowly—will inherit the earth. But none of us is perfectly like that either. Nevertheless we can be blessed and inherit the earth. How is that possible? It is because Jesus became meek. He says that he is "meek and lowly in heart" (Matthew 11:29 KJV).

But it was at the end of his life that he became "gentle," riding on a donkey rather than a warhorse (Matthew 21:5). He was like a lamb being led to the slaughter, yet he did not even open his mouth (Isaiah 53:7). He was stripped of everything; they cast lots for his garment. But because of his perfect, saving meekness, if we believe in him, we will inherit a new heaven and new earth (Romans 8:18–21).

Where have you seen an example of the quiet, kind, and meek person inheriting honor and power?

Prayer: Lord Jesus, you taught us that the way up is down, that the way to be rich is to give away. That seems stupid to the world, but I constantly see that it is the meek who in the end have the most power and influence. In my daily life I tend to grab for power rather than serving. Help me be meek, as you were. Amen.

December 30

Blessed are those who hunger and thirst for righteousness, for they will be filled. (Matthew 5:6)

RIGHTEOUSNESS. Proverbs calls the wise to seek righteousness, of course. But no one knows how bad they are until they try very, very hard to be good. Anyone who thinks of themselves as righteous in themselves not only is deluded but also has no idea what it really is. But the call to thirst after righteousness remains. Is it hopeless? Not at all. Paul says we can be filled with a righteousness from God that comes, perfect but unmerited, through faith (Romans 3:21–22; Philippians 3:9).

And how can we be filled? It is only because on the cross Jesus said, "I am thirsty" (John 19:28). Jesus was treated as the unrighteous deserve so we can get the treatment that only the righteous deserve (2 Corinthians 5:21). When I realize that through Jesus I'm already accepted, that changes my motivation for righteous living. Now I don't obey God merely because I have to, in order to get things from him. I obey also because I *want* to, to please, know, and resemble the one who gave me a free salvation.

Have you moved from obeying God solely out of duty toward obeying him out of desire and love?

Prayer: Lord, once I tried to serve you only out of duty. Later I lived to serve myself. Both were paths filled with thorns. Only now, in small ways, am I experiencing the unique motivation of serving you out of love and gratitude for a free salvation. It is an energy that does not exhaust me. Grow it in my heart! Amen.

December 31

Blessed are the merciful, for they will be shown mercy. Blessed are the pure in heart, for they will see God. Blessed are the peacemakers, for they will be called children of God. (Matthew 5:7–9)

EVERYTHING YOU NEED. Proverbs tells us to be merciful to our enemies (25:21). We can't forgive someone if we feel superior to them, if we think we have no sin. But in the gospel our hearts are humbled out of our pride. Why will we be shown mercy from God? Only because Jesus in his death got none: not from Pilate, not from the crowd, not even from his Father. When we see that, we can be merciful to others.

Why will we someday be able to see God? Because he was perfectly pure in heart, without sin (Hebrews 4:15). We will someday see God face-to-face because on the cross Jesus lost the face of his Father. Why will we have peace? Only because the whole world, including his Father, warred against Jesus Christ, attacking him. There is no peace for the wicked (Isaiah 48:22), and on the cross Jesus got what we deserved so we could have the eternal peace that he earned for us. And that, of course, equips us to be peacemakers.

In Jesus we receive everything we need to live in wisdom. Do you know him? Do you desire to be wise?

Prayer: Lord, I have learned that wisdom is only a by-product of wanting something more than wisdom—to see God! Aim at knowing you, and you get wisdom thrown in. Aim just at wisdom—in order to be successful—and you get neither. At last I see it. It took me long enough. I praise you for your patience with me. Amen.

ACKNOWLEDGMENTS

As usual we have many people to thank. First and foremost, we thank our patient editor at Viking, Brian Tart. After having completed a yearlong devotional on the Psalms, we thought that doing the same kind of book on Proverbs would take exactly the same amount of time and effort. It did not. Each proverb had to be analyzed, then categorized, then meditated on, and finally selected and arranged in a good order for reading and learning. When we finally faced the inescapable fact of how much time and energy it required, Brian rearranged schedules and made it work. Thanks for being long-suffering, Brian. (There's a proverb about that.)

As always, many friends upheld us in the most practical ways as we wrote this devotional book. Again we worked while being hosted at The Fisherbeck by Ray and Gill Lane in Ambleside, Cumbria, UK. This time Jane and Brian McGreevy went above and beyond the call of duty to help us with our South Carolina writing and travel. And we spent two great weeks working on the manuscript at Janice Worth's home in Florida. Thanks also to Lynn Land, Liz Santiago, Graham and Laurie Howell, and all the others who supported us in ways large and small.

Tim first learned to understand Proverbs through a little commentary by Derek Kidner, and his continued indebtedness to that volume is evident in the endnotes. Perhaps the two best and most substantial commentaries on Proverbs today are those by Tremper Longman and Bruce Waltke, great biblical scholars with whom Tim had the honor of serving on the faculty of Westminster Theological Seminary in the 1980s.

Finally, we want to thank our agent, David McCormick, who has now given us his wise and encouraging counsel for nearly a decade. Thanks for everything, David.

NOTES

1. Raymond C. Van Leeuwen, "The Book of Proverbs," in *The New Interpreter's Bible*, vol. 5 (Nashville: Abingdon, 1997), p. 27.
2. Derek Kidner, *The Proverbs: An Introduction and Commentary* (Downers Grove, Ill.: InterVarsity Press, 1972), p. 176.
3. Bruce Waltke, *The Book of Proverbs: Chapters 1–15* (Grand Rapids, Mich.: Wm. B. Eerdmans, 2004), p. 117.
4. Ibid.
5. Bruce Waltke, *Book of Proverbs: Chapters 15–31*, (Grand Rapids, Mich.: Wm. B. Eerdmans, 2005), p. 532.
6. "There are details of character small enough to escape the mesh of the law . . . and [be] yet decisive in personal dealings." Kidner, *Proverbs*, p. 13.
7. Marcel Proust, *In Search of Lost Time*, vol. 2, *Within a Budding Grove*. C. K. S. Moncreiff and T. Kilmartin, trans. (London: Chatto and Windus, 1922), p. 513. Quoted in Jonathan Haidt, *The Happiness Hypothesis: Finding Modern Truth in Ancient Wisdom* (Cambridge, Mass.: Basic Books, 2006), p. 152.
8. Kidner, *Proverbs*, p. 37.
9. Ibid., p. 310.
10. See Kidner's study of "The Scoffer," in *Proverbs* at pp. 41–42, and Waltke's study of "The Mocker," in *Book of Proverbs: Chapters 1–15*, p. 114.
11. C. S. Lewis, *The Abolition of Man* (New York: Collier Books, 1955), p. 81.
12. See Waltke, *Book of Proverbs: Chapters 1–15*, p. 528.
13. Winifred Gallagher, "How We Become What We Are," *The Atlantic*, September 1994, available at www.theatlantic.com/magazine/archive/1994/09/how-we-become-what-we-are/303534/.
14. These could be summarized as the options of (a) retreat, (b) attack, or (c) win through diplomacy. Kagan's argument is that each of us is born with a temperament that makes one of these instinctive and, therefore, we are prone to use it in situations where it is not practical and can even be destructive.
15. Kidner, *Proverbs*, p. 39.
16. J. D. Vance, *Hillbilly Elegy: A Memoir of a Family and Culture in Crisis* (New York: HarperCollins, 2016), pp. 6–7.
17. Kidner, *Proverbs*, p. 60.
18. Ibid.
19. Albert Camus, "The Wind at Djemila," in *Albert Camus*, ed. Harold Bloom, Bloom's BioCritiques (Philadelphia: Chelsea House, 2003), p. 59.
20. The first clause is Bruce Waltke's translation. See Waltke, *Book of Proverbs: Chapters 1–15*, p. 467.
21. W. McKane, quoted in ibid., p. 114.
22. Waltke, *Book of Proverbs: Chapters 1–15*, p. 97.
23. Van Leeuwen, "Book of Proverbs," p. 38.
24. This is my own free translation of this verse.
25. John Newton, *The Works of the Rev. John Newton*, vol. 1 (Edinburgh: Banner of Truth, 1985), p. 585.
26. Van Leeuwen, "Book of Proverbs," p. 40.
27. Proverbs 3:10 observes that, in general, a generous spirit tends to lead to more prosperity. Some people see this as an absolute promise that the more

you give away your money, the more money you will make. But that is to misunderstand the character of a proverb, which is an observation of how life generally goes in the world. Derek Kidner writes, "If it [verse 10] were more than a generalization (as Job's comforters held), God would not be so much honored, but invested in, by our gifts." But, as we will see tomorrow, adversity can bring "better prizes than prosperity." Kidner, *Proverbs*, p. 64.

28. Van Leeuwen, "Book of Proverbs," p. 50.

29. For an extended case for interpreting these verses in this way, see Waltke, *Book of Proverbs: Chapters 1–15*, pp. 266–67.

30. John T. McNeill, ed., *Calvin: Institutes of the Christian Religion*, trans. Ford Lewis Battles, Library of Christian Classics, vol. 22 (Philadelphia: Westminster, 1960), p. 696.

31. Kidner, *Proverbs*, p. 77.

32. Quoted in Waltke, *Book of Proverbs: Chapters 1–15*, p. 401.

33. Kidner, *Proverbs*, p. 77.

34. Ibid.

35. This is why it could be said that any thriving civil order (verse 16) or economy (verse 18) deploys at least some of the elements of wisdom. It is "indispensable . . . for civil or social order." Van Leeuwen, "Book of Proverbs," p. 91.

36. J. R. R. Tolkien, *The Fellowship of the Ring* (1954; repr., New York: Houghton Mifflin, 2004), p. 468.

37. Thomas Cranmer, "Collect for the Fifth Sunday After Trinity" in Paul F. M. Zahl and C. Frederick Barbee, *The Collects of Thomas Cranmer* (Grand Rapids, Mich.: Wm. B. Eerdmans, 2006), p. 78.

38. See Jonathan Edwards, "Beauty of the World" and "Images of Divine Things," in *A Jonathan Edwards Reader*, ed. John E. Smith, Harry S. Stout, and Kenneth P. Minkema (New Haven, Conn.: Yale University Press, 1995), pp. 14–21. Edwards's theory of beauty is that beauty consists mainly in seeing relationships between things. This, he believed, was based on creation being done not by a unipersonal divine being but by a triune God who consists of intimate relationships. It is because there was more than one divine person involved in creation—in relationship as creation occurred—that we long for and delight in relationships. See also Belden C. Lane, "Jonathan Edwards on Beauty, Desire, and the Sensory World," *Theological Studies* 65 (2004): 44–72.

39. Oliver O'Donovan writes: "Wisdom is the intellectual apprehension of the order of things which discloses how each being stands in relation to each other. . . . 'Delight' is the affective attention to something simply for what it is and for the fact that it is." Quoted in Van Leeuwen, "Book of Proverbs," p. 99.

40. Ibid., p. 104.

41. Isaac Watts, "The Hill of Zion" (hymn), 1707.

42. Kidner, *Proverbs*, p. 83.

43. Van Leeuwen, "Book of Proverbs," p. 104.

44. Christian Smith, *Lost in Transition: The Dark Side of Emerging Adulthood* (Oxford, UK: Oxford University Press, 2011).

45. See Derek Kidner, "Subject Study: Life and Death," in *Proverbs*, pp. 53–56.

46. John Murray points out, "The fear of God which is the soul of godliness does not consist . . . in the dread which is produced by the apprehension of God's wrath. . . . The dread of judgment will never of itself generate within us the love of God or hatred of the sin. . . . Even the infliction of wrath will . . . [only] incite to greater love of sin and enmity against God. Punishment has of itself

no regenerating or converting power. The fear of God in which godliness consists is the fear that constrains adoration and love. It is the fear which consists in awe, reverence, honor, and worship." J. Murray, *Principles of Conduct* (Grand Rapids, Mich.: Wm. B. Eerdmans, 1957), pp. 236–37.

47. The quote is from John Calvin, who in *Institutes* 1.2.2. writes: "This mind restrains itself from sinning, not out of dread of punishment alone; but because it loves and reveres God as Father, it worships and adores him as Lord. Even if there were no hell, it would still shudder at offending him alone." See J. T. McNeill, ed., *Calvin: Institutes of the Christian Religion*, trans. Ford Lewis Battles, Library of Christian Classics, vol. 20 (Philadelphia: Westminster, 1960), p. 43.

48. The two aspects of the fear of the Lord can be seen in places where it is treated as a synonym. In Psalm 19 "the fear of the Lord" is a synonym for the law, statutes, precepts, commands, and decrees of the Lord (Psalm 19:7–9). So to fear God is to recognize God as an authoritative law giver; it is to say, "Thy will, not mine, be done." In Deuteronomy the fear of God and the love of God are often used interchangeably to express the kind of motives that should empower our obedience (Deuteronomy 5:29, 6:2,5, 10:12). So the "fear of the Lord" is obedience out of love of God for who he is in himself; it is loving him for himself alone. See Waltke, *Book of Proverbs: Chapters 1–15*, pp. 100–101 on "The Fear of the Lord."

49. Kidner, *Proverbs*, p. 110.

50. Walter C. Smith, "Immortal, Invisible God Only Wise," 1876.

51. Tremper Longman, *Proverbs: Baker Commentary on the Old Testament Wisdom and Psalms* (Grand Rapids, Mich.: Baker Academic, 2006), p. 328.

52. Kidner, *Proverbs*, p. 32.

53. Ibid., p. 146.

54. Miroslav Volf, *Exclusion and Embrace: A Theological Exploration of Identity, Otherness, and Reconciliation* (Nashville: Abingdon, 1996), pp. 303–4.

55. What does "holy" mean? Many think of it as "moral," but were the angels crying "Moral, moral, moral is the Lord!" in Isaiah 6? "At its core, *holy* is almost an adjective corresponding to the noun "God." God is God. God is holy. He is unique; there is no other. Then, derivatively, that which belongs exclusively to him is . . . holy." D. A. Carson, "April 8," in *For the Love of God: A Daily Companion for Discovering the Riches of God's Word*, vol. 1 (Wheaton, Ill.: Crossway Books, 1998), n.p.

56. Consider reading R. C. Sproul, *The Holiness of God*, 2nd rev. ed. (Wheaton, Ill.: Tyndale House, 2000).

57. Derek Kidner, quoted in Waltke, *Book of Proverbs: Chapters 1–15*, pp. 407–8.

58. See Longman, *Proverbs*, pp. 82–86, for an excellent discussion of this subject. This day's devotional is largely taken from it.

59. Lesslie Newbigin, *Sin and Salvation* (Eugene, Oreg.: Wipf and Stock Publishers, 2009), pp.11–15.

60. Kidner, *Proverbs*, p. 80.

61. Ibid.

62. "This better-than saying limits the status of wealthy by placing wisdom and righteousness above it." Van Leeuwen, "Book of Proverbs," p. 197.

63. Ibid., p. 114.

64. See Graeme Goldsworthy, *Gospel and Wisdom* in The Goldsworthy Trilogy (Carlisle, UK: Paternoster, 2001). This understanding of God's order

perceived (in Proverbs), confused and disrupted (in Ecclesiastes), and hidden (in Job) is laid out by Goldsworthy on pp. 409–58. These terms I employ are his. See also Longman, "Proverbs in Conversation with Job and Ecclesiastes," in *How to Read Proverbs* (Downers Grove, Ill.: InterVarsity Press, 2002), pp. 79–91.

65. Helen Wilcox, ed., *The English Poems of George Herbert* (Cambridge, UK: Cambridge University Press, 2007), p. 102.

66. Longman, *Proverbs*, p. 62.

67. Tolkien, *Fellowship of the Ring*, p. 146.

68. The opening words of each episode of the *Cosmos* television series, hosted by Carl Sagan, were "The cosmos is all that is or ever was or ever will be."

69. Thomas Cranmer, "Collect for the Fourth Sunday After Easter," in *The Book of Common Prayer 1559*, John E. Booty, ed. (Charlottesville, Va.: University of Virginia Press, 1976), p. 63.

70. Michael Eaton, *Ecclesiastes: An Introduction and Commentary* (Downers Grove, Ill.: InterVarsity Press, 1983), p. 63.

71. Sinclair B. Ferguson, *The Pundit's Folly: Chronicles of an Empty Life* (Edinburgh: Banner of Truth Trust, 1995), p. 41.

72. Derek Kidner, *A Time to Mourn, and a Time to Dance: Ecclesiastes and the Way of the World* (Downers Grove, Ill.: InterVarsity Press, p. 98.

73. Ibid., p. 99.

74. Goldsworthy, p. 432.

75. Anonymous, "How Firm a Foundation, Ye Saints of the Lord" (hymn), 1787.

76. Helen H. Lemmel, "O Soul, Are You Weary and Troubled?" (hymn), 1922.

77. Francis I. Andersen, *Job: An Introduction and Commentary* (Downers Grove, Ill.: InterVarsity Press, 1975), p. 210.

78. Ibid., p. 73.

79. The original author of this well-known quote is uncertain.

80. *Agatha Christie's Miss Marple: The Body in the Library* (originally broadcast on BBC in 1984), available at www.youtube.com/watch?v=crds2h4a3rk (28:00–29:20).

81. Van Leeuwen, "Book of Proverbs," p. 226.

82. Ibid., p. 185.

83. This translation of Psalm 36:1 was used by C. S. Lewis in his preface to *The Screwtape Letters and Screwtape Proposes a Toast* (1961). There is no consensus about this rendering (see T. Longman, *Psalms: An Introduction and Commentary*, Tyndale Old Testament Commentaries, vols. 15–16 (Downers Grove, Ill.: InterVarsity Press, 2014), p. 175.

84. Kidner, *Proverbs*, p. 104.

85. Van Leeuwen, "Book of Proverbs," p. 145.

86. Waltke, *Book of Proverbs: Chapters 15–31*, p. 181.

87. Longman, *Proverbs*, p. 257.

88. Van Leeuwen, "Book of Proverbs," p. 229.

89. Elisabeth Elliot, "Epilogue II," in *Through the Gates of Splendor*, 40th anniv. ed. (Carol Stream, Ill.: Tyndale, 1996), p. 267.

90. Thomas Brooks, *Precious Remedies Against Satan's Devices* (Philadelphia: Jonathan Pounder, 1810), p. 60.

91. Richard Baxter, "What Are the Best Preservatives Against Melancholy and Overmuch Sorrow?" in *The Morning Exercises at Cripplegate*, vol. 3, ed. James Nichols (London: Thomas Tegg, 1844), p. 253.

92. Waltke, *Book of Proverbs: Chapters 1–15*, p. 541.
93. Kidner, *Proverbs*, p. 108.
94. George Herbert, "Joseph's Coat" (poem).
95. Wilfred M. McClay, "The Strange Persistence of Guilt," *Hedgehog Review* 19, no. 1 (spring 2017), available at www.iasc-culture.org/THR/THR_article_2017_Spring_McClay.php.
96. Kidner, *Proverbs*, p. 168.
97. On 21:2 Longman writes, "Humans do not define standards of virtue: God does." Longman, *Proverbs*, p. 390.
98. This paraphrases Kidner, *Proverbs*, p. 129.
99. Ibid., p. 114.
100. Ibid., p. 155.
101. Ibid., p. 165.
102. Longman, *Proverbs*, p. 307.
103. Quoted in Os Guinness, *The Call: Finding and Fulfilling the Central Purpose of Your Life* (Nashville: Thomas Nelson, 2003), p. 124.
104. Ibid.
105. This discussion is in C. S. Lewis, "The Great Sin," in *Mere Christianity* (New York: Macmillan, 1959), pp. 121–28.
106. Lewis Smedes, *Love Within Limits: A Realist's View of 1 Corinthians 13* (Grand Rapids, Mich.: Wm. B. Eerdmans, 1978), p. 34.
107. Waltke, *Book of Proverbs: Chapters 15–31*, p. 485.
108. William Shakespeare, *Troilus and Cressida*, act 2, scene 3.
109. Waltke, *Book of Proverbs: Chapters 1–15*, pp. 585–86.
110. D. A. Carson, *The Difficult Doctrine of the Love of God* (Wheaton, Ill.: Crossway, 1999), p. 39.
111. Lewis, *Mere Christianity*, p. 99.
112. Donald B. Kraybill, Steven M. Nolt, and David L. Weaver-Zercher, *Amish Grace: How Forgiveness Transcended Tragedy* (San Francisco: Jossey-Bass, 2010).
113. Ibid., p. 181.
114. Van Leeuwen, "Book of Proverbs," p. 133.
115. Shakespeare, *Troilus and Cressida*, act 2, scene 3.
116. Kidner, *Proverbs*, p. 157.
117. C. S. Lewis, *Reflections on the Psalms* (Orlando, Fla.: Harcourt, 1958), pp. 93–95.
118. Dorothy L. Sayers, *Creed or Chaos?* (New York: Harcourt, Brace, 1949), p. 81.
119. Kidner, *Proverbs*, p. 136.
120. Waltke, *Book of Proverbs: Chapters 15–31*, pp. 126–27. Waltke is quoting F. S. Fitzsimmonds from the *New Bible Dictionary*.
121. Benjamin Schmolck, "Open Now Thy Gates of Beauty" (1730), trans. Catherine Winkworth, 1863.
122. "Craving refers to aspirations rooted deeply within his personality, but its unclear specific objects could be his inordinate desire to do nothing but sleep or, more probably, his passion for the necessities of life such as food and drink." Waltke, *Book of Proverbs: Chapters 15–31*, p. 188.
123. Sayers, *Creed or Chaos?*, p. 81.
124. Kidner, *Proverbs*, p. 156.
125. Sayers, *Creed or Chaos?*, p. 51.
126. "What is sanctification?" *Westminster Shorter Catechism*, question and answer 35.

127. Kidner, *Proverbs*, p. 109.
128. Katharina A. von Schlegel, "Be Still My Soul" (hymn), 1752, trans. Jane L. Borthwick, 1855.
129. Van Leeuwen, "Book of Proverbs," p. 153.
130. C. S. Lewis, *The Four Loves* (New York: Harcourt, Brace, 1960), p. 94.
131. Lewis, *Mere Christianity*, p. 81.
132. Brooks, *Precious Remedies Against Satan's Devices*, p. 16.
133. Van Leeuwen, "Book of Proverbs," p. 72.
134. Waltke, *Book of Proverbs: Chapters 1–15*, p. 320.
135. Kidner, *Proverbs*, p. 46.
136. The Hebrew word in Proverbs 5:19, *sagah*, is translated here as "be intoxicated." But the verb literally means to wander and get lost. The verse then tells the young man to "lose himself" in his wife's love.
137. Van Leeuwen, "Book of Proverbs," p. 81.
138. Dietrich Bonhoeffer, "Self-discipline," quoted in ibid.
139. Thomas Cranmer, "Collect for Peace," U.S. *Book of Common Prayer* (1928), http://justus.anglican.org/resources/bcp/1928/MP.htm.
140. Charles Wesley, "Let Heaven and Earth Combine" (hymn), 1745.
141. Kidner, *Proverbs*, p. 46.
142. Ibid., p. 42.
143. Lewis, *Four Loves*, pp. 66–67.
144. Waltke, *Book of Proverbs: Chapters 15–31*, p. 33.
145. "Since the tongue is involved so fundamentally in all the thoughts, imaginings, longings and plans which lie behind the whole of our earthly life, it leaves the mark of its own defilement everywhere." J. A. Motyer, *The Message of James: The Tests of Faith*, The Bible Speaks Today, Leicester, England; Downers Grove, Ill.: InterVarsity Press, 1985, p. 122.
146. Joy Davidman, *Smoke on the Mountain: An Interpretation of the Ten Commandments* (Philadelphia: Westminster John Knox, 1954), p. 111.
147. In 19:5, the Hebrew word *puah*, translated here as "pouring out," means literally "breathing" out lies. The image conveyed is that every time one speaks he is lying.
148. This entire reflection is based on a passage, partially quoted here, in Lewis Smedes, "The Power of Promising," *Christianity Today*, January 21, 1983.
149. Waltke, *Book of Proverbs: Chapters 15–31*, p. 541.
150. Charles Gabriel, "In Lovingkindness Jesus Came" (hymn), 1905.
151. Kidner, *Proverbs*, p. 45.
152. Ibid., pp. 44–45.
153. Longman, *Proverbs*, p. 238.
154. John 8:1–11 is not found in the oldest New Testament manuscripts, but many believe it is a reliable and very old account, from another source, that became attached to the Gospel of John. It also fits with all the rest of the accounts of Jesus' character. See D. A. Carson, *The Gospel According to John* (Leicester, UK: InterVarsity Press, 1991), p. 333.
155. Kidner, *Proverbs*, p. 92.
156. Van Leeuwen, "Book of Proverbs," p. 152.
157. Waltke, *Book of Proverbs: Chapters 15–31*, p. 8.
158. Waltke, *Book of Proverbs: Chapters 1–15*, p. 496.
159. *Westminster Confession of Faith*, 15.4.
160. Franz Delitzsch observes that "the door of penitence [from our side] . . . does not always remain open." Quoted in Van Leeuwen, "Book of Proverbs," p. 242.

161. Kidner, *Proverbs*, p. 155.
162. Ibid., p. 133.
163. Edward Shillito, "Jesus of the Scars," in *Masterpieces of Religious Verse*, ed. James Dobson Morrison (New York: Harper Brothers, 1958), p. 235.
164. Waltke, *Book of Proverbs: Chapters 15–31*, p. 11.
165. Ibid., pp. 358–59.
166. See discussion in Anthony C. Thiselton, *The First Epistle to the Corinthians: A Commentary on the Greek Text*, New International Greek Testament Commentary (Grand Rapids, Mich.: Wm. B. Eerdmans, 2000), p. 1059.
167. Michael Mann and Christopher Crowe, *The Last of the Mohicans* (1991), screenplay available at www.awesomefilm.com/script/lastmohi.txt.
168. Kidner, *Proverbs*, p. 151.
169. There are exceptional situations in which an immediate criminal investigation is called for. It is right to report illegal business practices or sexual and physical abuse to authorities directly ("whistle-blowing"). Individual citizens do not "wield the sword" (Romans 13:1–7). That is, they should not seek to handle criminal behavior—that is the task of the state. But in the vast majority of situations these rules apply: (1) don't jump to conclusions but carefully inquire when you hear complaints, (2) talk to parties personally and respectfully, (3) and if they won't listen to you, try to get others to speak to them whom they respect. If the parties are Christian you may ask church leaders to intervene (see August 10). But do all these things rather than the ordinary responses—quickly condemning them to others, trying to get them fired, trying to embarrass them online, or threatening lawsuits.
170. Kidner, *Proverbs*, p. 115.
171. Based on the quote "All courses may run ill" in J. R. R. Tolkien, *The Fellowship of the Ring*, p.94.
172. Lewis, *Abolition of Man*, p. 80.
173. Van Leeuwen, "Book of Proverbs," p. 133.
174. Lewis B. Smedes, *Mere Morality: What God Expects from Ordinary People* (Grand Rapids, Mich.: Wm. B. Eerdmans, 1989), p. 237.
175. These are true accounts of Christians who were trying to work ethically in their workplaces, related to the author.
176. Judith Martin, *Miss Manners: A Citizen's Guide to Civility* (New York: Random House, 1999), p. 62.
177. Van Leeuwen, "Book of Proverbs," p. 208.
178. J. R. R. Tolkien, *The Return of the King* (1954; New York: Houghton Mifflin, repr. 2004), p. 378.
179. Waltke, *Book of Proverbs: Chapters 15–31*, p. 61.
180. D. M. Lloyd-Jones, *Healing and the Scripture* (Nashville, Tenn.: Thomas Nelson, 1982), p. 14.
181. Van Leeuwen, "Book of Proverbs," p. 49.
182. Waltke, *Book of Proverbs: Chapters 1–15*, p. 247.
183. John Owen, cited in I. D. E. Thomas, *A Puritan Golden Treasury* (Edinburgh, Scotland: Banner of Truth, 1977), p. 192. But this quote is also attributed to Robert Murray M'Cheyne in D. A. Carson, *A Call to Spiritual Reformation: Priorities from Paul and His Prayers* (Grand Rapids, Mich.: Baker Academic, 1992), p. 16.
184. Lewis, *Mere Christianity*, p. 192.
185. Thomas Brooks, *Precious Remedies Against Satan's Devices* (Philadelphia: Jonathan Pounder, 1810), p. 17.

186. Van Leeuwen, "Book of Proverbs," p. 182.

187. Ibid., p. 183.

188. Ibid., p. 155.

189. From C. S. Lewis, "The Weight of Glory" (1942), http://www.verber.com/mark/xian/weight-of-glory.pdf.

190. Ibid., p. 196.

191. Kidner, *Proverbs*, p. 141.

192. Van Leeuwen, "Book of Proverbs," p. 246.

193. How should a single adult approach the reading of the coming weeks on marriage and parenting? There are three ways to understand the relevance of this material to you. First, if there is any chance of your ever getting married, Proverbs will give great insight into what is actually involved, so you won't be "flying blind" and either overly romanticizing or overly fearing marriage. Second, if you have friends who are married and are parents, this will help you to understand your friends and be a better support for them. Third, if you have living parents (or even if you do not), what Proverbs says about the relationship of parents to children will be illuminating and helpful.

194. The Bible does allow for divorce. Breaking one's marriage vow through sexual unfaithfulness or desertion and abuse is grounds for divorce. So even the marriage bond, as solemn as it is, is not absolute. See Timothy and Kathy Keller, *The Meaning of Marriage: Facing the Complexities of Commitment with the Wisdom of God* (New York: Riverhead Books, 2013), pp. 92–93, 298–300.

195. Waltke, *Book of Proverbs: Chapters 1–15*, p. 117.

196. Kidner, *Proverbs*, p. 46.

197. Ibid., p. 45.

198. If we remember that the original audience of Proverbs was young men, we can understand why the "kind of spouse to look for" texts always describe women. It would be just as right to hear these texts as warnings against "quarrelsome" husbands—who exist in large numbers.

199. William Gurnall, *The Christian in Complete Armor* (London: Blackie and Sons, 1865), p. 12.

200. John Newton, *The Works of John Newton*, vol. 1 (Edinburgh, Scotland: Banner of Truth, 1985,) p. 136.

201. For more on this very discussed subject see Tim and Kathy Keller, *The Meaning of Marriage*, pp. 191–218.

202. See Rachel Cusk, "Making House: Notes on Domesticity," *New York Times Magazine*, August 31, 2016.

203. Kidner, *Proverbs*, p. 184.

204. There are two reasons that in this illustration it is a woman who is depicted as a pig. One is that Proverbs was written to be training for young men. The other, however, is that it is men who are the most likely to objectify, dehumanize, and commodify women by evaluating them primarily on their looks.

205. These two views are laid out in Kenneth Keniston and The Carnegie Council on Children, *All Our Children: The American Family Under Pressure* (New York: Houghton-Mifflin Harcourt, 1978).

206. Waltke, *Book of Proverbs: Chapters 1–15*, p. 176.

207. Kidner, *Proverbs*, p. 46.

208. Waltke, *Book of Proverbs: Chapters 15–31*, p. 252.

209. Arthur Schlesinger, "Foreword," in Charles C. Brown, *Niebuhr and His Age* (Harrisburg, Pa.: Trinity, 2002), viii–ix.

210. See Carl K. Spackman, "Parents Passing On the Faith," (D.Min. diss., Westminster Theological Seminary, 1988).

211. Kidner, *Proverbs*, p. 80.

212. From Martin Luther King, Jr., "I Have a Dream," https://www.archives.gov /files/press/exhibits/dream-speech.pdf.

213. Waltke, *Book of Proverbs: Chapters 15–31*, p. 43.

214. C. S. Lewis, *The Great Divorce* (New York: HarperCollins, rev. ed., 2015), p. 118.

215. Waltke, *Book of Proverbs: Chapters 1–15*, p. 463.

216. Paul Krugman, "For Richer," *New York Times*, October 20, 2002.

217. Longman, *Proverbs*, p. 286.

218. Kidner, *Proverbs*, p. 93.

219. Ibid., p. 71.

220. J. R. R. Tolkien, *The Two Towers* (New York: Houghton Mifflin, 1954; repr., 2004), p. 550.

221. Here I follow Longman, *Proverbs*, p. 507, who does not think we should (as some do) read this verse as simply getting people to obey the Bible.

222. Waltke, *Book of Proverbs: Chapters 15–31*, pp. 16–17.

223. C. S. Lewis, *Prince Caspian* (New York: HarperCollins, 1951; repr., 2002), p. 220.

224. D. A. Carson, "April 11," in *For the Love of God*, vol. 2 (Wheaton, Ill.: Crossway Books, 1999), n.p.

225. Kidner, *Proverbs*, p. 177.

226. Kenneth T. Aitken, *Proverbs* (Louisville, Ky.: Westminster John Knox, 1986), p. 216.

227. All commentators point out that the phrase "the blessing of the upright" is ambiguous. It could mean either the blessing conferred on them by God, which spills over to the rest of the city, or the blessing the upright confer on their neighbors and fellow citizens. It is best to read it as teaching both. See Aitken, *Proverbs*, p. 200.

228. Van Leeuwen, "Book of Proverbs," p. 214. See Van Leeuwen's entire, excellent reflection on 24:10–12.

229. Quoted in Charles Avila, *Ownership: Early Christian Teaching* (London: Sheed and Ward, 1983), p. 50.

230. For the many versions of this famous speech and poem, see https://en.wikipedia .org/wiki/First_they_came_.

231. C. S. Lewis, *The Four Loves* (New York: Harcourt and Brace, 1991), p. 52.

232. John Stott, *The Cross of Christ* (Downers Grove, Ill.: InterVarsity Press, 1986), p. 160.

233. This is taken from Bruce Waltke, "The Superiority of Jesus Christ to Solomon's Wisdom," in *Book of Proverbs: Chapters 1–15*, pp. 131–32. Waltke concludes this section, "Nevertheless, even though Christ's wisdom is so much greater than Solomon's, we do not discard the latter any more than we would throw away a five-dollar bill because we also owned a twenty-dollar bill."

234. I am referring to the intertestamental book of Sirach, also known as Ecclesiasticus. See Longman, *Proverbs*, pp. 69–70. See especially Sirach 51:23–27 and how it compares with Matthew 11:28–30.

235. James Proctor, "It Is Finished" (hymn), 1864.

236. John Newton, "In Evil Long I Took Delight," in *Olney Hymns in Three Parts* (London and New York: T. Nelson and Sons, 1855), pp.205–6.

237. Edwin Hodder, "Thy Word Is Like a Garden, Lord" (hymn), 1863.

238. Longman, *Proverbs*, pp. 215–23.

239. William Cowper, "O for a Closer Walk with God" in John Newton, *Olney Hymns in Three Parts* (London and New York: T. Nelson and Sons, 1855), p. 21.

240. Isaac Watts, "Alas, and Did My Savior Bleed?" (hymn), 1707.

SELECT BIBLIOGRAPHY

Best books

Alter, Robert. *The Art of Biblical Poetry*. New York: Basic Books, 1985. See especially chapters 1, 2, 3, and 7.

Goldsworthy, Graeme. *Gospel and Wisdom*. The Goldsworthy Trilogy. Carlisle, UK: Paternoster, 2001.

Kidner, Derek. *An Introduction to Wisdom Literature*. Downers Grove, Ill.: InterVarsity Press, 1985.

Longman, Tremper. *How to Read Proverbs*. Downers Grove, Ill.: InterVarsity Press, 2002.

Best commentaries

Kidner, Derek. *Proverbs: Tyndale Old Testament Commentaries*. Downers Grove, Ill.: InterVarsity Press, 2009.

Longman, Tremper. *Proverbs*. Baker Commentary on the Old Testament, Wisdom, and Psalms. Grand Rapids, Mich.: Baker Academic, 2006.

Van Leeuwen, Raymond C. "The Book of Proverbs." In *The New Interpreter's Bible*. Vol. 5. Nashville: Abingdon, 1997.

Waltke, Bruce. *The Book of Proverbs: Chapters 1–15*. New International Commentary on the Old Testament. Grand Rapids, Mich.: Wm. B. Eerdmans, 2004.

———. *The Book of Proverbs: Chapters 15–31*. New International Commentary on the Old Testament. Grand Rapids, Mich.: Wm. B. Eerdmans, 2005.

REDEEMER

REDEEMER

The Redeemer imprint is dedicated to books that address pressing spiritual and social issues of the day in a way that speaks to both the core Christian audience and to seekers and skeptics alike. The mission for the Redeemer imprint is to bring the power of the Christian gospel to every part of life. The name comes from Redeemer Presbyterian Church in New York City, which Tim Keller started in 1989 with his wife, Kathy, and their three sons. Redeemer has begun a movement of contextualized urban ministry, thoughtful preaching, and church planting across America and throughout major world cities.